OUR LIFE IN GARDENS

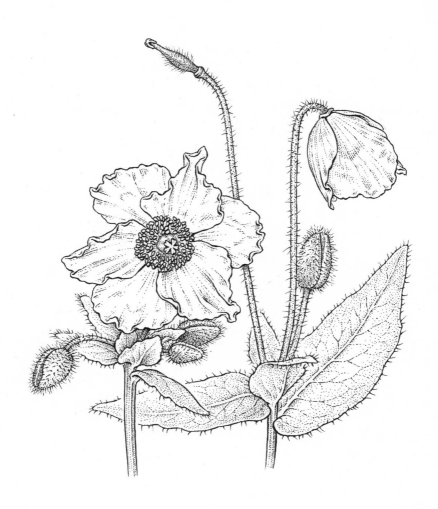

OUR LIFE IN GARDENS

Joe Eck and Wayne Winterrowd

Illustrations by Bobbi Angell

Farrar, Straus and Giroux   New York

Farrar, Straus and Giroux
18 West 18th Street, New York 10011

Copyright © 2009 by Joe Eck and Wayne Winterrowd
Illustrations copyright © 2009 by Bobbi Angell
All rights reserved
Distributed in Canada by Douglas & McIntyre Ltd.
Printed in the United States of America
First edition, 2009

Library of Congress Cataloging-in-Publication Data
Eck, Joe.
    Our life in gardens / Joe Eck and Wayne Winterrowd.— 1st ed.
        p.   cm.
    Includes index.
    ISBN-13: 978-0-374-16031-9 (hardcover : alk. paper)
    ISBN-10: 0-374-16031-7 (hardcover : alk. paper)
    1. Gardening—Anecdotes.   I. Winterrowd, Wayne.   II. Title.

SB455.3 .E25 2009
635—dc22

                                                            2008045349

Designed by Jonathan D. Lippincott

www.fsgbooks.com

3   5   7   9   10   8   6   4   2

For Jonathan

Contents

Preface   ix

Setting Out   3
Agapanthus   9
Annuals   14
Arborvitae   22
Artichokes   28
Bananas   34
The Bay Tree   38
Berberis   46
Biennials   51
Boxwood   59
Camellias   64
Colchicum   71
Corydalis   76
Cyclamen   82
The Daffodil Meadow   88
Forcing Branches   94
The Garden Trowel   100
Gentians   104
Hardiness   110
Hedges   118
Hellebores   125
Ilex   132

Leucojum   138

Lilacs   144

Magnolias   151

Native Groundcovers   157

Nerines   163

Pea Season   169

The Pergola Walk   176

Poppies   182

Pots   189

Primroses   194

Prunus ×'Hally Jolivette'   202

Prunus mume   208

Rampant Plants   212

The Rock Garden and Planted Walls   220

Roses   227

Sempervivums   234

Snowdrops   240

Sorbus alnifolia   246

Stewartias   250

Summer-Blooming Bulbs   255

Tender Rhododendrons   265

Time   271

Vegetable Gardens   278

Violets   284

Willows   291

Wisteria   297

Xanthorrhoea quadrangulata   303

The Future   308

Index   313

Preface

This is the third book we have written together, though separately we have written others, making a total of six. But to say
"written separately" makes no sense, for when two lives have
been bent for so many years on one central enterprise—in this
case, gardening—there really is no such thing as separately.
That is not to say that we do not divide up chores and tasks.
Much like piano duetists, we both have our separate parts to
play, though we are also concerned that the sound of our lives
be one seamless and complete whole. We hope our garden is
that, for we have known many gardening couples who divided
up their garden to avoid the quarrels we never seem to have.
We suppose that domestic harmony is bought in all sorts of
ways, when it must be bought at all. Fortunately, that has not
been an issue here.

We know that making a garden together is extraordinary
to many people. We further know that two people writing a
book about a garden seems even more impossible. Or at least
very bizarre. Indeed, there are people (even very experienced
writers) who claim that they can hear our different voices within
the text, and can tell which of us wrote an individual essay,
or even a single sentence. That is remarkable to us, for we
certainly cannot, and in the earlier books—when we glance
into them to see if we are perhaps repeating ourselves and
are saying something one time too many—the question is apt

to come to one or the other of us, "Did you write that, or did I?"

There is a deeper point here, however, than the silly surface question of figuring out who said what. Most people have difficulty with the idea that a couple can achieve anything in perfect harmony. So, for example, we are often told that Harold Nicolson was the architect of Sissinghurst, and Vita Sackville-West poked in all the pretty plants. We are hardly scholars of their relationship, but nothing in their correspondence or published writings supports that assertion. Indeed, many who knew them have assured us that the garden at Sissinghurst was never a bifurcated effort, even when it came into the capable hands of the two wonderful gardeners who followed Nicolson and Sackville-West, Pamela Schwerdt and Sybille Kreutzberger. Why can't two people make a garden?

Actually, that is the trumpeting assertion of Margery Fish's book *We Made a Garden*, and Mirabel Osler's wonderful *A Gentle Plea for Chaos* lovingly records such a joint effort—and its necessary dissolution when her husband, Michael, died. All Beth Chatto's books acknowledge the contributions made by her husband, Andrew, and she frequently expresses deep gratitude for the ways he saw and thought. We knew Linc and Timmy Foster well, and we also knew that perhaps some of their finest times together were spent in the joint creation of Millstream, their magnificent garden in Falls Village, Connecticut. They are both dead now, and the garden is gone, but Timmy left a wonderful memoir of its creation, *Cuttings from a Rock Garden* (with both their names on the title page), and Linc wrote an authoritative work on rock garden plants, *Rock Gardening*, with "Drawings by Laura Louise Foster."

Michael Pollan has said that sooner or later a writer who has a garden will write about it. We'd go further, to say that sooner or later two people who make a garden will write about it. Or at least we have. The point is this: When a book is written about a garden two people have made together, that book is really not about—or not just about—the garden they made. It is also about a relationship, and so it comes to be an autobiography of that relationship. It is for that reason, principally, that we write, and for that reason that we also find it so odd when someone says, as is the case with surprising frequency, "Come on! Who does what?"

This book is a mixed bag, a gypsy trunk of this and that. Within it, we hope the reader will find sound information about the cultivation of plants and their value in the landscape, and some perceptions about garden design, which is our profession. There are also essays about the various parts of our garden, and there are essays about particular plants—roses and lilacs, snowdrops and cyclamen. And vegetables. There are also essays on the development of the garden over time and the question that weighs on us most at this time, its probable demise.

Still, for all its mixed nature, this book has a coherence, for as we have tried to explain, it is really about us. Rather than apologizing for that implicit egotism, we would have to say that we may well shamelessly write another. We do not seem to be done yet.

OUR LIFE IN GARDENS

SETTING OUT

WE LIVED OUR FIRST YEAR TOGETHER on Beacon Street, in Boston. The apartment was impossibly grand, high and white and classically pillared, previously the ground-floor ballroom and formal dining room of a great private house. Its floor-to-ceiling bay windows faced the Public Garden, and that was our garden in a way, as was the magnificent *Magnolia ×soulangeana* that filled our tiny front yard. Sunlight flooded those windows, and in them we grew a collection of tender plants, some of which were permanent, and some of which were added as the seasons progressed. There was a ficus tree, a wide-spreading Kentia palm, and a staghorn fern mounted on a wooden slab.

To them we added cattleya orchids, pots of forced crocus and paperwhite narcissus, sweet-smelling hyacinths and bushy azaleas, all bought from Mrs. Fishelson's very costly flower shop on Charles Street just around the corner. We were prepared to make almost any sacrifice for beauty, though often enough we had only enough money left at the end of the month for pancakes. Still, there was always enough for flowers from Mrs. Fishelson.

We lived at 89 Beacon Street for three months short of a year. The plant collections grew larger, and at one point included a ten-foot-tall weeping willow tree forced in the high windows of the bedroom. But in the end, it was not plants that sent us to the country. It was chickens.

We can no longer remember how we came to visit a chicken show, but it must have been the venerable Boston Poultry Show, now in its 158th year. In any case, we came home with a trio of Mille Fleur bantams, a sturdy little red rooster all spangled over with white and black dots, and two meek little hens. The hens were of an age to lay, and so, shortly thereafter, on Beacon Street, we began to produce our own eggs, generally two every other day.

Even then it was probably quite illegal to keep poultry in a Boston apartment. At first we wondered how our landlord would react, and so we quickly fashioned a pen for our chickens in keeping—we felt—with the grand circumstances to which they had been elevated. It was a large cage, roughly six feet long and four feet wide, made of dark-stained wood and expanded brass wire, with a deep tray in the bottom for sweet-smelling cedar shavings. Tucked behind the Kentia palm at the sunny end of the great ballroom, it also had Chinese export-ware feed and water bowls, and was of course kept immaculately clean. Our landlord seemed, if anything, amused. We gave him some fresh-laid eggs.

But as all chicken fanciers know, chickens are addictive, and one can never stop at three. So many of our Saturday mornings were spent driving to the breeders of fancy chickens around Boston, our favorite of whom was Marjorie George, just over the Massachusetts line in Nashua, New Hampshire. Around Easter, she sold us a tiny cochin hen we named Emma. She was hardly the size of a cantaloupe, though her body was a cloud of soft, almost furry snow-white feathers. (We kept them that way, by weekly shampoos and fluffing out with the hair dryer.) She was the only chicken who had full run of the apartment, though she mostly favored the kitchen, where she had a nest box tucked privately in one corner. Soon she became broody, a skill for which cochins are famous, being generally considered the best of chicken mothers. Or foster mothers. For as Emma had no mate, her eggs were sterile. So we bought a dozen assorted fertile ones from Mrs. George, and twenty-one days later every one hatched.

Shortly thereafter, we had a morning visit from the chairman of the English department at Tufts, who lived in a beautiful house around the corner on Chestnut Street. Just at the moment he was lifting his cup of tea, Emma decided to show her brood the world. Perhaps seventy feet of dark, waxed oak parquet floor lay between the kitchen door and the couch where he sat. Emma proceeded that length, leading a stately procession of tiny, chirping chicks. She observed our guest skeptically, found nothing special in him, turned, and proceeded with her train the long way back. Good breeding kept him, we presume, from saying a single word about the extraordinary sight that had passed before him. But we wondered what Emma's perspective had been. Perhaps good breeding of her own caused her so politely to withdraw.

Figuring by May that we had perhaps reached the tipping point in our acquisition of chickens, we moved to a wonderful old rented farmhouse outside Boston in Pepperell, Massachusetts. Built in 1759, it preserved many of its original features, including a huge brick oven. Better, it came with a small barn that was more than ample for the thirty-five birds we brought with us, and then for the two hundred or so we soon acquired. We even kept a pig, named Morose, which was given to us a week before we left Beacon Street and which we had to keep in the bathtub there. Land came with this wonderful house as well, with pastures and woods and a stream and lots of space to make a garden. So we made the transition from being indoor to outdoor gardeners, starting first with an oval space fifty feet by thirty feet that lay in the center of the circular gravel drive.

Naïve, we were. On a trip to Lexington Gardens, where we had already begun to buy indoor plants, we filled the car with flats of annuals, a bit of this, a bit of that, in every imaginable color. We stripped the grass from the oval, tilled the soil, and filled it with our new plants. It was certainly the most colorful garden in town. Though thirty-six years have passed, we still remember what we grew. Salpiglosis was a particular thrill, with its felted petals, fantastically veined in contrasting colors over grounds of yellow and blue, chestnut brown and a purple almost black. There was also *Phlox drummondii*, which we still consider indispensable for the edges of beds, blooming softly all summer long in shades of cream and coral, mauve and pink and white. There were certainly snapdragons, in yellow and pink, mauve gomphrena, and red zinnias. We thought we were very sophisticated in knowing to plant drifts of one plant in one color. Now we feel the greater sophistication might have been to plant wildly, all mixed up like a flowering meadow, but that style, now so fashionable, lay far in our future.

We next turned our labors to a place to sit and enjoy the summer light. Flat fieldstone was abundant, and so we laid a stone terrace about ten feet by fifteen feet along the back of the house, and then made a screen around it of saplings cut from the woods. Into those we wove whips of privet hedge bought cheap in bundles from Lexington Gardens, and we planted bitter melon (*Momordica balsamina*) to scramble over the screen. Its bumpy, three-inch-long yellow fruits that split to reveal vivid scarlet seed and its dark lobed leaves all provided lovely contrast to the small fresh green of the privet. We still think the effect was surprisingly sophisticated, for the first garden we ever made together.

Success emboldened us. We bought a pair of handsome yews to flank either side of the front steps, and a dogwood to mark the corner of the ell. We dug laurels from the woods and planted them under the shaded living room windows. We also laid a fieldstone path from the driveway to the back door, on either side of which we made an herb garden, which even boasted a three-foot-high standard deadly nightshade tree. We fashioned a glorious espalier out of an old watermelon-red flowering quince we dug out of the front yard, and made another espalier out of pyracantha across the garage wall.

How quickly we grew in skill and knowledge. Everyone was nice to us. Allen Haskell, whom we met when we visited his magnificent nursery and garden in New Bedford, leveled the field between his lifetime of garden knowledge and our beginning ignorance by saying, "In this, we are all amateurs!" Plants he gave us then are still in our garden, having moved about with us for thirty-six years.

Our first autumn in Pepperell, we also planted bulbs, daffodils of course and crocus and tulips and hyacinths. The day in March when the hundred or so species of crocus we had planted near the doorstep bloomed was then, and remains, a curiously blessed moment in our life together. It was something we vowed would happen each year we were together, forever.

In all, we spent a little more than two years in Pepperell, gardening madly and also adding to our collection of animals, which eventually included two dogs, many more chickens, turkeys, pheasants, quail, pigeons and doves, miniature rabbits in several colors, and even a box tortoise. It was our peaceable kingdom. What is curious about that time is that it seemed to have been much longer than it actually was, in the way that children feel when they are very young and an eternity lies between birthday and birthday. When knowledge and experience expand at a rapid rate, time seems to stretch out. A year was as far into the future as we could possibly see, and yet we gardened as if we would be there forever, in an immediate pleasure in the moment that seemed to imply an inexhaustible future. Little of what we did there then remains, though the daffodils must, and that thought is very pleasant to us.

AGAPANTHUS

From a chance encounter, gardeners, like lovers, often form lifelong relationships of great intensity. You see a plant, your eyes widen, your pulse accelerates, and huskily you ask even complete strangers its name, importunately tugging at coat sleeves. More than once this has happened here, when visitors have seen an agapanthus for the first time. We smile on their quickening passion. For to someone newly in love, it is neither tactful nor appropriate to explain the difficulties that lie ahead.

It comes as no surprise that the genus *Agapanthus* takes its name from two Greek words, the first meaning "love" (*agape*), and the second, "a flower" (*anthos*). The genus—which contains about ten species and innumerable hybrids—passes in gardens under the popular name lily of the Nile. From a romantic perspective it suits them perfectly, for their flowers resemble the many renderings of papyrus in Egyptian hieroglyphics. It would not be hard to imagine Cleopatra on her golden barge, sailing languidly through tall stems of flowers of that shape, with colors ranging from clearest azure to lapis lazuli. Alas, the many species of agapanthus have nothing to do with the Nile. Though the genus occupies a wide geographic range, its origins are in South Africa, and the astral career of Cleopatra never took her that far.

Agapanthus africanus entered Europe as a cultivated plant in the late seventeenth century, but its huge popularity arose only after large glasshouses and conservatories became common in the nineteenth century. It then burst into popularity—for the effect of the flowers of agapanthus is always explosive—and large tubbed specimens shouldered against citrus, oleanders, and other tender glasshouse ornamentals used for summer display outdoors. Wealthy people continued to cultivate agapanthus—or to have them cultivated—well after World War II. Indeed, an elderly lady who visited here once explained to us in great detail how huge wooden boxes of them were stored over the winter in deep pits below the frost line on an uncle's estate in Brookline, Massachusetts. (He died, and it made her very sad that the agapanthus did not live long beyond him.) And anywhere they were hardy in the ground—Zones 9 and 10 in North America—they were planted with extravagance, in deep swirling beds and in large tubs and planters. Eventually, in sections of California and Florida, they soon became "groundcover," a term used to describe any weed-suppressing plant that can survive with little care and receives little admiration. In such places, agapanthus are as common as dirt, making it hard to explain to gardeners who live there why the rest of us covet them so much. But anywhere agapanthus may not easily be grown outdoors, "coveted" is a status they fully possess. Their great beauty when in flower makes it quite easy to see why; managing them over a long winter when they are not in flower does add a difficulty.

Agapanthus are clump-forming plants that grow from thick daylily-like rhizomes, producing strap-shaped leaves as much as eighteen inches long. Beneath is a mass of thick, spaghetti-like roots that will cling tenaciously to the porous sides of clay pots, making a plant that needs repotting impossible to turn out neatly. Further, agapanthus bloom best when slightly potbound. But if a specimen becomes too potbound, it will not bloom either, and that is a sign that it must be divided and repotted. We used to think there was no other way to do this than to smash the clay pot. Now we know that if the plant is allowed to dry out thoroughly, usually it will slip out easily. Still, division is a brutal process, often best done with an ax, chopping the plant straight through its heart, and then into pieces, each containing two or three rhizomes and as much fleshy root as possible.

Agapanthus are generally big plants, and so a pot big enough that one winces when lifting it is required. They are also very greedy feeders, though they demand perfect drainage, so compost for repotting should be humus-rich and gritty. For a year or two after repotting, new divisions will bloom poorly or not at all. Then they will proceed to become potbound all over again. For three or four years, however, you should reach the pinnacle of success with repotted agapanthus, with pots that produce at least one bloom scape for each fan of growth. In a large pot, that may be as many as fifty, blooming over a very long period from late June into early September. A splendid display like that makes being a sort of horticultural Lizzie Borden worthwhile.

Still, the great problem is how to store your agapanthus over the winter. If you have a sunporch or greenhouse or a well-lit guest bedroom, where temperatures can be kept hovering around 40 degrees, then the only effort required is lifting the heavy pots into such a place. Lacking these luxuries, however, a cool basement—again, hovering around 40 degrees and never freezing, even for a night—can be rigged with lights and the plants stored there. Plants must also be kept fairly dry, not so much that they shrivel up, but dry enough to force them into the rest period needed for good bloom.

If things are well managed, then your plants will look simply awful, with yellowed leaves and a sickly appearance. But as the days lengthen in March, water-soluble fertilizer such as Peters 20-20-20 should be applied weekly, at half the strength recommended on the package. As growth quickens, watering should also steadily increase, and the plants should be moved to the brightest indoor conditions one can manage. After all danger of frost is past, they may be moved into their permanent places outdoors. During active growth, it is almost impossible to overwater an agapanthus. Large pots should probably be watered daily.

From time to time, northern gardeners hear rumors of "hardy" agapanthus, special strains that might survive the winter even in Zone 5, "with protection." The famous Headbourne hybrids, developed by the Honourable Lewis Palmer at Headbourne Worthy, near Winchester, throughout the 1950s and '60s, are frequently mentioned. Palmer crossed species madly, ending up with a diverse swarm, rather like a barnyard of mixed bantam chickens. Some are very beautiful, such as the very dark blue 'Cherry Holley', the mid-blue 'African Moon' (the umbels of which spray out into tinier umbels, making it look like a lit sparkler), and 'Rosemary', colored the pale lilac-gray the late Rosemary Verey often wore. Incongruously, within the Headbourne hybrids is also 'Lilliput', the tiniest agapanthus of all, with six-inch-long, narrow leaves and flower scapes that scarcely reach a foot, topped by umbels of dark blue.

The Headbourne hybrids have achieved notoriety not for their considerable beauty, but because they are said to be the hardiest agapanthus of all. Hardiness is never a matter of mere winter lows, however, but is always something like a complex tossed salad. So it may happen—in a most privileged courtyard garden in Washington or even New York City, with perfect winter drainage, some evergreen boughs placed over the crowns in December, a good covering of snow, and perhaps an exposed basement wall that leaks heat and is just opposite the furnace—it *may* happen that some selection might live to see the spring and flower in summer.

But we remain skeptical. And so, to consummate an affair with agapanthus, we fear you must resort to shoving and hauling, smashing and splintering, to a cold bedroom full of nasty, yellowing foliage, always anticipating the pure bliss that will come. Not so very different, after all, from any other love affair.

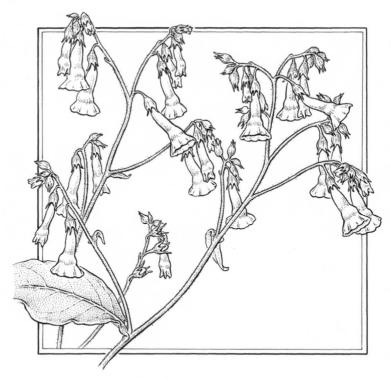

ANNUALS

A LADY WHO ONCE VISITED our garden showed a keen interest in *Begonia sutherlandii*. It is a lovely foot-tall plant with a graceful, mounded growth of gentle, watery green angel's wings into which nestle small, complex, four-petaled flowers of the clearest tangerine. We grow it among hostas, for which it is the perfect foil.

"What a marvelous plant! What is it?"

"It is *Begonia sutherlandii*."

"Hardy?"

"Well, it's a tender tuberous perennial. But not much trouble. In autumn you dig up the tubers and store them in a frost-free place. Then you start them back up in spring."

"Then you mean it is an *annual*!"

Over the years, we have come to recognize the scorn that can be poured into that word, and so we were ready for her next remark.

"I don't plant annuals! It is like pouring money into the ground." Our impulse was to remark, "When is gardening anything else?" But we held our tongues, and she swept on to pursue her tour of the garden, which we knew had already turned sour, for it was July and in her path lay many annuals.

Experienced gardeners know that the word "annual" should almost always be enclosed in quotation marks, as should the word "vegetable," for they are equally imprecise. In fact, many of the choicest annuals (and vegetables) are really half hardy or tender perennials, corms, tubers, rhizomes, sub-shrubs, or shrubs. A functioning definition of "annual" therefore is "any plant established for a single season with the expectation that it will not return the following year." Such a definition would hardly be acceptable to a botanist, however, or even to an experienced gardener. For with the proper facilities, many plants grown as annuals can be carried over for years of beauty—in greenhouses, in cold basements, or even on the famous sunny kitchen windowsill. The amiable *B. sutherlandii* asks the minimum, just a frost-free place to sleep out a long winter before waking in spring to offer incredible beauty of leaf and flower. It is hardly "pouring money into the ground." Rather, it is pouring money into an ever-greater number of clay pots, which seem to increase annually as plants need division, thriftily providing us with choice (and costless) birthday presents for gardening friends.

To the botanist, a true annual is a plant that goes from seed to leaf and stem and flower and then back to seed in one growing season. Within this group are some of the most charming plants that can be grown, such as zinnias, marigolds, sunflowers, nasturtiums, and poppies. Though they are often very beautiful in themselves, their charm resides to a large degree precisely in their naïveté, their simple sense of ease and well-being, just in themselves, just in what they are. It is true that their colors are often bold and unsubtle, usually in the part of the color wheel called "hot," which includes the hardest yellows, crimsons, and reds—but they are beloved by children, and to any adult they offer the same kind of lift to the heart that occurs when walking through FAO Schwarz at Christmastime. We always plant a few, most often in the vegetable garden, where the brashness of zinnias or marigolds accords perfectly with the fine green of bean leaves or radishes and lettuce. Nasturtiums snuggle happily at the feet of the finely crafted veined gray leaves of artichokes, and supply tender young leaves and flowers for salads, thus even crossing the divide between annual and vegetable.

Most gardeners we know maintain vegetable gardens, though perhaps not our lady visitor, who would almost certainly belong to the "Why bother? There's a very good farm stand near me" school of thought. But those of us who insist on vegetable gardens often have trouble maintaining a proper proportion of vegetables and annuals for cutting. Or for that matter, vegetables and perennials, for in autumn, at division time, there is always that row you just cleared of lettuces, and you can propagate extra dianthus there, of which you happen to have a handful, and which you vow to move out next spring, and don't. But this is always to be remembered: a vegetable garden is for growing vegetables. Whatever else happens there must be considered happy accident, and not main purpose.

The annuals we grow mostly in the vegetable garden—what might once have been called "chicken yard annuals" and now grace the fronts of many filling stations—are hardly the whole panoply of tender plants that can embellish the summer garden. Within the class of plants roughly defined as "annuals" exist many that are as elegant as the finest perennials, and further, will assist in maintaining the beauty of the perennial border throughout its three most difficult times: early in its life when little color is showing; in August, when something that all gardeners know to call the "August Slump" occurs; and then at the very end of the season, just before frosts come to cut everything down. These assisting annuals are very numerous, and each year brings others forward, either as hybrids or selections of familiar plants, or as completely new introductions discovered in faraway places. Many are already indispensable, and more are likely to become so as their special virtues establish themselves.

We start our annuals season with the gentle ones that bloom in late June, just as the large border geraniums are finishing. They are generally benders and weavers, little plants that can rise above emerging perennials, providing a tier of delicate flower when their sturdier neighbors are yet to bloom. Among those, a great favorite is *Nigella damascena*, which owns many popular names, according to the rule that the longer a plant is grown in gardens, the more popular names it will accumulate. Nigella was a common feature of Elizabethan gardens, and is known by at least five popular names, among them love-in-a-mist and devil-in-the-bush, the two conjoining to indicate where you end up when you start out. But it is also known as Chevre de Venus in French, from its fine, ferny leaves, and Catherine's wheels, as its flowers seem to resemble the wheel of fire on which Saint Catherine of Alexandria endured her martyrdom for refusing the advances of Emperor Maximinius. The fifth is Bluebeard, from the famous *bête d'extermination* in Charles Perrault's tale (published in 1697) who murdered seven wives and a few small boys in quick succession. These names hardly promise a charming plant, but in fact, nigella is wonderful, with a ragged ruff of pale blue petals surrounding a boss of green, filamented stamens that repeat its ferny leaves. The form called 'Miss Jekyll's Blue' is particularly fine, with a rich sky-blue flower that makes everything around it beautiful.

Another of these gentle plants is *Phlox drummondii*, in fact an American native and perhaps one of the most amiable plants that can be grown at the front of a border. It forms little loose bushes to about a foot tall, clothed in fresh, pale green leaves, each stem surmounted by a cob of recognizable phlox-like flowers in beautiful colors. The finest is the variety called 'Phlox of Sheep', which exist in various shades of biscuit brown, pale cream, and sometimes cameo pink.

Early to bloom, also, if you buy pre-started plants, is *Tweedia caerulea*, another American native that always creates excitement at the front of a border. It is quite different in effect from Drummond phlox, with stiff, two-foot-tall stems clad in bladelike, bluish-green, hairy leaves at the top of which forms a loose umbel of blue five-petaled stars. But to call them blue is an injustice, for buds begin pink and then fade to that shade of turquoise so much loved in the 1950s, for cars and ties and prom jackets, though the flowers eventually change to a deep, purplish blue dotted over with red freckles. Each blossom merits the closest study.

The list of annuals that act almost as glue in the late-season garden, holding its frayed parts together, is long. But at the very top is *Verbena bonariensis*, a plant without which we simply could not imagine the autumn perennial border. Though the plant was discovered in Buenos Aires in 1826 and given its species name after that city, the name is still a sort of pun, for it would be impossible to imagine any plant more airy. That is one of its great values in the perennial garden, for it is so slender of form that young plants may be inserted between perennials anyplace that a few inches of bare ground exists. From a few dark green, narrow basal leaves ascends a much-branched four-sided stem about four feet tall, surmounted by a flat, two-inch-wide corymb packed with flowers hardly three times the size of a pinhead, and of the purest lavender shaded to dark purple. They float above other perennials, and for this reason, *V. bonariensis* should always be used pointillistically, dotted here and there throughout other plantings to create a kind of purple haze in autumn. It will never get in another plant's way, and though it is a wonderful cut flower, as many corymbs of flower as possible should be left in the garden, for they are seldom unvisited by monarch butterflies, providing essential nourishment for those remarkable creatures before they make their long trip from Vermont to Mexico.

It seems that all species of nicotiana are valuable in the garden, including even *N. tabacum*, the smoking tobacco that has been humanity's bane, and the much older *N. rustica*, cultivated as a sacred herb by Native Americans from prehistoric times to the present. *Nicotiana tabacum* was much prized by Gertrude Jekyll, for its huge rosettes of rich green leaf and its ascending cobs of flowers to five feet in autumn—white or rose red or pink, according to variety. *Nicotiana rustica* is a much lower, cobby plant, to about three feet, with fleshy, celadon-green leaves and flowers that are arranged in a blunt, club-shaped panicle and tinted pinkish green. Both plants might be grown in the autumn garden for what one might call historical interest, or for other purposes. But neither would be as beautiful as several other species of nicotiana, among which our two current favorites are *N. langsdorffii* and *N. mutabilis*.

Nicotiana langsdorffii is a native of Brazil and Chile that has been cultivated in gardens for many years, but it has only recently become what one might call frequently grown. For one thing, its inch-long tubes of flowers are green, and green is a color most gardeners prefer to see in grass. But the flowers are of such a fresh and lively green that one should really call it chartreuse, and if you turn up a bell and look inside, there are five cobalt-blue stamens. From handsome rosettes of six- to eight-inch-long leaves, branched, wiry stems emerge, beginning their flowering in late July and continuing until frost. Hummingbirds adore the flowers, and a planting is never free for long from the whirr of wings and the flash of a ruby-red throat. Transplants bloom earliest, though self-seeded plants, which will occur around the garden every year after the plant has once been grown, provide a fine late show, lasting well into first frosts.

Nicotiana mutabilis was unknown until about twelve years ago, when it was discovered in open forest clearings in southern Brazil. It is a wonderful plant, with hefty rosettes of dark green, arrow-shaped leaves about two feet wide, from which emerge much-branched flowering stems as tall as five feet that produce hundreds of tiny, half-inch-long tubes that end in tiny, five-petaled stars. There are two miracles to this plant. The first is that flower stems appear quite late, not until the middle of August, when even a charitable estimate of the garden would have to call it tired. The second is that flowers start out white, fade to light pink, and then to deep rose, creating an iridescent shimmer over each plant. (Hence the species name, *mutabilis*, which generally means "changing in color.") But the plant is mutable in other ways, for no two individuals seem to behave in exactly the same way. Transplanted in June, some will bloom in early July, and some will gather force and bloom taller and freer in August, and some will wait until September, and then be giants. It is not a bad thing for plants to express individualism. Not everyone can be a marigold.

We would further say that it is annual and tender plants that do the most to keep our interest in the garden alive, season after season. They are not mere garnish, the pickled red crab apples beside the turkey that nobody eats. The idea that a garden would consist only of perennials that return faithfully from year to year to year is actually frightening to us. Annuals and tender plants are the growing tip, a chance to experiment and learn, but more important, to play. The very fact that they are not permanent additions to the garden is part of their vitality to us.

All this we would have explained to our visitor, had she had ears to hear it and had chosen to linger long enough over our *B. sutherlandii.*

ARBORVITAE

RECENTLY, we found ourselves committing a crime in broad daylight. We pilfered five cuttings from an arborvitae growing at a rest stop on the New Jersey Turnpike. The plant was an old acquaintance. It wasn't any arborvitae we knew, not the lance-shaped 'Holmstrup' or lustrous 'Green Emerald' and certainly not the elegant old 'Pyramidalis' or winter-black 'Nigra' or fat, serviceable 'Techny'. All are excellent in their way, for there is no such thing as an ugly arborvitae unless it is sick or mistreated. But the specimen that attracted our attention was extraordinary—about five feet high, a dense dark green and breathtakingly healthy, and as conical as an upturned paper watercooler cup. We experienced a lapse in morality and took some of it.

We wonder, though, whether another plant could have so quickly lured us into crime. Probably. And especially if it was the right season to take cuttings and we knew they would root easily. We certainly recall the dubious origins of several boxwoods in the garden, though we swear not one of them was taken from either Mount Vernon or Monticello. In our early years as gardeners we committed worse crimes too, with assorted groundcovers and even greenhouse plants. The morals of young people are often a little loose, and we suspect—actually we know—that the morals of young gardeners are the loosest of all.

Arborvitaes have been special to our garden from its very beginning. In as cold a garden as this, various cultivars of *Thuja occidentalis* are the only dense and narrow evergreen we can count on. The species (hardy from Zones 2 to 8) is native all along the eastern seaboard, but it favors the colder states. If you drive up I-89 through Vermont, at a certain point you will see it growing out of rock outcroppings and forming dense thickets near the edges of ponds. And that is another of its values. For though naturally occurring specimens in thin, rocky soil or with their roots almost in water are never very attractive, they still survive, indicating tolerance to an unusually wide range of cultural conditions. The native eastern arborvitae is a very rugged plant.

This innate toughness also seems to have earned the whole species scorn from people who think of themselves as discerning gardeners, for the rarest forms of eastern arborvitae are as easy to root and grow as the straight species. They all transplant readily, with relatively small burlapped root balls, and unless they are really abused, they settle easily into place—almost any place—and do what they were bought to do. These character-istics have made them both bread-and-butter plants for nurs-erymen and the darlings of developers, who can instantly dress up a raw new house with a pair at each corner and another pair flanking the front steps. Anyone who buys such a house should immediately move those arborvitae to a place where their in-nate nobility can freely develop. And any gardener who con-siders them common is just simply a fool.

There are more wonderful cultivars of *T. occidentalis* than we know, but a handful (sometimes, alas, literally speaking) have been very important in the development of our garden. A loose folded hedge of ten *T. occidentalis* 'Nigra' was planted along the roadside edge of our perennial garden to screen it from view, and over the years they have grown to towering, thirty-foot-high trees, though still branched to the ground. They have eaten the telephone wires along the road that were such an affliction when we started to make our garden. An equally monumental trio forms the defining barrier between the lower lawn and the rock garden, hiding it from view so it seems a complete surprise, as should any special part of any garden. And though we do not think thirty years is such a very long time, all these specimens of *T. occidentalis* 'Nigra' give the garden a sense of permanence and settled age. They are not really black, as the cultivar name seems to indicate, but they do remain a handsome, healthy grass green all winter, avoiding the rusty, yellowish pigmentation that disfigures wild roadside plants.

Early in the garden's history, Eleanor Clarke gave us a rooted cutting of 'Holmstrup', still unaccountably rare in trade though it is perhaps the handsomest of all cultivars of east-ern arborvitae, looking—when it is old and well grown—very like the Italian cypresses in early Renaissance paintings. Over twenty-five years, our original plant has become an elegant twenty-foot-tall spire behind the thyme terrace, where we sit most times in summer when we sit at all. We took cuttings of it when it was about as tall as we are, and they taught us a strange thing. Cuttings taken near the top have grown into equally imposing spires throughout the garden, serving as markers and transition points. But those we took from lower down on our original plant have produced only fat little blobs, cute in their way and very useful, but still blobs. So, unless that is what you want, harvest cuttings from upright growth high on any plant so that the columnar or pyramidal shape for which arborvitaes are mostly valued will occur.

Our love of Wagner's operas first commended 'Rheingold' to us when it was a smug yellow pyramid sitting in a black plastic nursery can. We also treasured its golden foliage— scales really—which kept their clear color summer and winter alike. It is still precious for that, since gold in any form is valuable to a northern garden, always bringing in sunlight, even on days drizzly with rain. What we didn't know was that 'Rheingold', as it develops, forms secondary spires of varying heights, making little landscapes all by itself. That characteristic gave us a clue to the use of other evergreens. We frequently plant single specimens in clumps to form not one spire of growth, but many, in a thicket. It is always a magical effect, like mountains piled in front of one another. And we are not the first to admire it, for Gertrude Jekyll noted in her book *Wood and Garden* that junipers tipped to the ground by storms made similar beautiful thickets, as if many trees had sprouted from one place.

We were very slow to discover *T. plicata*, the western arborvitae. But when we look at it now we wonder what took us so long. You'd of course know it for an arborvitae, from its conical growth and its branches, cinnamon-colored with age and covered with deep green scales when young. Its twigs have the fingered look it shares with its eastern cousin. But it is potentially a much bigger tree than any eastern arborvitae, growing to two hundred feet in the Pacific Northwest where it is native, but closer to thirty feet in the other places it is willing to grow. It also has the miraculous capacity of being deerproof, though the near famine conditions of the eastern American deer herd make us doubt that anything will be that, eventually. We have found it invaluable for its stately, dark presence, which can harmonize outbuildings, mask offensive views, provide logical turnings for paths or terminus points in the garden. Standing as a single specimen on a lawn or against a woodland edge, it is perhaps the most splendid evergreen tree that gardeners in Zones 4 and 5 can grow.

There are other arborvitae throughout the garden. Comfortable, two-foot-tall pillows of *T. occidentalis* 'Woodwardii' are scattered about, and there is a stately single specimen of 'Elegantissima' that provides a full stop to the rose path before the stones turn and become the back woodland walk. It is a broad pyramid about twenty feet tall, and though it is chiefly prized for its delicate pale gold growth in spring, that quickly turns to green with summer's warmth. But the sweet-smelling autumn clematis (*Clematis terniflora*) has threaded its way through to the very top, and in September flows downward in a lacy fragrant cloud. That arborvitae, at least, was bought from Weston Nurseries, and came on the very first truck of plants to arrive here, in 1977. The clematis, on the other hand, was a gift from nature.

We should blush, we suppose, in confessing how many arborvitae came here as pilfered cuttings—dwarf, gold, thread-needled, variegated, or weeping. But we know that all gardeners live in sin. Who among us is free from the Seven Deadly Sins of Pride, Covetousness, Lust, Sloth, Anger, Envy, or Gluttony? It is that last and worst sin, for gardeners, that caused us to pilfer more cuttings of that arborvitae on the New Jersey Turnpike than we really needed. We actually took ten. But if they all root, we can share our excess with other gardeners, thus easing some of the burden on our guilty conscience.

ARTICHOKES

REALLY FRESH FOOD IS BETTER than any other food. Like most people who live and garden in the country, we long ago accepted the strict rule that a large pot of water should be at a rolling boil before you even go out the screen door to pick the corn. It is an absolute truth that the shorter the interval between harvest and cooking, the better the corn will taste. We have found that's just as true for other things—for beans and carrots, spinach, and certainly for peas. And, usually, the difference between vegetables harvested straight from the garden just before they are cooked and those bought from markets is revelatory. Why should that not be true of artichokes as well?

For many years, we didn't have an opportunity to judge. The artichokes in supermarkets grow principally in California and are tender perennials. Their immature flower buds are harvested in winter, after the plants have spent a long, mild growing season bathed by fog off the Pacific Ocean. None of that promised much success to the home gardener in Vermont. But one September noon we were standing in the kitchen of Great Dixter (Northiam, Rye, East Sussex), the home of our friend Christopher Lloyd, when he entered with a trug of freshly picked artichokes. We were astonished he could grow them at all in England, but he answered our surprise with the promise of a greater one when we ate them. "Far better than the store-bought thing. You will see." On food, Christo was never wrong. The artichokes he served us, twenty minutes after picking them, were sweeter, more tender, and more succulent than any we had ever had before.

When you eat something really good—especially a vegetable—you become determined to grow it yourself. Or at least we do. So we did a lot of research and discovered that artichokes could in fact be grown in "northern gardens" (whether that meant Vermont we were not sure) and would flower if one resorted to a few tricks. So we started seed of standard perennial sorts such as 'Green Globe' and 'Violetto' on or around New Year's day, and grew the seedlings under halogen lights in the basement until March, when they were set out in cold frames for six nervous weeks. The idea was to keep them as chilly as possible without freezing them outright, so we were constantly opening and closing the frames, sometimes shading them on warm sunny days and, on really cold nights, bustling them into the greenhouse. The whole point of this drill was to convince the little plants they were experiencing a California winter, so that when we set them out in garden rows in June they would believe they were a year older than they actually were, and would decide to set bud. We wouldn't have minded all this bother if the system had worked. It didn't. Artichokes are no fools.

Though botanically artichokes are miles away from broccoli and cauliflower, it is the immature flower buds of them all that you eat. But artichokes are true perennials, which means they really need a full year of vegetative growth before they flower. But then, luckily, some clever breeder developed 'Imperial Star', a variety that somehow bypasses an artichoke's genetic code, to flower in its first season. That season must still be a long one, however, so the seed should be sown quite early— in late February at the latest—and the young plants grown under cool greenhouse conditions until the end of May, when the weather settles and it is safe to plant them outside. Bud set is not abundant, but there will always be one large artichoke on a single central stem, and frequently two or three much smaller ones will form from side buds, candelabra fashion. Those are delightful to harvest young and eat whole, boiled until tender and then marinated in oil and vinegar or, for a brighter taste, lemon juice, as Greek cooks do. Memories of one's first thrilling experience with anything can of course be deceiving, but still we'd have to say that the flavor of our 'Imperial Star' is not so fine as a fresh-picked 'Gros Camus de Bretagne' at Great Dixter. Still, the 'Imperial Star' is as fine an artichoke as can be eaten straight out of the garden in Vermont, which is to say, finer than any supermarket specimen. A finer one may someday come along, and we will be alert for it.

Artichokes are great fun to eat, since they must be deconstructed leaf by leaf in pursuit of the best bits, which lie hidden in the heart. If the artichoke is not aged and wisened, a good length of the stem is also edible, and one begins there, in a sort of prelude. Then each leaf is torn away and pulled through the teeth to extract the tender flesh at its base. The closer to the center, the more of what is tender clings. That is satisfaction enough, though you can also do something artful with the spent leaves, arranging them in swirls and full-blown roses and other patterns, rather than just tossing them into a heap in a bowl. This can be done separately by each person at the table, in a kind of competition, or it can be a group activity. Either way, the whole process of eating an artichoke is about as refined as finger painting—a sort of play—and that makes artichokes delightful to children who may scorn spinach or broccoli because they are green. The intensifying sensation is quite wonderful as you work along, especially when you are able to pull the most hidden petals out in a clump and eat them together, and then separate the hairy "choke," the heart of the flower, from the cup-shaped base, which is pure delight.

There is great controversy about what to serve with an artichoke by way of sauce, since something is always needed. At Great Dixter, a bowl of warm melted butter was offered, into which each petal was dipped before the meat was extracted. There's much to say for this, especially if the artichoke itself comes to the table quite warm. And as eating artichokes is, after all, an indulgence, why not go all the way? However, at our table we favor a light vinaigrette, made simply of good condiment-quality olive oil and a little balsamic vinegar, the dark, smoky taste of which seems to compliment the metallic richness of the artichoke itself. One thing is certain: wine is not to be served in any form, for the interaction between it and an artichoke will make you think you are eating a tenderized tin can. A glass of pure, clear water is all you should have, and maybe a little bread.

Artichokes are members of the vast Asteraceae, or daisy,

family, the second largest on earth (Orchidaceae is the largest), so vast that its more than twenty thousand species are divided into "tribes," twelve of which are acknowledged, though some botanists insist on a thirteenth. Artichokes, botanically speaking *Cynara scolymus*, belong to the Carduus tribe—the thistles—which includes at least one other edible plant, the cardoon (*C. cardunculus*), and a great many noxious weeds. All thistles, looked at carefully, are beautifully crafted plants, and artichokes are certainly no exception. Whether one gets an edible bud or not, the leaves are still wonderful, formed into a silvery-gray fountain that lacks only a smooth marble shaft to look like the stylized capitals on Corinthian columns. Though many vegetables are beautiful plants, to us, despite the persuasive arguments of our good friend Rosalind Creasy (*Cooking from the Garden*), a cabbage or a lettuce, however beautiful it may be, looks a little startling in a perennial border. Artichokes, however, seem perfectly at home there, their large, dramatic leaves providing striking accents to the finer, more fiddly growth of most perennials.

If you grow them there, and they form buds, you face a difficult choice. Those buds either can be thrown into the pot and boiled until just tender for succulent delight, or they can be left to develop as an ornament to the garden. If you restrain your culinary hand, the completely recognizable artichoke bud will eventually open into a rich violet thistle, perhaps six inches across, surrounded at its base by a ruff of the pointed green "petals" you could have eaten. It is quite pretty, and flower arrangers seek it at that point to use fresh in large arrangements and because it dries perfectly into a fine russet-and-ivory flower. We have seen beautiful wreaths of them, in California, where they are plentiful enough for that extravagance.

It is a difficult choice. Make up your mind about it early on, because if you waver, the choice will be made for you, and you will get either a very tough artichoke or a very pretty flower. We ourselves would fill a large pot with liberally salted water, bring it to a brisk rolling boil, and then go out with our secateurs.

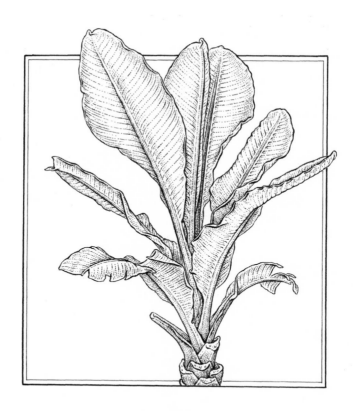

BANANAS

Improbability is not a quality we value in landscapes. Ponds on top of hills with little waterfalls gushing into them, however well constructed, simply look odd and out-of-place. Those tumped-over whiskey barrels spilling forth stunted marigolds shout just the opposite of their intent, painful contrivance rather than accidental abundance. Nothing can be said in defense of red bark mulch, which surely is as poisonous to the touch as it is to the eye. And flower beds made inside old iron bedsteads are simply a joke told too often.

No garden is a natural thing, of course, and people who garden as a way of getting in touch with Nature are actually only getting in touch with fantasy. Gardens are, by definition, contrived. Still, contrivance is one thing, and improbability is quite another. Improbability occurs when a plant or an effect is so alien to its surroundings that a willing suspension of disbelief still doesn't make us feel it fits. If the most precious of all garden qualities is harmony, improbability is bound to fracture it. And one knows what it is when one mutters, "What the hell is that thing *doing* there!"

So, though we love them hugely, we have to wonder what two banana trees are doing in our garden. The garden is after all in southern Vermont, many hundreds of miles from any place where a banana would actually be comfortable. Or rather, comfortable all the year, for our two trees certainly present a thriving appearance during the period they inhabit the garden, roughly from the first week of June until the last week of September. For the rest of the year, they miserably inhabit a rented plastic tube house as truncated logs, occasionally throwing a single, wan banner of leaf.

Bananas are a miracle of construction. Their most beautiful feature, their great sails of leaf, produce a wide-spreading palm that collects rainfall and funnels it into the heart of the plant, so the root zone need not quest very far in search of moisture. Each leaf actually originates at ground level, creating a pseudostem, which seems like a tree trunk—and is as sturdy as one—but is made up of many stem layers that produce tremendous tensile strength. Further, if you cut into one of the stems, you will find that it is not solid, but constructed of honeycombed tissue, offering even further strength. That is a necessary attribute in the places bananas are native, which is chiefly Southeast Asia, where they are often lashed by intense tropical storms. In such conditions, the great leaves will shred, reducing vulnerability to toppling wind, though in most

American gardens the leaves stay intact, as two down-sweeping, ribbed wings originating from a central spine.

Technically, all bananas are evergreen clumping perennials, producing offsets at their bases, either when the mother "tree" is cut down or, more likely, when she flowers, produces fruit, and dies. Though that death is dramatic—as it is for agaves, for example, which flower only after twenty or more years of growth—it is not so different from the behavior of any border perennial. In northern gardens, the fruit that causes this demise will never be produced, and so our plants simply pass from year to year, perhaps in maternal dreams that never will materialize.

Some of that dreaming has to occur in the depths of winter, when our plants are shipped off as cumbersome potted logs. Digging them is a hard day's work, and we try to put it off as long as possible. Often, they still look quite fine by the end of September, and like the grasshopper in the fable, we ourselves are still floating around, enjoying the garden. But we pay more anxious attention to weather forecasts, and we watch the indoor-outdoor thermometers more carefully. At some point, we always know that it is time to dig the bananas. We always hope we get enough notice.

The very structure of bananas assists us in saving ours, because for so large a plant, a banana hasn't got much root. Its funneling leaves and stems provide it with moisture, and possibly with nutrients (bat droppings? dead night moths? We could hardly guess). So a "tree" as tall as ten feet need only have a storage root ball the size of a bushel basket. It is a comfortable fit.

If frost has not already wizened the great leaves, the hardest part of this process is severing them. But each year we think we might have a happier solution, by wrapping thick chunks of cod in the leaves after marinating the fish in garlic and oil and ginger, and steaming them over an open fire. Somehow, there is never enough time.

But come spring, there'll be a wan leaf or two, extending out of the sheaf of truncated leaves. They won't make it into the spring air, and so should be chopped off as well, before the plants are reestablished in the garden, and offer a second chance to that steamed cod idea. The trees will then greet the new growing year pretty much as they departed from the ending one. That is the chain on which all gardening is strung.

And it offers an answer to the question with which this essay began. Why grow bananas? Especially, why grow them in southern Vermont, so far from where they could reasonably be expected to look appropriate? The first answer is . . . simply because we can. And the second is because bananas can make a contribution to the beauty of a garden, though not if they are used randomly, here and there—promiscuously, like marigolds. We have found that they look best not in the borders themselves but in outer places, under the window where guests can sleep above the lower greenhouse and be shushed by their leaves, or improbably, across the stone path from the calf stall, where we administer bottled rations of real milk for his short life.

This is the point. Tropical accent plants of any kind— whether bananas, cannas, hedychiums, or any other—are best associated with domestic buildings and with domestic activities, be it a swimming pool, an outbuilding, or even an animal stall. In that way, they will seem part of human contrivance on the land, pass-downs and pass-alongs, rather than something merely plunked down for showy effect.

THE BAY TREE

Ask a small child to draw you a picture of a tree, and chances are pretty good that you will get a brown trunk as straight as a broomstick, surmounted by a green blob as round as a childish hand can make it. Refrigerator doors without number have been ornamented by such drawings. As children, we probably made some ourselves. But the most interesting thing about this original idea of a tree is that it remains in the minds of gardeners, though as they become more sophisticated, they learn to call them "standards."

Almost any shrub that forms a woody stem can be made into a standard. The great contemporary master of this art was most certainly Allen C. Haskell, who died in 2004, but whose nursery in New Bedford, Massachusetts, was for over fifty years a place all good gardeners visited. In his years as a nurseryman, there was almost no woody plant that Allen hadn't run up into a standard. We remember plastic tube houses filled with rows of diminutive thymes and rosemaries, fuchsias, pelargoniums, coleus, tender azaleas and camellias, myrtles and bays. Once, one of us noticed a large potted bush of *Osmanthus fragrans*, the wonderful Sweet Olive of Deep South gardens, which scents the air in winter with its tiny white flowers. "Have you ever made a standard of that?" we asked. "No . . . but I will, the minute you are out the door!" was Allen's reply.

Standards became the signature of Allen's nursery, and if you saw a perfect little myrtle tree ornamenting an expensive room in a popular shelter magazine, that plant almost certainly originated in Allen's nursery. It would be straight of trunk and surmounted by a green globe of leaves, shaped as round as a baseball, and always in a fine, mossy clay pot. Thousands and thousands were shipped from his greenhouses each year, and every one was perfect. But in fact, the nursery was also always the best place to go for any wonderful plant, hardy or tender, and also to see the most imaginative use of them in the garden surrounding the nursery that was kept to the highest pitch of perfection. A family of rare miniature chickens was apt to cross the antique Belgian block path before you, or the scream of a peacock might startle you while you contemplated the ivory-berried form of *Ilex verticillata* 'Ivorine'. All this was the more extraordinary because Allen C. Haskell & Son is buried in a modest, shabby (and we were told, crime-ridden) section of New Bedford, on Shawmut Avenue.

It was from Allen that we bought our standard bay tree,

which we have owned and tended for twenty years and, there-fore, for which we take much credit. Still, he gave us a great start, and once (on pain of total excommunication from his good graces if we repeated the information) he explained the trick by which so many other standard bay trees he sold were made. As Allen is gone, we feel we can now share it. But we confess that we do so with a bit of trepidation, for though Allen was a good friend to us for over thirty years, we knew, like all his good friends, that his angers were not to be taken lightly.

Bay trees (*Laurus nobilis*) are easy to root from the current year's mature growth, but typically they will want to grow at first in irregular ways and not as the perfectly straight trunk you want for a standard. So, after the first year of growth, Allen cut down the young bush to about an inch above the ground. Almost inevitably a single, straight shoot would then emerge, and it could be trained upward to make a trunk of whatever height before stopping it by a pinch at the top. That first flexible stem could also be trained into a corkscrew, and Allen had a system for this also, though we paid no attention because the form seems excessively baroque to us, a violation of the dignity a bay tree ought to possess.

But about the height of the trunk Allen was very particu-lar, and so are we. Potted bay trees will be stood on a terrace or other outdoor garden room in summer, where they will con-tribute a wonderfully suave note of formality. If they loom too high, however, they seem ungainly. And if they are too squat, most of their elegant dignity is forfeited. The best height (al-ways including the pot itself) seems to be about the height of an average man, around six feet and perhaps an inch or two taller. So the trunk should be allowed to develop to about forty-two inches, and then pinched to induce branching. Eventually the head should be in proportion to the pot, not more than half again its diameter, for if it is larger, there is an unsettling, top-heavy look, such as might be seen on the terraces of Roman aristocrats, who did not grow their bay trees, but inherited them.

The pot in which our tree has grown for all its life with us measures nineteen inches in diameter and is only fourteen inches high. Those are unusual dimensions for a clay pot, but they offer a squat, stolid effect that nicely anchors the tree to the ground. Nevertheless, a six-foot-tall standard bay tree is a sail in any summer wind, crashing to the ground and possibly fracturing its pot. To prevent this, a four-foot length of rebar (concrete reinforcing rod) is hammered firmly into the ground, extending above just to the rim of the pot. Fence wire is then tied to it and looped around the pot just below its rim. The wire and the rebar rust quickly, creating much more a sense of good garden care than of hysterical remedy. We use this system for any plant stood outside that is likely to blow over. Since these are large plants, generally, they are positioned at the edges or corners of terraces, where the rebar can be unobtrusively driven in.

Developing a standard bay tree isn't of course a quick process. It takes at least four years to create a trunk and an acceptable branched head. But after that process is complete, one owns a treasure that only gets more beautiful with the years. Still, those years must be of careful tending, as with any fine thing. Watering must be faithful, for though bay trees are native to the dry Mediterranean shores, their questing roots run deep in search of summer moisture. In a pot, they will be entirely dependent on the gardener, and the older they get, the more this will be true. An old tree will have very dense roots and an extensive canopy of leaves that transpire moisture. As with bonsai (which an old bay tree resembles, in essence if not in appearance), two or three days in hot sun with no water may be fatal.

Careful fertilizing is also crucial, for you will hopefully end up with a rather massive plant in a proportionately small pot. During winter, no fertilizer is required. But at the turn of the year, just as spring growth begins to emerge, liquid fertilizer should be applied weekly, at half the strength recommended on the package.

Bay standards also require pruning, of two sorts, neither of which can be neglected if the tree is to remain shapely and ornamental. Top pruning is done during winter and consists of shortening last year's growth to within an inch or two of the point of emergence from the previous year's growth. The work can be done bit by bit over the whole winter, thus providing fresh bay leaves for stews, soups, and braises. (Use about twice as many fresh leaves as dry, for the strength is weaker, but the flavor is incomparably more delicate.) All pruning should be completed by late March, and if your tree begins to show pale green buds, pruning should be hurried to completion, and the extra clippings given away to friends.

The second form of pruning required by all standards is root pruning. Many gardeners find that hard, for though they seem to have no trouble taking a good chop at over-vigorous top growth, they are nervous about messing with the roots. Still, it is a necessity because one cannot keep moving any plant into bigger and bigger pots forever. There's a limit somewhere, if only for portability.

Root pruning is a technique well known to masters of the art of bonsai, and venerable four-hundred-year-old trees that enjoy the status of being Japanese cultural treasures annually survive it. It must always be done when the tree is still fully asleep but just approaching its flush of spring growth. The plant is removed from its pot, and the earth is gently teased from its roots, using a chopstick or some other sharp implement in a sort of scraping-clawing motion. Only about two or three inches of old soil need be removed, leaving roots dangling in wisps and hairs all around the root mass. Those are clipped cleanly away against the remaining soil, using scissors or sharp secateurs. As much as four inches may be sliced from the base of the root mass. Then the tree is repotted, with a layer of fresh potting compost placed over the crocking at the bottom, and additional compost forced down the two- to three-inch gap left on all sides. Eliminating air pockets is essential, and the end of a wooden kitchen spoon is best for that. It is satisfying work, once you get your courage up.

For most American gardeners, the greatest problem posed by a standard bay tree will not be in its care, pruning, or repotting, but in where to keep it over the winter. *Laurus nobilis* is reliably hardy from Zones 8 to 10, which means that when winter temperatures reach a low of around 20 degrees, it begins to suffer. If the trees are potted, they are dead, since the roots of a potted plant will reach the temperature of the ambient air, freezing long before roots in the ground experience even a chill. So throughout most of North America, winter quarters must be found. Ideally, bay trees want to experience a cool, moist winter, with nighttime temperatures hovering around 50 degrees and daytime ones about 10 degrees higher. Frequent drenching of the foliage keeps leaves green and shiny, whereas dry air tends to crisp them. These are not, obviously, the conditions in the average American living room, and so bay trees, for all their old-world elegance, will never take the place of a potted ficus tree.

Sometimes houses are lucky enough to have a sunporch

kept just above freezing, or a bright hallway or seldom-used guest room, where a bay tree—and perhaps other wonderful things—can settle down for a long winter's sleep. (Gardeners who have such guest rooms do not have guests, any more than they park their cars in the garage.) Failing any of these possibilities, however, our only and best advice is to build a greenhouse, or better, a winter garden or cool conservatory attached to the house. But do not think of it as a place to read books in shirtsleeves or serve lunch to friends and sip a convivial glass of white wine. If such a place does not require you to wear one or two sweaters in the dead of winter, you have simply built yourself another sort of living room, just the right place for another ficus tree.

We know we run the risk of sounding smug, but our bay tree, now with a smooth, iron-gray trunk measuring nine inches in circumference, has the perfect place to spend the winter. It sits just to the left of the three steps leading down to the winter garden and just across the stone path from the *Camellia sasanqua* 'Yuletide' that produces three-inch-wide cherry-red flowers all winter long. In spring, when all danger of frost is past, it is muscled out the French door, through the kitchen, and onto a corner of our planted terrace, where it serves as a marker post, defining the entranceway to the back garden.

There is something deeply satisfying about a long association with any plant and particularly with a portable one in a pot. Our bay tree is both one of the oldest plants we grow in a pot and the oldest one historically grown by western gardeners. As with several other plants that may be sheared into imaginative shapes, such as box and myrtle, its cultivation extends at least to Egyptian gardens in 4000 B.C. Roman gardeners loved it, for it offered just the sort of architectural dignity they believed was gardening at its best. In the Middle Ages, when utility was a necessary excuse for any plant otherwise grown for pure pleasure, its leaves had many culinary uses, and tinctures of its leaves and bark were employed to treat aching joints. Where it was not hardy, it was always among the collections of eighteenth-century orangeries, for it takes extremely well to tub culture, and it withstands severe clipping indefinitely. And—as any eighth-grade French schoolgirl knows—its leaves are obligatory in many dishes and always best when harvested fresh. So our bay tree has many claims on our attention. We do not neglect any of them.

BERBERIS

EXCEPT FOR THE FOREST TREES, the oldest plant in our garden is a single specimen of *Berberis vulgaris*, the common barberry. It stands at the back of the property, marking the point at which a fieldstone path makes a turn before leading to the stream and beyond. Though it has stood in full sun for almost thirty years now, it grew in the shade of large old maples and beeches when we came here. They had to be felled to form our back lawn, leaving only a fringe of them to mark the boundary between our garden and the neighboring hay field. Maybe because it has passed most of its life in shade—or maybe simply because it is very old—the barberry has grown to about seven feet tall, forming a congested, fountainlike bush of many corky gray stems. It isn't a comfortable plant to be near, because those stems are armed with hard little brown spines that can get deep into your fingers like splinters from rough old wood. So it is kept trimmed well away from the path and that is a process that never fails to startle us, because the inside of each stem is a beautiful canary yellow, unlike the pith of any other shrub we know.

The plant itself is not very beautiful. In fact, it could fairly be called homely. And anywhere in the rural parts of North America, barberry has a very bad reputation. Cattlemen and dairy farmers hate it, because it forms dense wiry mounds in pastures, too spiny for cows to nibble. In wheat country it is the alternate host to wheat rust, so if a barberry bush is growing near a wheat field, dull red streaks will show up on the leaf blades of plants growing nearest it, and then spread relent- lessly through the whole field in a sort of russet wave. And hunters moving through the edges of woods curse it for its sometimes impenetrable growth and wicked spines.

We half believe that we spared this particular plant because its species is so unloved. In us, that same quixotic impulse ex- tends to other hated plants, to Japanese knotweed (*Polygonum cuspidatum*), for example, which we grow in a beautiful varie- gated form we rescued from Beth Chatto's compost heap. Or simple plantains, amiable weeds that nestle at the Virgin's feet in paintings of the Annunciation to indicate her great humility. But this one barberry was also in a perfect place, offering the perfect reason for the necessary turn of the path. Also, it must have been well over fifty years old when we came, making it now eighty. That alone seemed to give it a claim. Besides, we just didn't have any other big bush then.

Like so many other plants that have come to impinge in

unpleasant ways on humans, *B. vulgaris* has had a very interesting history. The genus name carries an exotic sound, suggesting lurching camels and priceless rugs, so it is no surprise
that it is based on an ancient Arabic word for a shell, describ-
ing the small cupped leaves of most species. A native of eastern
Europe, *B. vulgaris* was widely cultivated from the Middle
Ages until well into the nineteenth century for a host of purposes. Until the discovery of synthetic dyes, stabilized infusions
of its dried inner bark yielded a fine yellow for tinting linens
and leather. All parts of the plant have been employed medicinally for the treatment of many internal diseases—for sore
throats, reduction of fever, and even the curing of gum diseases. Infusions of its fruit were especially valued for treatment
of illnesses of the liver, explaining one of its popular names,
jaundice berry. Its highly acidic fruit, consisting of numerous
and persistent pea-sized elongated bright red berries too sour
for birds to eat, can be boiled with equal parts of sugar to make
a clear, brilliant red jelly.

Chiefly for this reason, barberries were valuable plants to
early North American colonists, providing a condiment rich in
vitamin C that was also helpful in digesting fatty meats and often useful in concealing less than fresh flavors. The plant also
grows well in dry, rocky ground without much attention, and
so would thrive at the edges of gardens hard-won from stony
forest soils. The first barberries therefore entered North America as agricultural and therapeutic plants, and have managed
to stick around ever since. So every despised plant in fields,
hedgerows, and ditches could trace its lineage back to some
early New England dooryard garden. We once mentioned all
this lore to a dear old friend—a many-generations-back Vermonter who had paused scornfully before our barberry—and
she replied, "Well, in those days they had to eat just about anything they could find."

We have only this one bush of *B. vulgaris*, but there are many other berberis in the garden. Zone 6 is pretty much the cut-off point for the most elegant members in the family, the beautiful evergreen forms such as *B. wilsoniae*, *B. julianae*, or *B. ×stenophylla*. But *B. thunbergii* thrives here in many forms, all of them hardy to Zone 4 at least. First discovered in western China by Carl Peter Thunberg (1743–1828), the green-leaved species has produced a swarm of beautiful progeny, all of which are very valuable garden plants. The burgundy-leaved form, *atropurpurea*, grows to about five feet tall and is effective as a contrast to the antique roses. Its pygmy form, 'Atropurpurea Nana' (often called 'Crimson Pygmy'), is planted at regular intervals in our perennial garden, where its dense mounds of growth to two feet tall and its brooding, purple leaves make everything around it look prettier. On the woodland walk there are three specimens of *B. thunbergii* 'Aurea', with bright gold leaves that introduce sunshine to that area even when no sun is shining. Several years ago we were given a single specimen of 'Helmond Pillar' by Dan Hinkley, with red leaves and amazingly upright growth. It is now about four feet tall but less than a foot wide, and is wonderful as a vertical marker at the beginning of a secondary path in the rhododendron garden. But our favorite among selections of *B. thunbergii* may well be 'Rose Glow', with new foliage splashed pink and cream and then fading as it ages to red. A low hedge of it runs along the foundation of the winter garden, providing a fascinating backdrop to the vivid annuals grown there in summer. *Salvia horminum* in the clear blue form called 'Cambridge Blue' looks particularly fine in front of it, but so has *Cuphea lanceolata*, with scarlet, purple-centered flowers that look like the face of a tiny bat, or perhaps Mickey Mouse.

Sometimes we have a fantasy that eventually the forests will reclaim our garden, beginning perhaps at the far edges.

One by one the outlying sections of it will have to be abandoned, and the forest that we disturbed when we came here will steadily move forward. Some catastrophe may even eliminate the house itself, and then there would be no reason why the encroaching woods should not come up to its very foundations. All this may happen, for gardens are fragile things created out of the will and the energy of their makers, and domestic gardens such as ours, with no great house at its center, are not the kind that get preserved by organizations like the Garden Conservancy. But this image of eventual reclamation does not distress us, and we are amused to think that certain sturdy things—lilacs, vinca minor, and our *B. vulgaris*—will be here long after everything else has vanished. It was here before us, and if barberries can laugh, it may well have the last one.

BIENNIALS

Gardeners quickly learn that the neat divisions of the plant world into trees, shrubs, sub-shrubs, perennials, and annuals is far tidier than it is accurate. So much depends on where one lives. For shrubs can grow into small trees, perennials can be annuals, shrubs can be perennials, and "annuals" can be almost anything that is planted for one season with the expectation that it will not return the following spring. Nowhere is this classification more confusing than with biennials. Technically, they are all plants that require two full seasons to mature, building up reserves of leaf and root for the first one and flowering the second. But some, if encouraged by good culture and deadheaded promptly to prevent seed production, can slide into the fuzzy category of "weakly perennial," returning for at least a second season of bloom, and possibly a third, though it is seldom as strong as the first. Others, if started early and bred to do it, can function essentially as true annuals, flowering the first season from a late winter or very early spring sowing. Then there are some, such as clary sage (*Salvia sclarea*) or Canterbury bells (*Campanula medium*), that may actually be "triennials," producing strong rosettes of basal growth for two years and then flowering magnificently the third. And where, precisely, one puts those plants that may take scores of years to get their vegetable feet beneath them before soaring into bloom, like agaves or bamboos, depends a bit on one's expected life span, though botanically speaking, they are "monocarpic," meaning that after they flower and produce seed they die, even at a very great age. This much is certain, however, though novice gardeners sometimes suppose it: biennials are not plants that flower every other year.

Within the group of plants classed as biennial are some of the most treasured in gardens, not for their rarity, certainly, but for their homely, simple charm. Usually, they are considered "cottage flowers," and their ranks include hollyhocks, forget-me-nots, dame's rocket, sweet william, Saint Barbara's weed, and foxgloves. Like all cottage flowers, they seem to carry resonances far beyond their individual beauty, suggesting fine June country mornings with casement windows flung open to bright sun and the sound of bees at work. Somewhere near them there will always be an old, well-waxed table spread with good, fresh things, and the chance to linger in the garden, to work perhaps, or just to sit and stare. These flowers' very names are redolent of antique association, and even the most snobbishly Latinate of gardeners would think something was lost if they were called, respectively, *Alcea rosea*, *Myosotis sylvatica*, *Hesperis matrionalis*, *Dianthus barbatus*, *Barbarea vulgaris*, or *Digitalis purpurea*.

Despite the tug at the heart exercised by many biennial plants, they are seldom seen in gardens in all the perfection they can achieve, for several reasons. First, many gardeners are enamored of permanence, accepting the false assumption that you can buy a perennial and put it in the ground and expect years of beauty with little effort. "Aunt Alice had this beautiful patch of bearded iris and it bloomed every year. She didn't do a *thing* to it!" Well, perhaps, though Aunt Alice may have been a better gardener than she ever let on. Very few perennials will flourish indefinitely without appropriate seasonal attention, and the very few there are, such as peonies and . . . well, peonies . . . hardly make up a garden, or the excitement that may be had from it. One must go to the trouble, if indeed "trouble" is the right word, of overseeing the growth of plants and bringing them into flourishing leaf and stem long before one sees any blossoms at all. Biennial plants may thus be a sort of benchmark of committed gardeners, who will have ceased to think of plants, in Russell Page's telling phrase, as "so much flowering hay." They will ask you to admire the pale, gray-green rosettes of a lusty juvenile foxglove, or a swarm of thick-clumped, paddle-leaved forget-me-nots, a mere green carpet beneath the shrubbery, and they will say, "*Think* how fine they will be . . . next June!"

The pleasures of anticipation always depend on careful planning, and with biennials, that may be the big problem. Most biennials require twice the effort asked by any annual plant, but they are no more permanent as additions to the garden. Many annuals—not always the nicest—can be expected, marigold-fashion, to give two or even three months of nonstop bloom. Few biennials will flower over so long a period, and then they will die ungracefully, either ripening seed the gardener hopes to save for another flowering (two years hence) or simply needing to be cleared off. Either way, their shabby post-bloom occupancy in the garden or the bare patch they leave behind—usually in high summer when things need to look their best—can amount to a sort of garden hangover, causing one to feel one bought their pleasure at too dear a price. If their great beauty, and beyond that the resonances they carry of Grandmother's garden (or even of a fanciful grandmother's garden remembered only from the childhood books illustrated by Tasha Tudor), did not justify the effort they require, then certainly biennials would be grown only by cranky, obsessive gardeners who also cultivate rock gardens and maintain a greenhouse full of species orchids.

Probably the best biennials will always grow in very large old country gardens that are not given to much tidying up. In them, seven-foot-tall hollyhocks might grow against the weathered siding of a barn, showing saucers of pale pink or peach or cherry red or even black-red, so beautiful that one hardly notices their shabby leaves encrusted with rust disease, to which all forms of *Alcea rosea* are so sadly prone. (*Alcea ficifolia* and *A. pallida*, though not so varied in the color of their flowers, are rust-resistant.) Rust and the attendant defoliation, leaving bare shanks behind, is somehow acceptable in the high grass out by the barn, though not in the garden, up close. Dame's rocket can make its gentle way at the edges of woods or in partly shaded ditches, competing with weeds and making them glorious in mid-June, with three-foot-tall branched candelabra of little, four-petaled flowers in beautiful shades of purple, pink, and white, blended together like the colors of an old, much-bleached housedress. The smell is better even than that of fresh laundry, a rich, spicy, powdery sweetness elusive to Chanel or any other parfumier.

Forget-me-nots will colonize almost anywhere that is not overly worked, as, for example, under old shrubs or in flower borders where a reasonable amount of ground is kept clear by light cultivation. Even as infant plants they are cute, with down-facing, fuzzy green mouse ears, and with thick clusters of buds by late April or early May. Their limpid blue flowers throughout early summer justify their popular name, for seeing them, who ever could forget them? Pink-flowered ones and pure white ones occasionally show up in old gardens, and we have thought that the white one particularly ought to be isolated to come true from seed, to have its fresh icy coolness in a patch of ferns. But we, like so many gardeners, have a strong preference for any flower that is blue, particularly so limpid and winsome a blue as forget-me-nots. Even there, however, we have noticed that there are blues and there are blues. On our acid soil, flowers are the color of a pale June sky, though on more alkaline soils, they approach a deep cerulean blue. Either way they are lovely, particularly as each flower, of whatever tint, is set off by a golden eye. We are also not the first to notice that forget-me-nots are indicators of soil conditions, for when they are pale, more lime is asked for, and when they are rich blue, acid-loving shrubs will need some help. If ever the leaves are pink or purple in early spring, then there are serious problems, either of drainage or of trace elements all plants need to grow well. Old gardeners considered forget-me-nots to be as much instruments that measure the health of a garden as flowers, and old gardeners were seldom wrong.

Among biennial plants, foxgloves probably are the reigning queen, not just for the cunning shape of each individual flower, which simply asks for an index finger to be stuck in it, but more for the great vertical rods of bloom, a shape always precious in any garden where so much is flat or rounded. In the genus *Digitalis*, to which all foxgloves belong, there are many wonderful garden plants, almost all of which waver uncertainly between being biennial and being weakly perennial. But the most loved is certainly *D. purpurea*. It is native to much of central and northern Europe, but it has in some sense been appropriated by the English, in whose woods and gardens it flourishes. In its native form, it produces three-foot-tall, slightly bowed spires that are thickly hung with deep pink bells all on one side of the stem. Many English gardeners are sentimental about their wildflowers, and they will tell you that is the only true foxglove, though in fact there are better garden forms, all of which have more than a tincture of American blood in them. Half a century ago, a single plant was discovered in this country bearing pure white flowers on spires taller by about a foot than the wild form, with larger bells, somewhat more out-flaring, but most significantly, arranged all around its perfectly straight stem. It became the parent of the 'Excelsior' strain, which produces elegant, four-foot spires in early summer (five in good culture) in an unpredictable but always lovely range of shades from soft pink to white and ivory, the paler shades marked inside with freckles of tan and brown. Out of it have been bred other beautiful strains, some, like 'Giant Primrose', almost yellow, and the wonderful 'Sutton's Apricot', which is pink faintly warmed by orange.

Though each year we plant a few flats of foxgloves in the shadier parts of the garden, white for preference and probably some descendant of the 'Excelsior' hybrids, many of the foxgloves that bloom here early each summer are self-seeded plants, almost always appearing in places we would have planted foxgloves if we had thought of it. Over many generations some have reverted to the original one-sided form, and we do not find it homelier than the preferred garden varieties.

These and all other familiar biennial plants can be had in abundance in the right kind of garden, or with the right kind of effort. If a garden is large and perhaps a little relaxed around its edges, seed can be sprinkled, or even ripened plants thrown and scattered, to produce a reliable next generation. That is the good old country way, and it unquestionably produces the finest foxgloves, forget-me-nots, Hesperus, and hollyhocks. But such old-fashioned gardens are very far from most suburban plots, which are limited in extent and must—or at least should—be kept tidy at all times of the year. There is nothing particularly untidy or unattractive about a juvenile biennial, though it will not offer what is usually called "flower interest" that first year. One must wait for that, and a lack of space more than a lack of patience can make that rather hard. An easy solution is either to buy young plants in their second year, when they are preparing to flower, or to grow them in that mythical "out of the way place" all gardens are supposed to have, an extra row in the vegetable garden or behind the garage or wherever such very scarce space may be come by.

Foxgloves, forget-me-nots, and even hollyhocks transplant readily if a generous amount of earth is taken with each plant. The conditions under which transplanting of any kind should be done—a dank, cold drizzly day that only a gardener would find optimistic—are particularly important with biennials, which, after all, are intended to settle in where they have sprouted. In transplanting dame's rocket, the weather makes no difference at all, for it cannot be done, even if you get up in drizzly rain in the dead of night. That plant will simply not comply, and so had best be scattered as seed in damp, wooded places in dappled light, and with hope in one's heart. The cheerful part is that once one has succeeded, even with one plant, more are sure to appear.

Beyond all the obvious resonances of biennial plants, the most special one has perhaps become clear. They are as far from tidy, manicured, crisp-edged, freshly wood-chipped suburban gardens as one can possibly get. The values they carry, of ease, of abundance, of lightness of heart and settled history, are equaled perhaps only by distinguished old shade trees and the little bulbs that have seeded everywhere, even in every crack of the pavement. All seem to say, "We have been here a very long time, and we will be here for a while more." In any garden, that is a voice much to be treasured.

BOXWOOD

When we first began the garden we have occupied for thirty years, a boxwood came with us. There are yellowed snapshots of it sitting in its large clay pot in a sea of raw mud, just at the back corner of the house. It is still there, and has been for what startlingly amounts to just about half our whole lives. It may well survive us too, for boxwoods can live a long time. There are individual specimens in England and France, and in Virginia and Maryland, that can only be described as ageless.

Our particular boxwood, however, will need a bit of help. It may even need some sort of trust fund or endowment. But we should really say "they," for there are fifteen, all grown from cuttings of the original plant, which are now as large as their parent. That is to say, about five feet wide and as tall. They are all English boxwoods, *Buxus sempervirens*, and any good general garden reference will tell you that it is reliably hardy "only to Zone 5, with protection." In the beginning of our garden we tended to skip over that hardiness part—for North Hill is located squarely in Zone 4 (or at least used to be), and that seemed to eliminate so many wonderful shrubs and trees. We took our chances.

We are not sorry, for these sixteen boxwoods have never been more than lightly pruned in spring, and they have all grown into magnificent dark green pillows. Three of them, including the parent plant, form a sort of loose barrier or dividing point between a little terrace and the Rose Alley, just on the east side of the house. The others march in a regular rhythm up one side of a path planted with antique roses. They give form to that important section of the garden, for rosebushes, taken even at their best (without black spot and Japanese beetle and mildew and all that), never have much form of their own.

But they ask a lot from us. Specifically, each must be protected in winter by its own huge, clumsy wooden box. Burlap will not do, because it does not offer enough wind protection, and the biggest limit to the hardiness of boxwoods is not cold, but bitter wind and winter sun, both of which desiccate the leaves and twigs at a time when roots locked in frost cannot replace vital moisture. So the advice is often given to locate boxwoods on the north or west side of buildings, where shadows will fall on them all winter long. But that is no place for roses, and we wanted them growing together.

In the beginning, we simply used large crates we knocked together from any odd boards. But now the plants are so huge that we have to construct boxes in place over them, contraptions made of sheets of plywood held together by standard hooks and eyes, the kind on screen doors. It is a lot of work. And as we usually defer it until Thanksgiving, it is work generally undertaken with frozen fingers. But the alternative—to leave them to the mercy of our harsh climate without protection—would surely result in loss of much of the top growth, and even the death of the plants themselves. That is unthinkable.

We used to believe that there was no substitute for English box, but now we know there is. It isn't the much hardier Korean box, *Buxus microphylla* var. *koreana* (now *B. sinica* var. *insularis*), also called "littleleaf box," for we have also had plants of that from the garden's beginning, rooted from a basket of hedge trimmings given to us by a friend. They now form a tidy little hedge around three sides of a small terrace. They are beautiful at all seasons, even when their foliage pigments display a warm golden brown with the arrival of cold weather. Most people object to that, however, and so a form that remains green all winter has been developed, appropriately called 'Wintergreen'. It is also a very fast grower, excellent for low hedges, but its leaves are as small as most Korean box—hardly more than one-third inch wide and long, and so it cannot compare in nobility with true English box, the leaves of which are almost three times as large.

The best alternative to English box is one of the remarkable hybrids developed by Sheridan Nurseries in Ontario, Canada, beginning in the late 1960s. They are all crosses of *B. sempervirens* with the much hardier *B. microphylla*, and all have the word "green" in their name—'Green Gem', 'Green Mound', 'Green Velvet', and 'Green Mountain'. They are all excellent plants, but the first three are mounded and relatively slow-growing, and so are useful for low dividing hedges in parterres and ornamental potagers. The last, 'Green Mountain', is upright and attractively pyramidal, and it grows as rapidly as English box. It is perfect for freestanding specimens or for taller hedges. We have had plants in the garden here in all exposures for ten years without protection, and all have come through that many winters in good condition. That is more than we could say for *B. sempervirens* 'Vardar Valley', collected in a very cold part of Macedonia in 1934 and often praised not only for its hardiness but also for its hazy blue young foliage. Here at least, it has withstood winter cold no better than ordinary English box.

A beautiful boxwood developed at Chicago Botanic Garden in Glencoe, Illinois, sometimes called 'Chicagoland Green' and sometimes *Buxus* ×'Glencoe', has done wonderfully here, never suffering a sign of winter damage. We have three plants from the original test plants sent out years ago, and from small rooted cuttings they have developed into upright, vase-shaped plants each about four feet tall and of great beauty. But their leaves are small, and their growth tends naturally to be in loose, open sprays—wonderful in its way—but not a look-alike for the box we love best. Their wood can also be brittle under heavy snow, so plants are best cinched up by heavy twine in late autumn. That is a good precaution to take with any boxwood left uncovered for winter, for it is heartbreaking, come spring, to find that a perfectly hardy specimen has been split apart by snow or ice.

Over the years, we have grown many other forms of boxwood, some of which have been quite satisfying, and some, duds. *Buxus sempervirens* 'Graham Blandy' captivated us originally by its rigid, upright growth, which in ten years reached a height of about five feet but was no more than eight inches thick. It was a startling vertical accent, and it was also so easy to protect, because burlap in many layers could simply be wound about its slender form. Still, it had an irritating habit of growing skinny side branches that splayed outward, spoiling its one reason for being. When it contracted a bad case of boxwood mite, we did not treat it, but simply chucked it.

All the suavity that a boxwood can bring to the open garden seems increased when it is grown in a pot. Over the years, we have accumulated several potted specimens, trimmed into large globes or pyramids that provide weight when used with groups of potted flowers, and quiet distinction when stood alone. (Since, in winter, all potted boxwoods ask is a cool, frost-free place to sleep, we are apt to accumulate more.) With patience, boxwoods can be trimmed into almost any shape, and so we also have three standards in pots, little mop-headed trees on slender stems. The smallest, now about thirty years old and only a foot and a half tall, is one of the original Korean box rootlings that just seemed to want to grow that way. Almost as old is a much larger standard of *B. sempervirens* 'Vardar Valley', the cultivar that disappointed us so in the open garden. In a beautiful old square terra-cotta pot, standing four feet tall and with a head as round as a basketball, it carries an air of quiet sophistication wherever it stands.

But our favorite of the three is a three-and-a-half-foot-tall standard of *B. sempervirens* 'Elegantissima', with small, oval creamy-white-edged leaves on dense, short twigs. It was given to us twenty years ago as a cutting by the late Marshall Olbrich, co-founder of Western Hills Rare Plant Nursery. It is both beautiful in itself and also a living reminder of a very dear friend. 'Elegantissima' is the tenderest and most fragile of all English boxwood varieties, and so we take especially good care of it, in the hope that we can leave it in our turn to someone else.

CAMELLIAS

IT IS NOT REALLY SURPRISING that Georg Josef Kamel (1661–1706) never saw even a dried herbarium specimen of a camellia. He was a Moravian apothecary, who in our eyes more than doubled the value of his calling as a Jesuit missionary by cataloging the medicinal plants of the Philippines, where he began to botanize in his late twenties. How many souls he may have saved for the Roman Catholic Church has not been recorded, at least on earth. But his brilliant botanical discoveries, sent to his English correspondent John Ray, were published by Ray in 1704, and constitute the first systematic study of the rich flora of the Philippines. They appeared under the Latinized form of his name, as was then customary—*Camellus*—which the great Linnaeus (born a year after Kamel's death) assigned to the genus *Camellia* in tribute to Kamel's work. Linnaeus was always gracious and free-handed with the honors that were his to bestow, and so Kamel's ignorance of camellias matches that of many other distinguished botanists, such as Leonard Fuchs (1501–1566), to whom a living fuchsia would have seemed a miracle.

The genus *Camellia* contains approximately two hundred and fifty species, widely extended from northern India and the Himalayas throughout China and Japan and into Indonesia. They are among the oldest of cultivated plants, not only for tea, evidence of which exists well before the third millennium B.C., but also as a fermented "green food" that could be left in the ground all winter and then prepared with garlic, oil, and dried fish as part of the desperate attempt to fill the hungry gap between autumn's plenty and spring's abundance. The wood of camellia trees is strong, close-grained, and hard, making it suitable for carving into utensils and tools. Venerable, treelike plants also provide an unusually high grade of charcoal, if one can bear to think of them that way. The seeds of camellias, particularly *C. japonica*, produce oil of great medicinal and cosmetic value. In its various species, then, the camellia was so useful that its cultivation has been ensured from most ancient times to the present. And if, as eighteenth-century philosophers argued, beauty follows use, then the camellia is almost without compare among garden flowers, a fact that the earliest Asian literature noted.

Plants, like words in poetry, are both beautiful in themselves and also for the associations they trail behind, the histories they have in the world and in one's own life. Our own history with camellias stretches back over thirty years, when we bought our first four plants in promising bud in early autumn at the old Heimlich's Nursery, in Boston, and brought them back to pot up in Vermont. We bought the pots too, fine honeyed-orange ones that flared from the base to a roll at the top, one of which still remains with us and still holds a camellia, though not any of the original ones. They were the blood-red, anemone-flowered 'Professor Charles S. Sargent', the old informal pink 'Debutante', the formal double 'Alba Plena' of stunning white, and 'Pink Perfection', another formal double with petals that looked as if they had been carved of the clearest inner parts of the shell of some sea mollusk.

Of those first four camellias we grew in Vermont, we would still defend three, leaving out perhaps only the redoubtable 'Debutante', the pink of which has a shade too much blue in it, and the flowers a little too much looseness. We regret not having kept the others, because when a camellia can be made happy it is happy forever, and thirty years is nothing in its life. But we moved on, to other plants, even to other camellias. When, from indifference or some minor unintended failure of theirs (or ours!), they grew poorly, or we simply got greedy for another pretty face and tossed them away, their individual beauty continued to tug at us, long past the grave. 'Pink Perfection' is doing that, though it has been twenty years since we had it in a pot.

The first camellias we grew in the ground at North Hill were part of our general conviction that whatever else our brutal newly adopted climate brought us, we would still have a bit of the mildness of San Francisco here in Vermont, however tiny it had to be. We wanted to step out the side kitchen door into that dewy freshness and flower, even if it was only one step, even though the real world out the front door was howling with sleety ice and bitter cold. So we designed a small winter garden protected by poured cement frost walls and with rich soil open to the living earth. Camellias were important there from the first, planted in the ground with a fine cherry-red leptospermum, a ceanothus pinned to the wall, jasmines of several sorts, tender rhododendrons, and even a *Magnolia grandiflora*, the very compact cultivar called 'Little Gem', because we thought it might be important, in a room hardly fourteen by twenty-four feet, to be thrifty with space.

Most of all that has gone now, as we shifted to new plant interests such as *Daphne bholua*, with its rich floral scent at Christmastime, or the gaunt old wisteria, a huge, ten-foot-tall bonsai in an old clay tub that occupies the coldest corner and will rain fragrant ivory flowers come late winter. But there will always be camellias there, and now some of them would be the envy of any established southern garden.

There's an eight-foot-tall 'Yuletide', a *sasanqua* actually, with bleached-bone trunks and small, inch-long laurel-black leaves in which the flowers nestle, blood red and flattened around a boss of golden stamens. It is the first to bloom, and on a clear November day it smells gently of tea, a reminder that its near relative, *Camellia sinensis* var. *sinensis*, is the source of that ubiquitous beverage. Across from it is a Higo camellia, one of the so-called snow camellias of Japan, anciently cultivated because their relatively low stature, to five feet or so, allowed them to be covered by mountain snow until the mild weather of spring, when they bloom with unusual freedom. All Higo camellias are single, and ours, called 'Yamato-nishiki', is variegated, as the word "nishiki" always indicates, with rich carmine-red stripes staining in random widths its broad, rounded white petals. They begin by cupping a two-inch-wide boss of many stamens of the clearest golden yellow, which loosens into a sort of pillow as the petals flatten to reveal a pea-green eye, actually the fertilized ovules.

Midway down the house and across the fieldstone path

from 'Yamato-nishiki' is a broad, four-foot-tall bush that bears the rather inelegant cultivar name 'Berenice Boddy'. We always did think it would sound better if given a strong French pronunciation (*bay-ray-niece bo-die*), but the lady in question is known, having been the wife of the founder of one of the most remarkable camellia plantings in North America, Descanso Gardens in Los Angeles, where many fine camellias were hybridized. In a good year, Mme Boddy can produce hundreds of flowers from mid-September until the end of February. They are technically semi-double, which means that three rows of petals will overlap to produce a somewhat cup-shaped flower. They are of clear, luminous pink, the special quality given by washes of deep and light pink over a white, crinkled base.

The only other camellia in the winter garden is 'Katie', a very tall-growing upright variety that has now achieved ten feet in the highest far corner of the lean-to structure, and produces its flowers, visible from the open window over the sink, quite late for a camellia, usually not until February. They are formal doubles, with many petals laid in alternating layers to create a flattened, perfectly crafted flower that most people would imagine the ailing heroine of Dumas's play *La Dame aux Camellias* to have worn. Poor 'Katie' has an almost embarrassing vigor, however, and must receive a severe annual pruning just after flowering to keep her from bursting through the roof into a world she would not find to her liking. But flowers are abundant as a result, and of a pretty bright pink, perhaps with a shade more blue in them than should be, without which 'Katie' would be put into real competition with our still-mourned 'Pink Perfection' (and to accommodate which, she may soon be shouldered aside).

Four mature camellia plants are hardly enough for a long winter, even if they are joined later by tender rhododendrons and azaleas, orchids, fragrant daphnes, jasmines, and wisteria, with the quiet comfort of our venerable standard bay tree and several old standard tubbed boxwoods tucked along the path. So we found we were acquiring new camellias, grown in pots that found winter lodgings sometimes in the winter garden, sometimes in the lower greenhouse, and once (with disastrous results, for camellias hate house temperatures maintained for the comfort of humans) in what we thought was a rather cold spot in front of the living room French doors. When we had acquired ten or so fine bushy plants in fifteen-inch clay pots, and come to love their extra flowers, always in the darkest time of our year, we realized that we had a collection—a passion, actually—that required attention. This happens often, and we have learned over the years not to ignore the signs. For that is where joy lies.

Finding a suitable place to over-winter a rather large collection of potted camellias turned out not to be so very difficult. Almost from the first construction of our simple house, a narrow little building connected it to the barn, providing a unified front and helping to gentle the precipitous slope down to the stream. We called it the woodshed though it never did much but float between the two larger structures, ripping away from the one and pushing against the other, and so we were cautioned by builder friends not to load it up with too much firewood. It therefore became a storage shed, which simply meant a place to put anything you could not find a place for otherwise. It housed breeding pigeons at one time, and a brood of guinea keets as they careened toward even more manic maturity. Mostly, however, it was a mess. And it continued to wiggle sideways, no matter how light a burden of domestic detritus it was asked to bear.

In aspect, this small building is hardly desirable for greenhouse space, for though its exposure is east-west, it is low and dark, and further, is shaded on the east side by the house and barn, and by a towering and much-treasured old yew tree on the west. For camellias, however, it seemed ideal, since they have the engaging quality of blooming when they are essentially dormant, in winter. They also demand only minimal heat—somewhere between 45 degrees at night and 10 degrees higher in daytime—which could be supplied by pipes beneath a paving of antique brick, which, in addition to being a pretty surface on which to stand the pots, served as a sponge, providing the plants with their only other winter requirement, enough humidity practically to grow moss on the windowpanes.

So far, thirty potted specimens, including a tea plant grown as bonsai, have found winter quarters in a space barely twenty by twelve feet. There is no way into it except through an outside door on the east side, which is hardly the first compromise we have made with what real estate agents call "accessibility." But on a blustery winter day, there is something quite splendid about opening the heavy plank door and entering a world fecund with earth and mold and rich with flower, glowing against black-green leaves. We think, by the use of pressure-treated four-by-fours of varying heights stood on end, we can increase the number of our collection to perhaps fifty plants, maybe more. After that—so strong is our addiction—we are not sure quite what we will do.

COLCHICUM

SOMETIMES WE FIND AUTUMN a melancholy season. What we had eagerly anticipated a mere six months before—the first snowdrops, hosts of daffodils, a garden drenched with the scent of roses, the first fresh peas—has passed so quickly. And what lies ahead are shorter days, cold winds, snow and ice, a world bereft of color. So it is a happy fact that among the last flowers of our garden, a few seem almost to be the first flowers of spring. *Crocus speciosus* and *C. sativus* delight us with their limpid blue flowers centered by golden anthers, a late feast of beauty for us and a real one for the autumn bees. Along the conifer border, colchicum also begin magically to appear, studding bare ground with chalices of vibrant lilac magenta, just the color that looks best with tawny autumn leaves. A single bulb catches the eye from a great distance, and a full drift, in rich warm pink, with perhaps a tawny maple leaf or two caught among them, is the last best thing in the garden to look at.

We find it puzzling that colchicum are unfamiliar to so many gardeners, for the genus is rich in virtues. First of all, most thrive under a wide range of cultural conditions, from the severe winter cold of Zone 4 to the torrid summer heat of Zone 9. Possessing natural repellents, they are free of diseases, insect pests, and predators, including deer and rabbits. Though single bulbs can be breathtakingly costly, up to twelve dollars apiece, colchicum are exceptionally easy to divide. We began with twenty-five, and now perhaps there are two thousand along the front of the conifer border, all from divisions in early spring, just as the green snouts appear above ground, or in mid-summer when the leaves die down. It is easy and satisfying work, and our initial investment has paid huge dividends.

The genus *Colchicum* includes approximately forty-five species native principally to stony hillsides around the Mediterranean, but extending well into northern India and even western China. (The genus name is classical, from Colchis, the ancient Roman name for the Black Sea region of Georgia.) In their native habitats, one species or another will be in flower from August to April. Still, the bulk of the genus flowers from mid-September to early October. They are all a play on shades of lilac mauve, some deepening almost to magenta, others washing out to pinkish gray. There are a few doubles and a sprinkling of precious albino whites. All are beautiful in their subtly different ways, and all are gifts, for the time in which they bloom.

The first colchicum to appear here is *C. agrippinum*, showing its flowers just as the August drought gives way to September rains. Each flower is checkered over, the deeper mauve ground hashed with lighter lines. Botanists call this pattern "tessellation," and it is most familiar to gardeners on the petals of the snake's head fritillary, *Fritillaria meleagris*. Do not, however, expect too much precision in this design. For if dishevelment is part of the charm of autumn, it is certainly part of the charm of colchicum, and *C. agrippinum* possesses that to a rather large degree. Its six or so pointed petals stand about four inches tall, when they don't flop over, and the pattern is often blurred to dots. Still, it is beautiful. And the first.

On the heels of *C. agrippinum* is *C. byzantinum*. A much more vigorous species, it can produce as many as two dozen blooms from a single bulb, each standing five or so inches tall, and each making way for the next by falling over on its side, a habit that irritates tidy gardeners. The petals are rather watery, and so the effect of a bulb in bloom is of a puddle of soft pinkish lilac, or when several bulbs are grown together, a pond. A very fine white form exists (*C. byzantinum* 'Album') that is equally vigorous, and manages somehow to be a little more upstanding. We have planted both in adjacent drifts, for the white is very clear and pure, and the lilac very moody and autumnal, and each seems prettiest when allowed to create its own effect.

Sometime in early October, just as the woods that surround our garden turn to their full autumn splendor, *C. speciosum* comes into bloom. To say that it is the most commonly cultivated species is not to detract from its great beauty, for it is perhaps the jewel of the genus. It bears the largest flowers of all, chalices up to seven inches tall, with oval, rounded, overlapping petals clasping yellow anthers. Buds emerge pale ivory, but quickly color up to a rich, pinkish purple. And though flowers are not born in the profusion of *C. byzantinum*, their size and the intensity of their color more than make up the difference. Surprisingly, this colchicum is fragrant, though the great early-twentieth-century gardener E. A. Bowles found in its scent an underlying smell "like that of a stable." No flower is perfect.

But as close to perfection as one can get is the white form of *C. speciosum*, *C. s.* 'Album', which is the pearl of the genus. It is pristine white, a beautiful cup of six petals held perfectly upright, no matter what insults autumn storms may deal. It is odd anywhere in gardening to find the albino form of a flower with more substance than its colored counterpart. Here, however, it is so, and this might be the colchicum above all others to plant, were they not all so wonderful in different ways. We have no idea whether it also smells of stables, but if it did, it would hardly matter.

The last of the commonly cultivated colchicum to bloom is *C. autumnale*. Actually, however, though it usually brings up the end of the parade just as autumn leaves begin to fall here in mid-October, it sometimes gets out of step and overlaps its cousins. It is a neat plant, producing six or so blossoms about five inches tall, all at once from each bulb, a tight little bouquet. Though other colchicum show off best on bare ground in bays of shrubbery or the sunny edges of woodland verges, *C. autumnale* always looks best in rough grass, as its popular name, meadow saffron, indicates. It is an effect we would love to have here, but as we have no rough grass except the high, rank growth of the meadow that gets brush cut at just about that time, all our *C. autumnale* mingle with our other colchicum in one great sweep. There is a very fine white form of *C. autumnale* also, 'Album', which again is best kept adjacent to, but not mingled with, the rose magenta of the typical form.

We have somewhat ambiguous feelings about the three double forms of colchicum, 'Waterlily', 'Pleniflorum', and 'Alboplenum'. All three emerge quite late, as if their quadrupling of petals required more energy to push above ground. Because the essential form of a colchicum flower is so elegant, they can all look rather odd, like penwipers, and it must be said that their numerous petals seem to attract the splashed mud of autumn rains. For this reason, we grow all three of them far away from their slim relatives. 'Waterlily' is planted in an open bay of the rhododendron garden, where its many pointed petals of lilac pink bunch tight against mulched ground. 'Alboplenum' is similar in form, but snow white, and its flowers rise higher and tumble over quickly from their own weight. It grows in an open patch of one of our woodland walks, where, if we forget to visit it, we find it no great loss. 'Pleniflorum' grows in the rock garden, surrounded by gravel mulch, where its pale lilac blossoms are actually quite beautiful.

There are gardeners—and we are unabashedly among them—for whom the knowledge of a genus of mostly hardy plants of easy cultivation and aristocratic demeanor, with subtle permutations from species to species, creates an insatiable appetite. Give us two species within any such genus, and we must have them all. Rarer species and hybrids begin to appear each year on the more adventurous bulb lists. There are dainty colchicum like *C. baytopiorum*, whose flowers are half the size of those of *C. autumnale* and would be wonderfully suitable hovering against a granite stepping-stone. There are even colchicum that flower in spring, *C. hungaricum* being perhaps the easiest, producing up to eight goblet-shaped pale, pinkish-mauve, three-inch-tall blooms per bulb. A rare white form of it also exists.

But perhaps the rarest of the spring colchicum is the only yellow-flowered species in the genus. *Colchicum luteum* is native to northern India into Tibet. Though said to be abundant there, and hardy to Zone 4, it is perhaps the rarest in the trade. We are certain to run it down, sooner or later.

CORYDALIS

FEW GARDENERS can resist a fern, or something that looks like one. So all by themselves, the delicate, finely divided leaves of corydalis always win hearts. But unlike ferns, corydalis produce dainty racemes of four-petaled tubular flowers that look like little stretched-out snapdragons, or possibly like schools of tiny fish swimming just above the leaves. Their delicate beauty suggests fine porcelain or a rare botanical print. Even the name (pronounced *co-RI-da-lis*) is pretty, from the ancient Greek word for "lark" because each flower bears a nectar spur at its base that resembles the spurred feet of that bird. Collectively, the genus carries the very old popular name Fumitory, from the

Latin *fumus terrae*, "smoke of the earth," because the leaves of many species are a delicate shade of blue-gray or purplish blue.

Many corydalis are notoriously cranky to establish and keep in the garden. But fortunately, many years ago, we started out with *Corydalis lutea*, one of the prettiest and easiest to grow. It produces clumps of ferny leaves about one foot tall, and its three-quarter-inch-long flowers are a blend of yellow and white, like quickly scrambled eggs. It is never so happy as when it can find a crevice in an old stone wall, where it will flourish seemingly only on dust and air. In fact, however, old stone walls usually have a core of rich humus within, made up of years of decomposed leaves and debris falling on and through them. We had no such walls on our property, but we knew how to fake them. And we had plenty of fieldstone, usually at least one with every shovel-thrust into the dirt. So we constructed wall beds—"planted walls" as they are called by rock gardeners—across the front of our lower greenhouse and on its shady side. The stones are essentially a veneer, behind which is a core of stiff gravelly soil. The lichens that come quickly on exposed fieldstone increase the impression that the walls are very, very old.

We planted a single *C. lutea* halfway up the wall on the shaded side of the greenhouse, since we had read that it would flourish in cool, shady rock crevices. All corydalis are unwilling transplanters, and the usual advice is to buy a plant, set it in its pot near a likely place, water it all summer, and wait for seedlings. But we were impatient, and more than a little cocky in our confidence, so we gently bare-rooted our first specimen and planted it directly in the wall as it was built. By luck or skill (probably the former), it took hold, grew vigorously, and within a year or two, small plants began showing up in other crevices along the wall, not only on the shaded side but also across the sunny greenhouse face. For once a single plant is well established, *C. lutea* is uncanny at finding the places it likes to grow. It has even made its way, somehow, up the whole length of the property to appear in the low retaining walls of the perennial garden. Experienced gardeners of a snobbish bent call it a weed because of its promiscuity. But if that is so, it is such a pretty weed that we are content to let it come where it will, most of the time. We yank it out only when its ferny growth, light as it seems, threatens to smother out a more precious plant.

Corydalis ochroleuca is quite similar to *C. lutea*, though it bears slightly pendulous flowers of creamy appearance, with more white than yolk in them. It is also as easy to grow, though it so far sits comfortably in a trough garden in back of the house and refuses to produce seedlings. We are sorry for that, because the two plants grown together would be a wonderful blend of creamy white and light yellow. A magical effect is always created when flowers of two or more closely related shades mingle. Perhaps it will happen yet.

There are seventy species in the genus *Corydalis*, most of which share the family birthright of grace and beauty, but many are very rare and can be quite fussy if their preferences are not exactly suited. Those preferences are usually—not always—for deep, humus-rich woodland soil that is constantly moist but never waterlogged. Light, dappled shade is best, such as would be provided by high old trees, but sometimes the canopy of a large shrub provides a perfect spot. They are not greedy feeders, and so fertilizers should be withheld, especially granular ones that can burn their sensitive roots. Still, a very dilute wash with liquid fertilizer, such as Peters 20-20-20, at half the strength called for on the package, can often encourage weak plants to catch hold and thrive.

Among the true woodland species, *C. cava* is the easiest to grow, producing airy, blue-green, fringy leaves topped by cobs of flower of a haunting misty lilac, making it seem especially fumitory. Even in the cool, moist shade it demands, it is apt to melt away in summer heat, causing anxious gardeners to fret. But it will usually reappear with the cool rains of either autumn or the following spring. *Corydalis solida* differs from it in that its tuberous roots are solid rather than hollow, a trivial botanical distinction that would not prevent most gardeners from thinking it just as wonderful. In the "pure" form (if such actually exists), it shares the predominately lavender or purplish color of *C. cava*, though it has given rise to many wonderful seedlings and crosses with pink, cherry-red, or even coral-colored flowers.

Corydalis dyphilla is also irresistible, not so much for its leaves, which are the least delicate of all, as for its upended dancing flowers. They appear in mid-spring, colored a pale whitish mauve with violet-purple lips and throat. Each flower, hardly an inch long, is carried loosely above the foliage in a panicle of six or eight others that seem to nod to one another in curious animation. All corydalis require good drainage at their roots, but give this one the best gritty soil you have, in light shade or morning sun.

As corydalis gain in popularity, more species and hybrids seem to appear each year. Among those recently made available, the present aristocrat is *C. flexuosa*. For one thing, its flowers are an electric blue, produced in late spring above foot-tall fringy growth, and to many gardeners blue is the best color a flower can come in. Several selections have been made, of which the best are 'Père David', with turquoise flowers; 'Blue Panda', almost gentian blue; and 'China Blue', with royal blue flowers animated at their tips by a spot of purple and white.

More than one gardener has noted that the flowers, with prominent upturned spurs and flared mouths, resemble a school of tiny, vivid blue tropical fish. We have grown them all, but we'd have to confess, not as well as we would like. Our best claim would be, perhaps, that they persist here, offering us enough encouragement to keep trying. Give all forms of *C. flexuosa* the coolest, richest spot in the garden, in moist, dappled shade, and when they go dormant in the heat of summer, pray for their return in spring.

The Russian *C. turtschaninovii*, though impossible to pronounce, is far easier to grow. At its best, as in the collected form 'Blue Gem', the flowers are bluer than any gentian or delphinium. In 'Eric the Red', the blue flowers are set off against copper-hued foliage for a frankly breathtaking effect.

Among the blue- or purple-flowered corydalis is the nicely named 'Blackberry Wine', which was introduced only in 2001 but has quickly become a sensation. Its name serves it well, for its flowers are a complex blend of deep and pale purple shading to blue. And though many corydalis possess a slight, delicate fragrance, 'Blackberry Wine' is rich in scent. To all its other virtues it adds ease of cultivation. Its parentage is vexingly uncertain, though its tolerance of heat and sun suggest our old friend *C. lutea*. If that is in fact one of Blackberry Wine's parents, whether it will seed about as freely remains to be hoped for.

Most corydalis cultivated in gardens are perennials—or at least, you hope they will be perennials—but the genus contains annual and biennial species as well. Among the annuals the most charming is *C. sempervirens*. It is a much-loved native American wildflower with a range from Nova Scotia to Georgia, and the only corydalis we know of that has its own popular name, rock harlequin. It is typically found growing on thin soils atop rocky ledges, but once established in gardens, it faithfully returns from year to year, its airy sprays of flower appearing on delicate, ferny plants up to two feet tall. The flowers are an engaging blend of color, each tube beginning pale yellow and then transitioning into hot pink, just the sort of costume Harlequin might wear.

All these corydalis grow in our Vermont garden, so their hardiness extends northward at least to a cold Zone 5, but southward only to Zone 7 or so, for they all dislike summer heat. Their greatest enemy is heavy clay, all too common in the upper South, the Ohio River Valley, and parts of the Midwest. If we gardened in those areas, we would have a bucket of sharp builder's sand ready to dig into the soil while the corydalis was still in its nursery can. Digging in a bucket of good compost or well-rotted cow manure is also always a very good idea, anywhere. All this is trouble, of course, but corydalis are worth it. For some, such as the wonderful coral-flowered *C. solida* 'George Baker' that has (so far) eluded us, we would dig in pearls, if we had them.

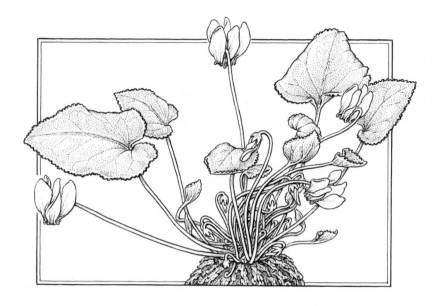

CYCLAMEN

At North Hill, from earliest September to late in April, the most watched and watched-over part of the whole garden is actually indoors, in a small quarter of the lower greenhouse. On its bench lives our collection of cyclamen, which includes many of the nineteen or so species in the genus. Cyclamen grow outside too, in the open ground, but sadly, only one species is truly hardy in Vermont, the ivy-leaved *Cyclamen hederifolium*. Though all the others relish a cool winter when they are in active growth, they need protection both from the arctic cold that sweeps over Vermont in winter and from its lush, wet summers. That is because all cyclamen are native to the

Mediterranean basin—southern Europe, Asia Minor, and northern Africa—and so, like all denizens of that world, they want a wet, mild winter balanced by a dry, baking summer. Fortunately, plants that crave a summer dormancy are among the easiest tender plants for the northern gardener to grow, since during the most active part of the year they can be stood outdoors in a dry place or left in pots in the then-emptied greenhouse. Ours remain just where they have lived out most of their long lives, in their section of the front bench in the lower greenhouse. There they sleep out the summer from late June until September, with no foliage, very little water, and internal temperatures that may reach 100 degrees on a hot summer day. Since the Aegean is not close by, that greenhouse is as near to Greece in the summer as any place in Vermont might be. Or Corsica, or Libya, or Lebanon, or Turkey. The comparison is even reinforced by an old potted grapevine, 'Datier de Beyrouth', which is trained up into the eaves and casts a light transparent shade over the bench.

Cyclamen are such tractable plants that we wonder why more northern gardeners do not collect them. But though ease of culture is always a plus for any plant, it is not the main reason we grow them. Quite simply, they have a charm all their own, with small dancing, inside-out flowers tinted white, pale pink, or deep rose, held pertly on long stems above their beautifully patterned foliage. Many of them are intensely fragrant, to the extent that when we open the greenhouse door on a wintry day, we become lighthearted. It is a complex fragrance—sweet, certainly, but with strong hints of fresh-cut lemons and honey. It is unmistakably Mediterranean.

All cyclamen are variations on a theme, differing one from another mostly in small but significant ways. Our friend Ellen Hornig, at Seneca Hills Rare Plant Nursery (from which some of our best have come), compares them to snowflakes, no two of which are alike. Our collection of fifty pots or so resembles a little village, where each face is recognizable both for its family relationships and its uniqueness. Each small clay pot, never more than six inches across and sometimes just two, contains an individual, with its own distinct personality and its own way of being in the world.

Most species form little rosettes of leaves not more than eight inches across, and sometimes much less, for every species seems occasionally to create a dwarf plant that is completely endearing, as tiny things are. Each leaf is only an inch or two long and as broad, and generally they emerge from the center of a fat, rounded corm that sits smugly on top of the compost— or ought to, if the plants are correctly potted and one expects a long life from them. With some, such as *C. coum*, old corms develop a dimple in the center, presumably to catch a precious drop or two of Mediterranean spring rain. But there are some, such as *C. rohlfsianum* and *C. africanum*, that shoot their sparse leaves outward from the central corm underground until they emerge at some distance from it, often on the very edges of the pot. Yet within that rough description, which covers most cyclamen, there are endless variations. Not so much of flower form, which certainly may vary in size or color or season of bloom, but of leaf. Leaves may be rounded or arrow-shaped, dark green, green with a finely etched zone of silver, all silver, or pewter-leaved. Some might even be called "leaden-leaved," though such a description robs them of the lightness that is always the most salient characteristic of species cyclamen.

There is one major exception to this general description. Even as a naturally occurring species, *C. persicum* is heftier, to perhaps a foot across, with marbled leaves three inches wide. But through selective breeding, it has reached Brobdingnagian proportions. It is the cyclamen you see in supermarkets, fattened with chemicals and swathed in tinsel, fleshy, out-of-shape, and destined for a very short life on a Christmas holiday table, or as an emergency hostess gift. Often these plants are as big as a potted azalea, and in colors far from the natural range of the genus, including ice white, brassy scarlet, sugary pink, and deep purple. There are even "picoteed" forms of some shade of pink or white marked with a stronger color at the edges of the petals. In our early years as gardeners, we often brought one home at Christmas, which we generally managed to keep blooming until spring by removing spent blossoms, fertilizing regularly, and growing it in a cold, sunny window. Quite cool, for no cyclamen on earth, even the overbred florist's sorts, will last for long in temperatures that exceed 60 degrees in the daytime and 10 degrees less at night.

But recently a race of miniature Persian cyclamen has become available, in the same color range as the giants, but much more appropriately cyclamen-like, with tufts of leaves eight inches wide, surmounted by delicate flowers on slender stems. Some are wonderfully fragrant, particularly the white ones. A few of these have been added to our collection, where, once carried over a summer dormancy and freed from fertilizer dependency, they assume a grace and character far closer to wild species than any giant Persian cyclamen can ever manage. One could make a collection just of them alone.

Even more collectible are other species, for though the colors of the flowers stay within the white to pink to purple range (never red), within each species there is an astonishing variation of leaf form and patterning. Most common among these is *C. hederifolium*, but we also grow many in pots on the greenhouse bench where their flowering can extend from the end of August until well into November. *Cyclamen hederifolium* blooms well before its first leaves appear, producing dozens of thin brown stems extending from the fat dark corms at soil level. The little white or pink bloom shows five swept-back petals revealing the puckered mouth of the perianth within, where bright yellow anthers are clustered. Just as the flowers fade the leaves begin to appear, rounded or heart-shaped, marbled or zoned, sometimes showing a shieldlike blazon, sometimes a feathered patterning of lighter green at the edges, and sometimes all silvered over. From Ellen Hornig at Seneca Hills, we also have two plants with dark green, very narrow arrow-shaped leaves, a variant that rarely shows up even in a large sowing of seed.

Though *C. hederifolium* is marginally hardy for us, all the rest are not. We know, for we have tried. And sometimes we have stumbled, accidentally and with great pain. More than fifteen years ago, when Nancy Goodwin was still running her remarkable nursery, Montrose, in Hillsborough, North Carolina, we got from her a single seedling of *C. africanum*, which we grew into a very large corm as wide as an apple that produced masses of small pink flowers every October. One year, we set it pridefully atop a stone wall outside the greenhouse, the better to enjoy its beauty. In the night, the temperature dropped slightly below freezing, and the next morning it was a mess of slimy leaves, its cell walls shattered by ice crystals it could never have experienced in its North African home. We learned a lesson then, in that painful and unforgettable fashion that is every gardener's hard experience, and from which, more than perhaps anything, good gardening is born. Happily, however, we whimpered to Nancy about our loss (begged, you might say) and another came to us in the mail as a gift.

Cyclamen africanum is another of the species that blooms naked, with leaves that follow and persist until spring. They are of such great beauty that they offer a reason to admire the plant just for them. Also, when the flowers are spent, the plants have the curious knack of curling their bloom stems under their leaves and inward, like tiny pig's tails. Minute cyclamen seedlings then sprout at the edges of every pot, and even on the greenhouse floor. Fortunately, even the tiniest are apt to show their identity from the beginning, and the tiny, pea-sized corms can be carefully dug out with the blade of a knife and potted on.

When you have two of anything you treasure, you are on the way to a collection. In our gardening life, this rule has proven true many times, but never so clearly as with species cyclamen. We have pots not only of *C. hederifolium* and *C. africanum*, but also of *C. balearicum* from the islands off Spain, *C. creticum*, *C. cyprium*, and *C. libanoticum*. *Cyclamen rohlfsianum*, from Libya, is especially precious, for though its slender, fragrant pink flowers born in autumn and even its leaves are sparse, they are large for a species cyclamen, and they look like little hands, with five distinct lobes. We have three pots, each with a different pattern of silver marked over the green leaves.

We are still some distance from having all the species in the genus, though we make up for that gap by growing many forms of *C. coum*, perhaps the most variable in the whole genus, new forms appearing in nearly every random seedling. As we find new forms, we do not seem able to give up any of the others, some of which have flourished here for fifteen years. Under good conditions, a cyclamen corm can live practically forever. We muse sometimes about how odd it is that just those conditions can occur in southern Vermont, so very far from the countries in which our plants variously originated.

THE DAFFODIL MEADOW

WHEN WE FIRST CAME TO VERMONT, building a house was about the last thing we had in mind. We wanted to *buy* a house, and we could easily picture exactly what it would look like. It would have some land, of course, because we intended not only to make an ornamental garden but also to raise vegetables, and we wanted to keep animals of all sorts, dogs and cats but also poultry and pigs and possibly even cows. We also hoped our land would have woods, enough that you could get lost in them, or at least have that impression. But there should also be an open, sunny meadow, or maybe two, one kept mown and one left to wild asters and goldenrod and brambles for gathering blackberries. As for the house itself, it should be old, at least two hundred years old, with as many of its original features preserved as possible—wide-planked floors, working fireplaces in most rooms, heavy timbered beams, and small-paned windows. This picture could be elaborated on endlessly, but that was the general idea.

It was not a realistic one. For though we had some resources—mostly supplied by kind parents—they were still far too limited for the house we had come to Vermont to find. We were the frustration of many Realtors, but one actually seemed touched by our optimism and promised, as he put it, "to do my damnedest." His name was Stub Burnet, and he is now dead. He was old even then, but he chose to travel around on a moped, and we now think he had a secret plan for us. He wanted us to build because land was still plentiful then, but a house such as we wanted was not to be bought for our meager ready funds. One day he putted up to the house we were renting and insisted we see a property. "No house. But lots of advantages. Twenty minutes is all you'll spend to look, anyhow." So the three of us piled into our little Honda, and he directed us to Readsboro, where, incidentally, we had been determined not to look at anything. Halfway up North Hill was "the piece," about twenty-three acres. It had plenty of woods, it had a sunny meadow far back into the property, and it also had the one thing we had dared not put on our list, a running stream. Besides, it was cheap even for that time, five hundred dollars an acre. "OK," we said to Mr. Burnet on the spot, "we'll build."

Two years of exhilarating misery followed that rash commitment, during which the house somehow got finished and the garden got begun. But it was very much a little house buried in the woods. Beautiful as the old beeches, maples, and ash were, there was a feeling of claustrophobia around us, and we began to feel the need for light and air. And though shade gardens are wonderful things, they are not the whole of gardening, and we did want the whole. So we agreed with a neighbor, Jim Sprague, to cut a meadow in exchange for half the timber for his winter firewood. Now that we have been rural people for over thirty years, we realize that a large portion of the deal was pure kindness on Jim's part. He was a crusty old fellow, with social prejudices that sometimes took our breath away. But he liked us and liked our land, which he had known for over seventy years, and liked the idea of clearing a meadow out of the woods. So we marked a roughly square section of about two acres, comfortably far from the new house to leave a fringe of woods, and Jim set to work. We did not even once pause to get sentimental about the splendid old specimens being felled. We had a plan.

Part of that plan was not to establish a meadow of naturalized daffodils. A meadow, certainly, maybe for livestock, and indeed, the first year we tethered two Nubian goats there to graze the thin grass which came that spring from a first seeding. They drove us crazy with their bleating, got loose over and over, and finally found their way into the stew pot. We cannot really remember when we decided that the purpose of that meadow, all along, had been to establish a fenced vegetable garden at the top, and plant the rest—probably about an acre and a half—with daffodils. For like so many other features of the garden that have given us great pleasure, it just seems always to have been, suggesting an almost Platonic assumption about our garden and our presence here, one of an infinite number of possibilities that may be realized in this space and matter. Just as we cannot imagine the incarnations that came long before, we will not obviously see those that will come long after. But it is a daffodil meadow now, at least for our fraction of an instant here, though that is already half a lifetime.

Having daffodils in the garden seems an almost elemental

need in gardeners. And not just a few daffodils, but as many as you can possibly cram in. It would be interesting to know what nongardening readers make of Wordsworth's great poem "I Wandered Lonely as a Cloud." But no gardener can fail to respond to his "host of golden daffodils." A host is certainly the right idea, since the richest experience with daffodils is when there are more of them than you could possibly count or even estimate.

"But how many are here?" the few visitors who see them at their peak on a raw April day always need to ask. "How many did you plant in the beginning?" Those are complicated questions because the first planting, of around two thousand bulbs, occurred at least ten years ago, possibly even fifteen. The initial idea was to border the wide mown grass path that runs through the meadow with drifts on either side, from the point at which it leaves the woods and proceeds up to the vegetable garden gate. Since the lane is about five hundred feet long, two thousand was certainly no more than a few, though that number would have overwhelmed a garden of average size. Every October in the following years, we added a minimum of two thousand more, and early on we began to divide congested clumps from the garden below to fill up bare patches in late spring when the daffodils were still in leaf, since bulbs transplanted while they are growing settle in readily, if the work is done carefully and in rainy weather. So the easiest answer to that question is "Oh, there are now maybe twenty-five thousand." At best, this must pass as a reasonable estimate.

Our daffodil plantings have now reached the edges of the meadow where it meets the woods. In the beginning, the idea was to plant each variety in an elliptical drift perpendicular to the path itself, each drift interlocking with its neighbor. That way, we could always identify each variety, and we could blend pale or deep yellow sorts with cream or white ones, and of course include the occasional double or pink form. As we have expanded outward we have adhered faithfully to that idea, because in any planting some underlying principle of order should exist—else the whole fabric will fall into a nervous chaos.

For that reason, we would never plant the inexpensive blends that nurserymen sell. They are simply leftovers from Holland bulb auctions all tumbled together, bought cheap and sold cheap. Worse, though it is a nice feature of daffodils that they bloom over a long season, here usually from the first week of April to the last week of May, each variety doesn't bloom that long. For there are early, mid-season, and late varieties, and each flowers according to its genetically programmed time. In the dooryard garden, that sequence is wonderful. But in a mass planting it isn't so wonderful, since early ones will pass before mid-season ones bloom, and both will linger in shabby completeness just as the late ones open. That results in a mess. So when we make additions to the daffodil meadow, we confine ourselves to mid-season sorts. For any others, such as the lovely and very late heirloom-pink 'Mrs. R. O. Backhouse' or the wonderful, long-cultivated double white called 'The Bride' (which actually will bloom in June if hot weather does not cause it to wither first), a place must be found in a remote and sequestered area off to the meadow's side or in the garden down below.

From the beginning, we have bought only the sturdiest old varieties for our meadow, and that is a practice we would strongly recommend to anybody. There is certainly always something wonderful about studying any daffodil close up, especially when it is an heirloom variety or one of the rarest new cultivars, with, for example, a corolla of clearest pink or lime green, an unusually neat arrangement of perianth, or a celebrated fragrance. We would never forgo that pleasure, and so each year we buy three bulbs, or perhaps five, of ten or so different varieties from Dave Burdick, who specializes in both classes. Those are potted up singly, sent through a winter chill in the bulb closet, and brought out in March to develop in the greenhouse. When they are in flower, they are set on the kitchen windowsill to study and to memorize. Just as they finish blooming, they are accustomed to outdoor living, and then, after daffodil season is done, each is slipped into a spot in the garden for future bloom.

But never in the meadow. For many of the most sought-after daffodil varieties are expensive, either because they are new breakthroughs or because they have been painstakingly rediscovered and multiplied. Many are also simply too fragile to compete with rough grass. Fortunately, however, there are plenty of wonderful ones to be had cheap, and the cheapest are often the sturdiest and the best for naturalizing.

So over almost thirty years our garden has become a sort of daffodil democracy, with each in its place but none lower than the other. The rarest daffodil on the market, at perhaps one hundred dollars or more a single bulb, will find a spot along the rose path, close to us for frequent admiration, and there it will probably multiply. But even the most beautiful of those couldn't rival the sturdy, snow-white 'Empress of Ireland', an old variety that has multiplied abundantly in the meadow, though always confined to its own personal drift. We'd be bereft without the annual reappearance of 'Ice Follies', its flattened face beginning pale yellow and fading to white, or 'February Gold', which we never see until April, but welcome always for its perky flowers of the deepest daffodil yellow. All these old varieties, and others, are sure to increase with little care, and that means they will always offer what daffodils should, the first abundance of the gardening year.

FORCING BRANCHES

In the middle of January, almost always, there comes a brief period of mild days so predictable from year to year that it has a name like any other season: the January Thaw. Those days are a tease, really, for the cruelty of February still lies before us, and even March can go out like the lion it came in as. But for a few days rain might fall, snows melt, and even night temperatures hover around 20 degrees, which any seasoned Vermonter would consider balmy. Our little stream roars, and we are lured out into parts of the garden we have not visited for two months because the drifts have been so deep. Our garden blood stirs, as surely as must the blood of our two tortoises, buried deep in the greenhouse earth to sleep out the winter.

But they don't stir. Their pinched, nostrilled snouts never appear aboveground, and ripe strawberries and slugs remain in their dreams. We are different from them.

Here in Vermont, the January Thaw does not hurry winter along, for we must still be in thrall to it for two or even three more months. If we lived in the coastal regions of the next state below us, Massachusetts, we might actually poke in a few pansies during these mild days or even plant a row of peas. But that would be quite foolish here, and so we continue to subsist on an indoor diet of forced paperwhite narcissus, supermarket cyclamen (the dwarf ones that proved fragrant and are saved from year to year), and our carefully cosseted collection of camellias. Later in the month, the jasmine in the winter garden will bloom, scenting the house with its magic fragrance.

These are all greenhouse flowers, and we could have more, by choosing from shrubs and vines that flower naturally in warm climates in winter. But to have flowers from the garden, only cheating will do. Cheating is a harsh word. "Forcing" is hardly less a one. But we engage in that activity every January, not to delude ourselves that spring is here, but only to secure a fleeting glimpse of it. When winter closes down again, the January Thaw will seem as much a distant memory as summer does. So we make the most of this briefest of all seasons. On treks through the garden, we are aware that buds have swollen and even twigs and branches have taken on a fullness they did not show for two months before. Briefly, the sap has risen, and though it will surely find its way back underground as soon as temperatures fall, now is the time to harvest branches of flowering shrubs and trees for forcing.

We are hardly experts at forcing branches, for there are skilled florists who seem able to force almost anything, at any time, by carefully manipulated temperatures and light. Their produce fills whole lobbies of expensive hotels with tree-sized branches of apple, magnolia, cherry, and peach. Such feats are beyond our abilities, but there are some stalwarts that seem willing to open indoors when cut just about any time after the New Year, and probably the best of them is forsythia. It may be true in fact that branches of it, hung thickly with four-petaled, down-hanging flowers, are more beautiful in a vase indoors in February than outdoors in the garden in spring. This is particularly true of crosses between *Forsythia suspensa* and *F. viridissima*, such as 'Karl Sax' or 'Lynwood', the profuse, almost violently yellow flowers of which can be a visual affliction in hot spring sunshine. But indoors and out, we far prefer the paler, more gently colored forsythia. So we have planted 'Vermont Sunrise', an extremely hardy cultivar bred from northern Chinese species at the University of Vermont, to form a loose hedge about eight feet tall at the far edge of the daffodil meadow. It flowers late, just about the same time the daffodils reach peak, and the two are beautiful together. But it also provides armloads of branches in winter, which come indoors looking scaly and chaffy and most unpromising, but which open pale yellow bells within a week. We have long been tempted to combine branches of 'Vermont Sunrise' with the so-called white forsythia, *Abeliophyllum distichum*, a much lower-growing shrub, to about four feet here, but our timing has always been off. We have forced abeliophyllum by itself, and its wine-colored buds and milk-white open flowers, identical to those of forsythia except for color, are both very beautiful and sweetly fragrant.

Fragrant also is *Viburnum ×bodnantense* 'Dawn', which is normally listed as hardy only to Zone 6 or even 7, though it has grown here in Zone 4 for at least twenty years. We cannot say it is a beautiful plant, for it has formed an angular bush eight feet tall, and its coarse, five-inch-long dark green oval leaves make little contribution to the summer garden. For these reasons, our one gangly bush of it has been tucked between the forgiving presence of a yew and a hemlock. But *V.* ×*bodnantense* does have the wonderful habit of opening little bunches of candy-pink bells on any warm day in winter. It is sure to be in bloom during the brief January Thaw, but branches may be cut on any day when daytime temperatures are above freezing, and flowers will quickly open indoors, scenting a whole room. Their very angularity also adds charm to any arrangement of winter-flowering branches.

It is no accident, we suppose, that shrubs which choose to bloom in winter or very early spring produce bell-shaped down-hanging flowers to protect their vital pollen against the wind and are often fragrant, since bees are scarce then, and they need to attract every one. The most fragrant of winter-flowering shrubs are the witch hazels, species and crosses of *Hamamelis*, but instead of bells, they produce curious flowers made up of one-inch-long threads, gold or acid yellow or amber, according to cultivar. Though the first timorous flowers of *V.* ×*bodnantense* 'Dawn' will be blasted by the return of real winter—to be followed later by others—the witch hazel petals simply curl back up over their centers and sleep a bit until warm sun causes them to unfurl again. We often know they are in bloom not by seeing them, but because their unmistakable fragrance lures us across the snow. Anytime after Christmas, whether their petals are spread out or furled, branches can be counted on to open indoors, and fragrance is assured.

Willows have been a passion with us from the very early days of the garden, when we struck twigs of almost every one we passed. In part we had a lot of space to fill, and almost nothing roots as readily as a willow. In fact, before the invention of root hormones, old gardeners used to brew willow tea in the belief that it encouraged rooting of other plants. We've never tried that, but the genus is valuable to us for vividly colored winter twigs, particularly selections of *Salix alba*. *Salix alba* var. *vitellina* produces brilliant, egg-yolk-colored stems, and two forms selected from it, 'Britzensis' and 'Chermesina', offer a blend of yellow and scarlet or bronze. Along our stream we grow several plants of each for winter beauty, though pollarding them on five-foot-high trunks both encourages vividly colored young stems and creates interesting accent plants for the summer garden. And in the dead of winter, a mixed arrangement made up only of their varnished stems is beautiful.

We grow other willows for the catkins they produce from mid-winter to spring. Most hardly need forcing, for they form little furry ovals up and down young stems out in the garden in the second half of winter, and may be cut for indoors on any day. Our native *S. caprea*, which grows in swamps and wet ditches all around us, will begin to show catkins by the January Thaw at least. But earlier than that, at Christmastime even, we can bring out the tiny, gray-blue catkins of *S. alba* var. *caerulea*. Long branches—almost limbs—can be cut from a ten-foot bush that has grown at the edge of our rock garden for many years where bog water gathers below the steep slope. Later, the large silver-white catkins of *S. ×chaenomeloides* will come of themselves, ready to cut by early January. *Salix gracilistyla* 'Melanostachys' will not bloom until March, but its ink-black catkins—the blackest flowers we know—can be encouraged to form indoors at least by the middle of February.

We must wait almost until mid-March to cut branches of highbush blueberry (*Vaccinium corymbosum*), and we always have a struggle then between two desires—the pleasure of clusters of tiny, scented lily-of-the-valley flowers on reddish twigs and the thought of the blueberries they would have produced. Our hunger in winter for flowers always wins out, and we steal a few branches, the oldest ones, with gnarled and congested stems. All blueberries require occasional restorative pruning anyway, and so will be the better for our theft. In any case, we have many bushes forming a five-foot-tall hedge across the back of our vegetable garden. They always produce enough berries for us, and so we substitute one form of greediness for another.

From the final leaf drop in autumn until spring, we admire the structure of many deciduous magnolias in the garden, especially *Magnolia* ×*loebneri* 'Merrill' and *M.* ×*loebneri* 'Leonard Messel', with their thick gray trunks and their graceful branches, the smallest twig carrying a velvet, mouse-gray bud. Those grow plump by late January, when each one sometimes wears a little cap of snow. They look as if they would force with the greatest of ease, but we have never succeeded until the first flowers are almost open. Still, their Japonesque beauty is wonderful in a vase.

In fact, every winter we have a fantasy that we will achieve one splendid arrangement. It would be made up of rods of tawny willow and pussy willow; branches of fully opened witch hazel, forsythia, and abeliophyllum in full flower; angular branches of *V. bodnantense*; and a few delicate twigs of fully opened blueberry, all from our garden. In all this variety there would be two harmonies: gray branches and the promise of spring. Such an arrangement would require some careful orchestration, for timing would be everything. But all gardeners know that any idea existing in the mind will sooner or later be attempted in the garden, or in this case, in a vase. Perhaps next January Thaw we can bring it off.

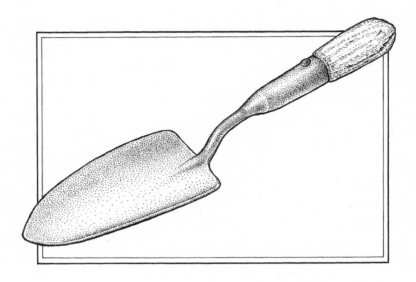

THE GARDEN TROWEL

WE KNOW GARDENERS who have really beautiful tool sheds. Wooden pegs protrude from rough paneling, and the tools hanging on them are as artfully arranged as paintings. There are rakes and hoes of several sorts and sizes, and spades and shovels for every purpose. Pruning tools are arranged in neat, graded ranks from giant loppers that can bite through a thick limb down to dainty Japanese shears for clipping bouquets of roses. Wooden handles are smooth and sanded, and the metal parts are scrubbed clean of dirt and glisten with a protective coat of oil. Always there is a selection of brooms, for we are talking here of a passion for neatness that can sometimes exist for its own sake. Brooms are of course essential to that.

We'd love to have such a tool shed, but we love a tidy garden as well, and that has proven to be enough demand on our time and energy. So the tool shed we have is in fact an extremely untidy corner of a very untidy barn, which is also used to store lawn mowers, the invaluable but unwieldy gas-powered wheelbarrow, firewood for the house, grain for the animals, and alas, all the empty wine bottles, dog and cat food cans, and other household detritus waiting for the next trip to the town dump. But though on a whim one of us may bring home a new rake or hoe on a grain run to the local Agway, mostly we buy a new tool when something wears out. Any old shovel or hoe will do, provided we remember where we used it last. And the answer to the impatient, long-distance shout "Where's the shovel?" is apt impatiently to be, "Up in the compost heap. Where you last used it." So much for neatness and order, at least among our tools.

But without question, the indispensable tool, for which there is no possible substitute, is a nurseryman's trowel. It carries no fancy brand name, but ours has always come from that sensible nurseryman's hardware store, the mail-order company A. M. Leonard. The trowel costs around fifteen dollars, not including postage, and is always proudly labeled "Made in the USA." When brand new, each trowel measures fourteen inches long, eleven and a half of which is taken up by a scoop and a long neck and socket, all made of a single piece of strong forged iron. A hardwood handle, comfortably rounded at the end, is firmly wedged into the socket, so that iron and wood make up one elegant, unified shape. The trowel looks antique from the first, or at least does after a day or two, when the label we never quite succeed in peeling away and the factory blacking have worn off from use, and a light patina of rust sets in. But within our collection, there are specimens of varying lengths, the tips of some having been worn down by hard digging and the wooden handles by hand friction. At any given time, our population of six or so contains one or two that are just right for whatever hand that grabs them. Eggs in a carton, you'd think they were, they are so similar. But not to the hand that loves one above all others, and so all of us respect the cry that can come from anyone who works here: "Who has *my* trowel?"

Though other tools may be scattered about the landscape or deposited (with luck) somewhere in the barn, all our trowels are inserted into the earth just outside the back door, at a point where almost all garden rambles and all work begins. It is just in front of a buried stone pediment that holds a potted standard fuchsia 'Hidcote Beauty', which in summer rains down its white and coral-pink flowers, almost hiding the ranks of trowels. One waggish visitor dubbed it the "trowel garden." It is an instinct with all of us at North Hill to tally up the number of trowels there at the end of the day and be sure our particular one is among them. If one is missing, it is of course not ours, and, both out of genuine concern and the day's fatigue, we are apt to whine, "A trowel is missing."

Two distinct lifts of the heart occur where the trowels are stored. The first happens after a busy morning of phone calls and client business, when we are finally free to go out and garden. The second, a moment after, occurs when we bend down and select our own particular trowel. No work in the garden, and no walk either, is possible without that comfortable presence in hand. As gardeners, we are simply not ourselves without this trowel, to the extent that when we travel, we each put one in our luggage, along with the obligatory dinner party sport coat. We even used to carry them on our persons, until airport regulations made simple gardeners into terror suspects. These days, for example, if you are randomly sent through the pouffer, you will register dangerous levels of nitrate, and it is no good, really, explaining that you have been fertilizing the houseplants and that a balanced 10-10-10 fertilizer is one-third nitrogen. Better just submit to the pat down and make no dumb jokes.

Why are these trowels so important that they are our only tool of preference? First, they are sturdy, almost indestructible, to the point that when one is lost in the shrubbery for two years or more, it will still be in good usable shape. They never bend or buckle, even when we attempt to dislodge a heavy buried rock in what is really shovel work—if only we knew where we left the shovel. The reach, of fourteen inches or so (a little less with wear), can scoop up the deepest-buried daffodil clump, or plant a tulip bulb at the desirable twelve inches, or quickly excavate a hole for a perennial in a one-gallon can. Most of all, however, they are simply comfortable, even when the blade is tucked into the right-hand rear pocket of a pair of Levi's.

Gardens are infinitely imaginable, and fantasies of one sort after another slide endlessly through our minds. Sometimes they occupy real ground, now or later, here or elsewhere. We will probably never have the imaginary tool shed with which we began this essay. But the making of any garden is unimaginable to us without this sturdy, sensible tool, the nurseryman's trowel. It brings us down to earth.

GENTIANS

FIFTEEN YEARS into the life of the garden we built a green-house, a little, rustic homemade building of barn sash windows and cedar siding. There were two reasons for its construction. The first was that our collection of tender plants had steadily grown, each winter trip to San Francisco adding one or two more agapanthus, another camellia, and rarer plants such as *Myosotidium hortensia*, the magnificent Chatham Islands forget-me-not with lustrous, hosta-like leaves and unforgettable blue flowers. The second was that the garden fell away to nothing down below, and seemed to require some terminus point, some full stop. We already knew that outbuildings, beyond their merely practical uses, could be powerfully effective in organizing garden space. For these reasons, it seemed a very good idea to build a greenhouse there.

The trouble, however, was that our hillside falls to the southwest, and there are no level spaces on it anywhere except what we have made. So a gently sloping bank had to be cut away in order to provide enough fill to create level space on which the building could sit. A lot of fill was required, as it happened, leaving us with a very ugly steep slope of red clay subsoil, and at first, we wondered what we had done. But as has happened so many times in our garden, what seemed a huge liability became a gift. In this case, the slope offered the perfect site for a rock garden. So, with much setting in of massive old granite boulders, half buried to seem natural outcroppings, and then a few dwarf conifers, we had the basic structure we needed. We dug gravel into the clay—clay is always more fertile than gardeners assume, if it can be broken up for free drainage—and mulched the surface with more gravel. The result was a more or less plausible high alpine garden, with the huge advantage of constantly percolating water. We discovered that we had more than a rock garden; we had that golden thing, a scree. The question then was, What to plant there?

Buried in every gardener's memory are plants he has seen or read about and vows to grow, or wishes he could grow, if only he had the right conditions. In our case, one memory went far back, to high school English classes in very different places, Shreveport and Philadelphia. Both of us had read D. H. Lawrence's poem "Bavarian Gentians," with the lines

Not every man has gentians in his house
In Soft September, at slow, Sad Michaelmas.

Bavarian gentians, big and dark, only dark
Darkening the daytime, torch-like with the smoking
   blueness of Pluto's gloom.

Early on, then, the plant was fixed in our memory, though we both think it odd that neither of our teachers brought in a picture of a gentian to show. Such pictures came much later, as we thumbed through garden picture books and encyclopedias. So when we could have gentians, they were among the first plants we sought.

Since we now had a rock garden, we joined the American Rock Garden Society, and we religiously attended meetings every Saturday, even though we were schoolteachers and Saturday was our only full gardening day. The nicest feature of those meetings was not the amazing spread of pastries made by the members, or sometimes even the featured speaker, who was apt to show slides of his last vacation in New Zealand or South Africa. What drew us back each Saturday was the plant sale, of seedlings grown by members. And in that way we acquired our first gentian, *Gentiana acaulis*. We were cautioned that it was difficult to grow. That of course added to its appeal, though we have not found it difficult at all. We planted it at the edge of the new rock garden, half shaded by a young magnolia 'Elizabeth'. Over fifteen years, it has become a large patch a foot or more across. When it flowers in late April or early May, hundreds of nearly stemless blue trumpets appear, a stunning deep blue shading to black-blue in their hearts, the five petals flecked over with green. We have never disturbed it and rarely fed it. We dare not congratulate ourselves on our luck, which is due to the site we were given rather than anything we have done.

Just as *G. acaulis* passes off, another gentian growing in the rock garden begins to flower, *G. decumbens*. From bold rosettes composed of eight-inch-long, lance-shaped leaves of a rich, polished green, flower stems emerge, upright at first but then sprawling out languidly and bearing small bunches of small but plentiful watery blue funnels. If it was the first gentian you ever saw, you would wonder what all the fuss is about. Reginald Farrar, in his magnificent book *The English Rock Garden* (1928), scornfully calls it "a weed," and even we would never call it particularly choice. But it has the amiable virtues of being very easy to grow, blooming faithfully and even seeding about. Perhaps we have too much of it, but it is very hard to weed up any of its handsome progeny, which appear here and there throughout the sunnier parts of the rock garden. And when all is said and done, it is, after all, a gentian.

Not all our gentians grow in the rock garden. Above the house, almost at the opposite end of the garden, *G. asclepiadea* has thriven without much attention for twenty years. It has a place much like *G. acaulis*, under the partial shade of a magnolia, and in constantly moist but well-drained soil above a bog. It is popularly called the "willow gentian" from its gracefully arching wands and its narrow, two-inch-long leaves. They really do look like sprays of willow, though their botanical name associates them with the god of medicine, Asklepios, because gentian roots were used by ancient Greek physicians to treat severe nervous disorders and provided an antidote to poison. We grow it for other reasons, chiefly for its grace and the surprise of its trumpet flowers, appearing in August on the tips of four-foot stems, bending them closer to the ground. Our original plants were blue-flowered, but one or two pure white ones have come of themselves. We think of where they grow as primarily a spring garden, planted to marsh marigolds in single chrome yellow, but also in a smaller, paler yellow double form and in white, and to *Primula florindae*, with two-foot stems topped by clusters of yellow bells. Because it is a bog, with percolating water running under it, all those flowers are precocious, and some years we enjoy them as early as late March. Later in the season, the bog is given over to foliage, to the four-foot-tall umbrella leaves of *Darmera peltata*, to selections of blade-leaved *Iris pseudacorus,* and to large-leaved hostas. So it is always a surprise, in August, when we stumble on *G. asclepiadea*, a quietly beautiful plant that waits its time to bloom. Then a whole part of that section of the garden comes back to us, with the full force of spring's first discoveries.

We grow—or, as gardeners so frequently say, "once grew"—other gentians throughout the garden. *Gentiana andrewsii* is native hereabouts, and we collected plants from our own land and grew them in the garden for years. The species is called the "bottle gentian" or "closed gentian" because its flowers, borne in late summer at the tops of erect, two-foot-tall stems, never seem to open. You keep thinking they must, but they don't, and so how the plant ever sets seed is a mystery. Perhaps some minute insect bores through unobtrusively, or maybe it is self-fertile, tending to all that business without assistance and in secret. We have lost it, largely due to the aggressiveness of the double-flowered form of *Houttuynia cordata*, one of the many pesky plants we love here. But we loved the bottle gentian too, and we must find it again.

Gentiana septemfida, the crested gentian, is not the last to bloom, but it comes very late in August, and marks the beginning of autumn here, for it will continue in bloom even when orange maple leaves fall about it, making a beautiful contrast to its dark blue, white-throated flowers. It grows in two places, down in the rock garden and at the edge of the little thyme terrace where we sit in the evening. Both locations offer it the full sun it requires, and individual plants have formed low mounds of congested growth, consisting of almost stemless laurel-green leaves each about an inch and a half long. The flowers are also about that size, and when they occur, their abundance almost obscures the leaves beneath. The species is native from Turkey to Iran, and is usually rated as hardy only to Zone 6. But as with many other plants that grow low to the earth, our abundant winter snow cover allows it to thrive here.

The gentian we love the most is the last of its genus to flower in the garden, and perhaps the last flower on any perennial plant we have. For it blooms when everything else is brown and faded—the colchicum, the tiny cyclamen, even the late autumn crocus, *Crocus sativus* and *C. speciosus*. When fallen leaves lie thick on our paths and even the fruit on the *Ilex verticillata* has begun to be stripped by robins on their way south, *G. scabra* chooses to bloom, its deep blue trumpets on semi-erect, two-foot stems almost lost in fallen leaves. It flowers so late that even its own narrow, two-inch-long leaves color too, in shades of faded rose and biscuit yellow and orange. There is something deeply touching about any flower that blooms so late, and we wonder how it has time to make seed. It seems forgetful of that necessity, and even, therefore, faintly tragic, or at least melancholic. But then, so is the season in which it flowers. Seedlings do appear, however, from time to time, close to the large flat fieldstones that make a path above the stream. We can only marvel at them and be grateful.

Gardeners who live in cool mountain climates such as ours can have gentians in bloom from late April to late October, one species stepping forward as another fades back. They are all quiet plants, somehow, despite an intensity of blue that is almost legendary, and that gave D. H. Lawrence the poem we have remembered.

HARDINESS

"Vermont?" a horticultural friend quavered when he learned we had decided to move there. "Why Vermont? It is so cold there. And the growing season is about fifteen days! You'll be lucky if you can even grow ferns and mosses."

Even then, thirty years ago, we knew that gardeners loved to exaggerate the difficulties of climate, theirs and yours. It is always colder than it is, or drier than it is, or hotter than it is, either because it feels that way, or because of some remembered, once-every-fifteen-years event. But we had also done a little research, and had determined that though winters in Vermont were certainly cold—as much as 30 degrees below zero at times—there was reliable snow cover that insulated the ground and protected the roots and crowns of plants. Better, Vermont also enjoyed cool, buoyant summers, with evenly spaced periods of sunshine followed by brief spells of summer rain, and a long, mellow autumn that was famous for its beauty. Soils can be dry and rocky in the northern part of the state, but the southern part, where we proposed to move, was glacial till overlain by a deep, well-drained, neutral to slightly acid loam, the "ideal garden soil" that is seldom met with.

We had also seen the land, twenty-three acres on a south slope at the base of the Green Mountains, high above the isolated and not very populated village of Readsboro. The land was beautiful, with old mature hardwoods of maple, beech, and ash and a sprinkling of somber hemlock. A five-acre meadow lay far in the back corner. Most wonderful, however, was a little stream that gurgled through the property, looking, on the first day we saw it, fresh and alive and somehow companionable, as if it welcomed us. Some people buy land because it is available as an investment or because they suddenly need to build a house someplace. We bought ours because we fell in love with it. And if, like a lover, it had all the characteristics we found desirable save one, we would learn to compromise on that.

Our feeling for our land has not blinded us to the real challenges and even difficulties of making a garden in such a cold place. They are considerable, and as some recede others step forward. There are always surprises, though we are happy to realize that they fall about evenly on the sides of success and of disaster. Over our years here, we have gained some wisdom about both, and that is what we wish to pass on.

In the first few years of our gardening life, we were too ignorant to assess our chances of success very accurately. So, like most beginning gardeners, we checked in references, which always list the probable hardiness of any plant. We had determined from the USDA hardiness map printed routinely at the beginning or end of most gardening encyclopedias that our garden-to-be lay geographically in Zone 4. Consequently, if we read for example in *Wyman's Garden Encyclopedia*—our bible then—that a certain tree or shrub was "Hardy to Zone 6," we did not add it to our dream list or, when we saw it in a nursery, give it more than an admiring wistful glance. Though many beautiful plants were designated for survival in Zone 4, many others were not. And as the costs of building left so little money for trees and shrubs, we were very conservative about taking chances.

We have since learned that though hardiness maps are a valuable resource and are constantly being revised to reflect more subtle geographic gradations in climate, they are at best a rough-and-ready guide to actual hardiness. They do offer parameters, but, with careful manipulation of other variables such as soil quality, drainage, water, fertilizer, mulches, and various winter protections, any gardener should be able to extend the range of his garden by perhaps two zones above his own. Plants now grow here that are generally listed as hardy to Zones 7, 6, and 5, and in fact, if all the plants listed to Zones 6 and 5 were eliminated from our garden, it would be a poor thing to see. So when an inexperienced gardener says to us, "But that's not hardy here!" we frequently reply, "Try it." We doubt, however, whether many of our plants in the warmer ranges would have survived here in the beginning, for several reasons.

The first is wind, for though the south-facing slope of our garden provides both abundant sunshine and good air drainage, bitter winds rake up and over us from below, and winter wind is the first enemy to hardiness. We are always a little embarrassed when asked by other gardeners to "admire the view," for in most gardens, views generally mean wind, and wind inevitably means the loss of all but the sturdiest plants, many of which must be natives adapted to withstand it. Our own views, though not spectacular, are—or rather were—very fine, particularly to the south of the garden, where thickly forested mountains rise up, part of the vast Green Mountain National Forest. From inside the garden, we now get only the merest peek at them, for they have been mostly planted out to strong-growing conifers that provide shelter from the desiccating winds of winter and early spring. Those conifers—mostly spruce, pine, and arborvitae—were planted early in the garden's life, as much to provide privacy and a sense of enclosure as shelter. But now most of them are perhaps thirty feet tall, and they have given us at least a full zone of hardiness, so we consider most of our garden now Zone 5, and a warm Zone 5 at that.

It is a general truth that as gardens grow older, they grow warmer. Most plants, after all, live in mutually sustaining communities, not isolated as a single specimen, as one sees too often in the middle of suburban lawns. As layers of plants build up, they offer protection for others. The tall hardy and wind-resistant evergreens shelter lower-growing, more tender ones, which in turn shelter delicate perennials, ferns, and woodland plants. In the case of plants that do not die down to the ground as perennials do, that protection is not only from wind, but also from winter sun, which can desiccate the exposed leaves of evergreens and the bark tissue of deciduous plants while their roots are locked up by frost and therefore unable to replace moisture. Such shelter belts provide pockets of the garden that seem warm even on the coldest days—or at least warmer. If they are occupied by something known to be perfectly hardy, it should be transplanted elsewhere to make a place for something marginally hardy. In fact, a large part of securing hardiness is shifting things about in a restless attempt to make everything, even plants of dubious hardiness, grow happily in the garden.

Houses also offer wonderful protection for marginal plants. Some evergreens will gain a zone of hardiness—or even two or three—if shaded in winter, a condition most frequently offered by the north or west side of houses or outbuildings. The wonderful thing about such spots is also that there may be a basement wall that leaks heat, a fact only a true gardener could celebrate. We treasure every inch of our foundation walls. On the winter-shaded sides, we have been able to grow a splendid specimen of the native American holly, *Ilex opaca* (leaf hardy to Zone 6), and a splendid clump of tall bamboo with glamorous golden stripes on its green culms, which now reach almost to the house roof. Even the sunny, windswept portions of the foundation have provided homes for sweet violets in many varieties, and—improbably—a single plant of *Nicotiana langsdorffii*, which came of itself and has stayed faithfully for seven years, behaving as the true perennial it is, though it is root hardy only to Zone 9.

Where there is percolating water under frozen ground, as, for example, beside our little stream, trees and shrubs that would otherwise perish in our winter lows manage also to flourish, provided they will accept swampy ground at their feet. Knowing early on (from references) that the native sweet bay tree, *Magnolia virginiana*, was essentially a swamp dweller (though reliably hardy only to Zone 6), we took a chance and planted one in a small bog that forms in the upper garden where the stream briefly divides. It has persisted for twenty-five years, rewarding us all summer long with four-inch-wide, creamy white fragrant blossoms. And, though it is quite hardy, a specimen of *Hamamelis* ✕ 'Brevipetala', the intensely fragrant Chinese witch hazel, surprises us each December with its precocious orange-rust thrums of flower. In another site here, it would perhaps bloom in March, but in December, it is most welcome indoors, as an alternative to the traditional sorts of Christmas flowers we never have.

There are other ways to play what might be called the "hardiness game." Chief among them is winter protection. In most years we can count on reliable snow cover, of a depth terrifying to most gardeners elsewhere but comforting to us. But one winter out of every ten will be what is called an "open winter." Then, no snow falls until March—if then—and the coldest temperatures we can endure occur in late December, January, and February. Early in the history of our garden, we had our hearts broken by these open winters, and since then, we have laid about two tons of evergreen boughs over sensitive plantings every year. Two tons is not so much as one might think from the sound of it, about four pickup loads, and farmers around us are glad to supply them for a little extra money between Christmas tree harvesting and sugaring. In fact, probably the best boughs are from the bottoms of Christmas trees, chiefly spruce, for pine is too loose and hemlock loses its needles. Spreading boughs is late October work, clean and efficient, and there is a comfort in tucking in heaths and heathers, rock garden plants, hellebores, and tender and newly established perennials under such a sweet-smelling blanket. In a normal year, snow would do this work. But we feel better for doing it ourselves, and we must assume the plants do as well.

It is a happy fact that the earth itself is always warmer than the ambient air, so if the air temperature is minus 20 degrees, it may be much warmer close to the soil. It is that warmth we hope to capture with our covering of evergreen boughs. But any marginal plant we can bend to the ground gets bent, and then covered with Remay, a wonderful horticultural cloth that traps soil warmth, and then by evergreen boughs. Such treatment is given to many of our roses, particularly the pillar roses, which would otherwise whip about in frigid winter winds and simply not be there come spring. It is nasty work, with every thorny cane hungering to rip into tender human flesh. But once done, it is done, and clouds of fragrant flowers are our reward in early summer. The taller bamboos are also bent to the ground and covered in the same way, and though they are generally kinder under our ministrations, their thick culms can creak and then crack, spoiling next year's show. Roses are mean and bamboos are meek, but both must be treated with great patience.

Then there is the use of clunky boxes and burlap and whatever sturdy thing might be left in the basement that has promise for this purpose. We know a very fine gardener in New Hampshire, in a zone as cold as ours or perhaps one below us, who once boasted that he had gotten winter protection down to a coffee tin and a rose cone. Not so here, for though our snow cover and our evergreen boughs will do for most winters, we have learned that certain important plants need a sturdy shelter to endure our winters. For example, English boxwoods are important features of the garden, and ours have now grown into great pillows five feet wide and as tall. Because they are evergreen, they have not a hope aboveground in our blustery winters. Burlap will not do, nor will Remay. Only boxes work, and we have now had to resort to a hinged affair, because there is no place here to store a box five feet wide and as tall. When the boxwoods are uncovered, their fine rich green in early spring is splendid against the daffodils.

Finally, we treat every broad-leaved evergreen with an antidesiccant marketed as Wilt-Proof. It is mixed with water and sprayed on with a backpack sprayer, just before temperatures begin to drop below 40 degrees, which in our garden is in late October or early November. Careful judgment is required, but if one should miss the moment first time round, there is almost always a second chance a week or so later. And we hope there is a third, when the January Thaw occurs, sometime toward the end of that month. All the rhododendrons are treated, including the most hardy, such as the Yakushimanums, for though they can perfectly well endure our winters, their beautiful apple-blossom trusses in spring are completely spoiled by winter-browned leaves. We want a ruff of fine green around each bouquet of flower, and we have it, this way.

Gardeners live for challenges, and playing games with hardiness is perhaps chief among them. There are no gardeners anywhere, even in the most privileged of climes, who do not long to grow something they cannot. All gardeners know Pride, Envy, Lust, Greed, and sometimes Anger, and manipulations of the hardiness of plants encourage all of those, though not Sloth. Still, try as hard as we will, sometimes we fail. We know with plants, as Marianne Moore said in her poem "The Student," that

> *Wolf's wool is the best of wool*
> *But it cannot be sheared because*
> *The wolf will not comply.*

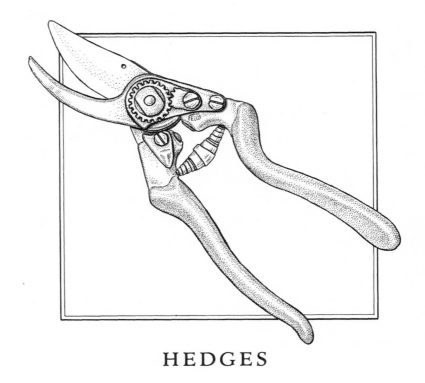

HEDGES

EARLY THIS SUMMER, a time that is really the prettiest in the garden, we finally accepted the fact that we had to do an act of violence to our great old yew hedge. It was planted in 1978, the first real year we began gardening here. The thirty balled-and-burlapped plants, each three feet high, were a special cultivar called 'G-4', which sounded to us like a cough syrup, or possibly some patching material for automobile bodies. But it had been highly recommended for its hardiness by our friendly salesperson at Weston Nurseries, in Hopkinton, Massachusetts, and since we had moved so far north of Boston, or so it seemed then, we were not yet ready to take chances, especially with a large order that had sorely taxed the small budget of two young schoolteachers.

We have never met with this cultivar again, and we know now, from many other forms of yew growing all through the garden, that we need not have been so cautious. Still, it is an attractive plant, differing from the commonly chosen 'Hicks' yew by a denser, slower growth, and from 'Hatfield' by the fact that it never forms a central trunk. For all these virtues we might have chosen it even without our fearfulness about hardiness.

When the yews arrived, we remember thinking two things. First, they seemed terribly lonely and insignificant, sitting in a huddle at the edge of the road, with a vast expanse of raw subsoil between them and the newly constructed house. Second, though we knew we wanted a yew hedge (Thalassa Cruso had told us so, in her masterful *Making Things Grow Outdoors*), we had no idea where to put it. As landscape designers for twenty-five years now, we have frequently dealt with this particular panic in others, and we would have welcomed someone whom we respected saying simply, "Just put it there!" But there was no one to do that, and so we thought first perhaps it should go off the corner of the house, and then perhaps it should screen us from the road. We finally settled on a compromise, which was to put it midway between the house and the road, creating a barrier behind which we could establish a vegetable garden. We thought at that time that it would always be "the Vegetable Garden," close to the back door and the kitchen, as conventional wisdom dictates. We had no idea then that this property would experience many "gardens," and that the vegetable garden itself would move five times before it settled in the daffodil meadow, where it has been for fifteen years.

The choice of where to plant that hedge was absolutely arbitrary, born of impatience, confusion, and our sense that our investment had to sit from weekend to weekend aboveground in the hot spring sunshine while we taught school and were making up our minds. It was our first mark on our land, and in one sense, where we put it was irrelevant. Some other garden would have grown out of some other placement, and occasionally we find ourselves wondering what that garden might have been like. It would have been different, certainly. Better? We cannot know. For though our garden vision has been able to stretch always to what might be, it is no good at what might have been. What difference would it make, anyway, since the hedge is now a towering nine feet high, could not be moved, and will never be chopped down, at least by us.

So the yew hedge got planted roughly where we decided, though we remember that an enormous buried rock forced us to put the opening in the hedge a third of the way up, and not dead center, as a slavish adherence to symmetry would have demanded. Like so many good things in a garden, that was a happy accident, a forced adaptation to a problem that could not otherwise be solved. Now one enters that space with a focus up, not both ways. We certainly would have chosen to put the opening just there, if we had known to choose.

What we did know was how wide to make it. Most gardeners realize that a certain generosity of space is an important part of a garden's beauty. Gates, paths, steps, terraces, and lawns should be wide and gracious. It is true, certainly, that more intimate spaces—stepping-stone paths through the woods, a tiny terrace with a bench just for resting and taking a breath of air, a narrow, single stone fording a stream—can be wonderful if they suggest room for only a solitary traveler through the garden. But access to major areas should be ample enough for two people, at least, to walk side-by-side, and not straggle out like a line of baby ducks. That is the practical side of the issue. But even when a garden is merely viewed, a sense of expansiveness, of wide reaches of space, must be preserved. We think we knew that instinctively, though perhaps we were influenced a little by the need to stretch our thirty bushes as far as they would go. However it was, we made a comfortable opening originally eight feet between the yews on either side.

But plants grow. And they do not just grow taller. Our ample entrance shrank first to six feet, which was acceptable, and then to four, which began not to be. When it reached three, we knew we had to take some sort of action. For it was clear that things were only going to get worse, until no opening was there at all. One would simply just have to slither through. So we took our tools in hand, cutting away a full three feet on the left side of the entrance. The results were grim.

For a mature hedge is essentially a green skin clothing a skeleton of gray branches. When the skin of green is removed, sunlight shining on the wood will awaken dormant growth buds that will develop into small shoots and eventually into well-leaved twigs that will provide another green skin. Hedges need not be of evergreens, of course, and many fine effects can be achieved from deciduous plants that will accept this occasional radical surgery, such as beech, hornbeam, Cornelian cherry, and even the much-scorned privet, which can look quite handsome when well tended. Even highbush blueberry can make a fine hedge, if you do not care about the berries, or lilac, if you do not care about the flowers. In fact, almost any woody plant that will accept hard pruning can be made into a hedge. We have even wondered whether willows might be struck as rods to provide a hedge both quick and cheap. Of course, such a hedge would require pruning practically weekly, but that would be no worse than lawn grass.

But evergreens are best, especially in the dark months of the year, when they step forward in somber magnificence. Among evergreens, from time immemorial yew has been the first choice for high hedges, and boxwood for low ones. The native arborvitae, *Thuja occidentalis*, makes a very fine hedge, if it is pruned very carefully. Beyond those, there are very bad choices, such as white pine, spruce, and hemlock, which, though often available just for the digging, will never rejuvenate new growth from hard wood. Nothing can bring a hedge of trimmed white pine, or spruce or hemlock, back into order once it is overgrown. But any hedge—any whatsoever—must be allowed a few inches of annual growth. So sooner or later, it *will* get overgrown. You can take it practically as a law of Nature. Still, there are hedges that have been handsome for a hundred years or more, and there are three secrets to their many decades of beauty.

First, they have been maintained according to the cardinal rule of hedge pruning, which is "Prune little and often," even from the first year of growth, because building up a branched internal structure—what gardeners call a scaffold—will matter later. Second, they have been battened, pruned on a slight slant from bottom to top so that sunlight falls evenly across the face of the whole hedge, preventing the base from becoming thin and straggly. Third, they have been kept in superb health by frequent fertilizing, and by dealing with insect pests and diseases as soon as they appear.

Of all these factors, probably good culture is the most important. Many hedges are too often planted, periodically hacked at when they look ragged, and then mostly forgotten. But they are not walls or fences. They are living plants, asked to grow far closer to one another than they would naturally grow. How close depends on the species, its rate and pattern of growth, and perhaps on the gardener's impatience. The best hedges are spaced widely, so that each individual roots deeply before it must compete with its companions on either side. Even so, sooner if not later they become congested, for hedges, unlike probably any other garden plants except lawn grass and groundcovers, are meant to crowd each other and fill the voids between.

Of the three rules for maintaining beautiful hedges over many years, we neglected two. We did not prune "little and often." We were too thrilled that our hedge got first twice as tall as the little bushes we put in, and then so tall that we could not see over it. But our second infraction was to give insufficient attention to the health of our hedge. On its own dropped needles, windblown leaves in its shanks, and the general richness of the garden soil around it, it seemed to be doing just fine. Fine, that is, until we had to cut it back hard. Then we wished we had paid more attention to it, for we were asking a lot, and we have not gotten as much as we hoped. Some of the stems, as thick as wooden spoon handles, have shown encouraging puffs of green shoots, and those shoots, cut back by half in early spring, will branch and spread, creating in time a new green skin. But we have spent a whole growing season anxiously scraping with our fingernails, and we know that many branches are dead. It may be that next year's hot spring sunshine will activate additional buds closer to the trunks and we will have fine new growth there. But a second pruning job awaits us early next spring, of cutting back pulpy dead branches that will never rejuvenate.

Many activities in a mature garden are best described as "biting the bullet." We are certainly not the first to discover this fact, for when Vita Sackville-West died, and the two brilliant gardeners she left behind—Sybille Kreutzberger and

Pamela Schwerdt—had to take over, their first task was to reduce the yew hedges essential to the structure of Sissinghurst, from their girth of twenty feet to five. Christopher Lloyd also said that the hedges at Great Dixter, planted by his father, Nathaniel Lloyd, more than one hundred years ago, had been reduced four times. Each time was a trauma, and Christo shuddered at the thought that soon it would have to be done again.

Knowing all that we now know about hedges, we have begun to make preparations. This autumn, as long as the weather allows, we will dig two buckets of composted chicken litter on each return from our morning chores, and spread it at the roots of our hedge. By winter's end, or in early spring, we will have supplied rich material its entire length. Then we will lime it, for despite the conventional wisdom that all evergreens like acid soils, yews enjoy a neutral to slightly alkaline soil. Once our hedge is in the best health we can manage, we will hack at it again. We do not expect the process to be either pleasant or attractive. But it must be done.

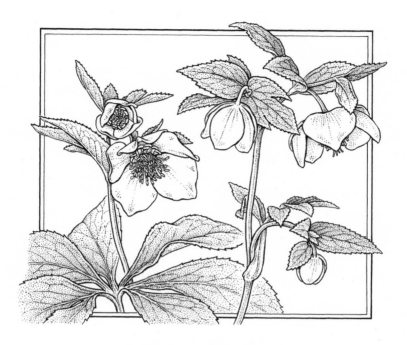

HELLEBORES

"IF POSSIBLE," the great English garden writer Margery Fish quaveringly suggested, "I think hellebores should be grown as separate clumps, so that each plant makes a picture with its flowers and leaves . . . I like to come across my hellebores in odd places" (*Gardening in the Shade*, 1964). Of course, she well knew it was not possible, for when one comes to love hellebores, those "odd places"—snug spots under the holly or against the cool stone steps of the garden shed—quickly run out. So wonderful are these plants that it is not hard for the whole place to go to hellebore.

Other people know that as well as we, like David Culp,

whose Pennsylvania garden contains (at last count) between four thousand and five thousand hellebores. We have never numbered ours. We are not sure we even could, for it would be a little like "Guess how many jelly beans are in the jar." But our fondness for them has made us break a cardinal rule in our garden, which is that each plant, no matter how splendid it is, should occupy its own place, and not be dotted about everywhere, thereby diluting its impact. So there are hellebores in the back garden along the woodland path, hellebores thickly clustered on either side of the pergola walk, and hellebores in the rhododendron garden. We are even beginning to contemplate a nursery row of them under the huge old blueberry bushes in the vegetable garden. Our appetite for hellebores seems to increase almost as rapidly as new crosses, unfamiliar species, and unusual colors become available.

It is always interesting to ponder the almost magnetic pull some flowers have on gardeners. In the case of hellebores, the unlikely season in which they bloom is the first of their many charms. In cold gardens such as ours, few plants flower between late December and early March. Those that do are mostly shy things—witch hazels that uncurl their fragrant threads of copper or gold on warm days, the tiny pink perfumed tubes of the winter viburnum (*Viburnum ×bodnantense*), or inch-high snowdrops piercing through crusts of ice. Hellebores are their companions, though by contrast, many are boldly beautiful, with flowers that would command as much attention in high summer as on a cold, raw day in March. If it could be forced to bloom later (God forbid!), the pristinely elegant *Helleborus niger*, the Christmas rose, would surely be coveted for a June bridal bouquet.

"Hellebore" is a mellifluous word, though it has a slightly ominous sound, seeming to preserve a shadow of its dark ancient Greek meaning, "food to kill." All species of hellebore are poisonous, none more so than *H. niger*, from which the old pharmacists brewed one of the most deadly poisons they offered. (It is called "niger," meaning "black," for its inky black roots.) It is happy, then, that the common names of the two most widely grown species have a more cheerful sound. *Helleborus niger*, the earliest to bloom, is called the Christmas rose, and *H. orientalis*, flowering a month or so later, the Lenten rose. Parkinson first made the comparison in the seventeenth century ("like unto a single rose"), and it fits, if one thinks of the wild, five-petaled English eglantine.

But you must not look for the delicious tea-sweet fragrance of that rose in any hellebore, or for that matter any smell at all, except in the aptly named *H. foetidus*. Sadly called, both in Latin and in English, the "stinking hellebore," it smells bad only when molested, and not all that bad either, something like the distant smell of skunk that some people find pleasantly redolent of spring. Its stout, persistent two-foot stalks are topped with beautifully fingered evergreen leaves and with masses of nodding green bells in early daffodil season. It is very beautiful, for all its unfortunate name, though we have largely given up growing it here. Its hardiness is listed only to Zone 6, and its fleshy, evergreen top growth seems unable to survive our cold winters, though we have occasionally had spontaneous seedlings from plants that managed to flower. Perhaps we will try again.

Also possessed of pure green flowers is *H. dumetorum*. It is among the first to bloom in spring, and its flowers are the smallest of all the species, an inch or so across, demurely nodding. Many gardeners pass over it in favor of showier species and hybrids, but we admire it just for its modest beauty. We grow it at the base of an old, rotting beech stump on the pergola walk, rather apart from its companion hellebores, the more to show off its shy and gentle charm. It is reliably hardy here, and perhaps one of the rarest hellebores we grow.

More common in gardens and hardy from Zones 3 to 9 is *H. niger*, and at its best it can be a stunning garden plant. In earliest spring, a well-established clump can form a perfect bouquet of as many as fifty snow-white, four-inch-wide flowers, looking as if some skilled hand had arranged them in a vase beneath the earth. But "well established" are the key words, for the Christmas rose is notoriously slow to settle in, and cranky in its needs, which seem erratic and even willful, but which certainly include a position in cool, dappled shade, a humus-rich, well-drained limey soil, and plenty of moisture. Still, it may pout like a sick child for some need it cannot name. That is its nature, and the great thing is not to fuss over it, but to do the best one can and be patient. Most certainly, once it is happy, it should never be disturbed, for though old plants can be divided, separated bits are even slower to accept a new life than young plants raised from seed or transplanted from pots. *Helleborus niger* has also been a shy parent to hybrids with other species, though a handful exist, most notably the wonderfully named *H. ×ericsmithii*, though who Eric Smith was is a mystery to us. It makes a fine, sturdy, fuss-free plant that bears cobs of abundant white flowers, which in bud look like thick clusters of grapes and which age to green and rose pink. It is not reliably hardy here, but we have had good success with it in a pot, over-wintering it in the coolest spot of our greenhouse.

As often happens in families, however, another hellebore, *H. orientalis*, has stepped forward to make good the deficiencies of its close cousin, in its good nature, its ease of cultivation, and—put bluntly—its readiness to procreate. "I fear they are all rather promiscuous plants," Margery Fish comments in her ladylike way, "but they are all very beautiful." She is of course right, for the commonest random seedling will show modestly down-turned flowers with a fine brush of green over a rose-tinted base, and when their faces are turned upward, a finer rose or pink, perhaps freckled over with russet. Such seedlings are always to be found clustered under established plants like tiny chicks under a mother hen, and if you are after positive sheets of hellebores—a woodland carpeted with them—then every tiny one will be worth transplanting. They should reach flowering age in their third year, and though the rarest, sought-out colors will probably not be among them, not a one will seem homely to you.

Helleborus orientalis is an entirely amiable plant, hardy from Zones 3 to 10, a range few other desirable garden plants can claim. Like the Christmas rose, it would prefer that moist, humus-rich, semishaded, and well-drained spot where so many other choice woodland plants will thrive. But it will put up with far less than its idea of the best, making a fine show in thinner, poorer soils and in deeper shade, or in cooler northern gardens even in full sun. Anywhere you can grow hostas, *H. orientalis* will be happy.

It is with the Lenten rose that breeders have had their greatest fun, for in addition to possessing a wide color range as a pure species, it readily accepts crosses with others in the genus, to the extent that the finest forms now available should really be called *H. ×orientalis*, or less ponderously, simply "oriental hybrids." The leaves will always be similar, made up of handsome, broad-fingered, dark green palms of eight to ten leaflets, each finger three to six inches long, each leaf standing on its own foot-high stem. A single clump develops slowly but surely over many years, eventually forming a circle of a hundred leaves, all facing outward from the center. One of the wonderful things about *H. orientalis* is that, like a peony, once it has made itself at home it is there forever. Unlike peonies, however, it seems quite unable to compete with other plants, particularly grasses, which soon will smother it out.

As a result of recent breeding, the flowers of *H. orientalis* can be almost anything, from five-pointed stars to perfect circles and cups and even (more and more) doubles. As for their color, there exists both a difficulty and a fascination. Most of the flowers could be called pink or red or white or deep purple, but as with fine wines, they always seem in need of more descriptive adjectives. So they are described as brick or carnelian or burgundy red, coral or cameo pink, ivory or acid green, steely slate blue or satin black. Even then, precise descriptions are elusive, for in all hybrid forms there are apt to be strange overwashes of other colors, shadings and subtleties, freckles and stripes. When a particularly fine plant occurs, it is given a name, such as 'Pluto' or 'Black Prince', 'Celadon' or 'Cosmos'. But hellebores are not bearded irises and still less, daylilies. All species resent root disturbance to a greater or lesser degree, and therefore named forms cannot be divided and redivided for rapid increase. So most breeders have chosen to concentrate on strains—of deep black or pure rose or clear green or white— and in flower forms with pointed or rounded petals, or doubled. More and more, a pretty face is simply described by its strain, as, for example, "Black Seedling Strain," and that, of course, allows nurserymen to sell young plants before growing them for three years to determine their precise color. Most will be within the range specified, though there are always surprises. Still, to repeat Margery Fish, "they are all very beautiful."

And so, in their way, are the random seedlings huddled under any mature plant. It is for that reason that we have contemplated a nursery row of them in the vegetable garden, a place for them to develop from the one tiny, three-lobed leaf that is their newly sprouted shape, to strong, youthful clumps that can then be carefully transplanted into our woods of old beeches and maples. Then, perhaps, we could share Margery Fish's pleasure, and "come across our hellebores in odd places."

ILEX

A FRIEND OF OURS writes often in the depths of winter, sometimes every day, to tell us what is happening in her garden, and to ask what we have happening in ours. It is a season in which one is desperate for news. And there is always something, even in the darkest days of December, in one or another of the greenhouses at least. But outdoors only the last bits of the native witch hazels still unfurl their threads of petal, dull mustard yellow but vivid against the prevailing white of snow and the gray bark of the trees. Outdoors, at this season, bark is mostly what one studies, and though the somber beauty of trunk and twig are all deeply satisfying, they also create a hunger for any speck of color that might be. So the blaze of berries on the *Ilex verticillata* always causes a shock of pleasure, even though we have been seeing them at this season for almost thirty years.

There are three bushes, trees really, since each is ten feet tall, spreading across the gray clapboards of the house and extending upwards to its cedar-shingled roof. Each of them is thickly hung with scarlet fruit, and because their twigs and trunk more or less match the gray of the house and roof, the berries seem spangled there. With snow thickly on the ground, and only the somber black of the yews and rhododendrons, winter in the garden might present a most melancholy scene. We are glad, then, for the brightness of the ilex berries, and treasure them for as long as they last.

We are hardly alone in our appreciation. For though we have few guests at this season, the garden is not unvisited. In early October, just before the weather gets crisp and the leaves turn, robins begin their flight south, and our garden lies squarely in their path. To us, it is a mystery that the robins prefer the three ilex across the front of our house to those growing in the wild, with berries so numerous on the twigs that they weigh the branches to the ground. We see such bushes all along the highway from the Canadian border well into southern New Jersey and beyond, and they are never robined. Perhaps house-grown berries are tastier, or perhaps the prevalence of well-stocked bird feeders has made the birds believe that the best things are often to be found around people's houses. Or maybe they are just eager to make us miserable, intruders, after all, in a world they knew long before us.

Whatever the explanation, they settle in flocks on our bushes and can strip them in a day, each bird gulleting down more berries than you would think its little body could contain. We sometimes impatiently call them "robbings," for they are greedy in really unseemly ways. We used to net our bushes, and one year we fired some sort of harmless gun in the air that had been given us by a neighbor whose boy had outgrown it. Now we just hope a sudden cold snap will encourage them to get on their way southward before all our berries have been taken.

But we are inconsistent. For after the passing of the New Year, beautiful little crested cedar waxwings will come, shyer than the robins, lingering only a little while to grab a berry or two before flitting away. We wish they would stay longer. And in February, when the bitterest cold we experience has turned the ilex berries to wizened black raisins, flocks of yellow and purple grosbeaks appear. That is the only time we see those birds, and we sit at the kitchen table, just on the other side of two big-paned windows, gladly watching them take every berry, for there must be little else for them at this season.

There always seems to be an improbability in this display, so brilliant and in winter so welcome to us and apparently to many other creatures. Most of the year, these bushes are unremarkable, at least to the casual eye. There is, to be sure, a handsome muscularity to their trunks and a pleasing intricacy to their interlacing branches. From the beginning, we have carefully eliminated suckers to leave each clump with only three or four trunks. Each trunk is now about five inches in diameter and looks like a stout young cherry tree. When the ilex are in full leaf, visitors sometimes wonder why we have let them block the windows and arch over the front steps. But when October comes to strip the leaves away, every eye lingers, both ours within and those of a thousand birds, it seems, without.

Any gardener is always mentally remaking spaces, wondering, "What would it look like if I took that away and put something else in its place?" We have never had such a thought about these ilex. We are a little sorry, perhaps, that the house front could not accommodate even more of them, for then we might have added an orange fruited one, a yellow, or even a rare white, in contrast to the prevailing scarlet. But the house isn't going to get larger, and we aren't going to crowd more specimens in front of it. So those others are elsewhere in the garden, secondary grace notes, making scrims of many colors against each other. They are nice there too, and oddly, the robins seem to leave them alone.

Much as we love *I. verticillata* for its naked beauty, there is another in the garden that keeps its leaves in winter, which we have cherished for many years. *Ilex opaca*, the native American Christmas holly, is usually rated from Zones 5 to 8. But both of us have loved it from childhood and with something much-loved we have been willing to take reasonable bets with hardiness ratings, especially if the upper limit is close to ours. So twenty-six years ago, a fine specimen came on the first truck from Weston Nurseries, a six-foot-tall female with an impossibly heavy burlapped mass of clay at its roots. We muscled it up the drive and planted it at the northeast corner of the house, hoping that there the house's shadow would prevent its broad, shiny leaves from desiccating in bright winter sun. That is the bane, we knew even then, of many broad-leaved evergreens.

Still, we gave our one holly extra protection. For many years a heavy pine box as large as the Volkswagen we then drove was maneuvered into place over it in early December. That was, of course, the season when it looked its prettiest, and we did somewhat wonder what sort of sense it made to cover it up just at its main season of beauty. But simply keeping it alive was satisfaction enough. That was true—and remains true— about so many things growing in this garden.

Eight years later we built our barn, attaching it to the house by a small building that was initially a woodshed (which is to say just another place for garden clutter) until it became a glassed-in, minimally heated space for winter-flowering camellias. The barn and woodshed created a small semi-enclosed courtyard that lay in the shadow of the house all winter long. So we moved our holly there, just under the living room windows. In its honor that space became the Holly Court and it became another sort of ilex to look at, from another window. Two, actually, for you can see into its center from the living room, and down into its top from the second-story bedroom on that side.

Here is a landscape pronouncement of possibly dubious value: Any ilex ought to be planted in front of or below windows for winter beauty, simply because you stare out of windows so much during that season. Even in a spring when bees are scarce, *I. opaca* will still look handsome just for its spiny, matte-green foliage, though it set never a berry. *Ilex verticillata* will still display its beautifully whirled and congested stems when picked quite clean by birds. On that theory, we planted a drift of *I. glabra*, the native North American inkberry, in front of the upper greenhouse and just at the feet of the *I. verticillata*. A more experienced gardening friend had told us that *I. glabra* "looks just like boxwood but is much hardier." Wrong on both counts. Ten winters turned the leaves of all our plants a sad brown, and the eleventh—an unusually severe one—took them down to the roots and we grubbed them completely away. We are not sorry, for in their place are super-hardy Sheridan hybrid boxwoods that never need protection and always look good throughout the winter and into spring, just as any evergreen should.

And we learned this important lesson: Never, ever plant

anything that is supposed to look like something else. It won't. And if it isn't pretty in and of itself, it cannot serve the garden well. So if we *could* grow *I. glabra* into a really fine big plant, then we would—and perhaps will—though not there, on the sunny south face of the house where winds are fiercest and winter sun the strongest. Instead, we would grow it in a sunny patch of the rhododendron garden in the open woodland along the pergola. We'd choose 'Ivory Queen', with beautiful white berries against the dark green leaves, reminiscent of mistletoe. But when we planted our first *I. glabra*, in the beginning of the garden, we didn't know enough to know all that.

LEUCOJUM

Earliest spring boasts many small bulbs of great beauty, scillas and chinodoxas, snowdrops and crocus, often in a rainbow of species and selected cultivars. In such a vivid crowd, the lowly leucojum is often overlooked, for it exists in only two species that are commonly grown, *Leucojum vernum* and *L. aestivum*, and of the two, only the former, the spring snowflake, possesses variants sufficiently distinct to have been given two varietal names. Besides that, everybody knows what a crocus is, and a snowdrop too. But most gardeners have never heard of leucojums. Yet in very early spring, on a wet March morning, clumps of *L. vernum* are not to be overlooked, whatever might be offered by treasured sheets of snowdrops, or a wealth of multiplying *Crocus tommasinianus* in translucent lavender. And that is so, for many reasons.

First, there is a curious sturdiness about *L. vernum* that contrasts pleasantly with its more fey spring counterparts. Seldom exceeding a height of six inches, it forms bold, leafy clumps of rich green that could never be described as wispy or grasslike. Almost simultaneous with this growth, slender flower stalks emerge, each bearing one or two down-hanging bells composed of six equal segments, all a pristine, waxen white that seems to reflect the mild spring sun. For all their modesty, however, there is something antic in the poise of the flowers, for each petal (sepal, actually) is curved outward at its tip, and sharp pointed, the point accented by a dot of acid green that, upon close examination, turns out to be chartreuse yellow shaded to deep green. (More chartreuse, and you have the distinction of growing *L.* var. *carpathicum*; less, and you may have *L.* var. *vagneri*. It depends on the day and the weather.) The flower looks like a jester's cap with out-flaring flaps, the green dots serving for the bells, and the effect, for so small a thing, is luminous. *Leucojum vernum* seems to make everybody smile.

And there's another special thing about *L. vernum*. Whereas the slow emergence of snowdrops is watched over and measured by the gardener in millimeters from early January to March, the spring snowflakes, true to their elfin nature, appear almost magically overnight. Suddenly, they are just there. This may be in part because the low-lying, shady hollows they favor are not the first places, in spring, a gardener looks. Actually, we often have to lift a thatch of partially decayed maple leaves from a crown, revealing almost fully grown leaves and flowers, all supine and butter yellow. But a day or two in the sun, such as it is then, turns them green and upright.

If *Leucojum vernum*, for all its charm, is somewhat rare in gardens, part of the explanation lies in the difficulty of establishing the dry bulbs in autumn, when most gardeners assume all bulbs should be planted. It can be done, though the life of bulbs dug from the field is short, and so they should be ordered for early delivery in late August or the first weeks of September. The bulbs should be planted singly, about six inches apart and two inches deep, in moist, even boggy soil, for it is a peculiarity of this branch of the family that they prefer such unexpected conditions. Even so, prepare for disappointment the first year, since some of the bulbs will never quicken, and others may seem to languish for a year or two until they become established. Far better to plant "in the green," while the plants are still growing in late spring. That is how ours came to us, when a friend, before having to leave her well-established garden in Connecticut, dispatched packages of bulbs in full growth, wrapped in damp paper towels. So beg a clump from a fellow gardener, and separate and plant the bulbs as quickly as you can, within a day or two. They never look back, and often bloom modestly the following spring, abundantly thereafter. Clumps will seldom need dividing, unless one is either greedy or altruistically inclined.

The other leucojum often grown by gardeners is *L. aestivum*, popularly known as the summer snowflake because it blooms much later, just as the leaves on the trees have unfurled. It certainly bears a resemblance to its spring cousin, but it is more remarkable for its differences, and therefore, for its different garden uses. It forms thick, black-green clumps of leaves to as tall as fifteen inches, among which the flower stems, only a little taller, nestle. Each stem is surmounted by two or more delicate, nodding bells, with characteristic outflaring petals and tips of green, though this time, they are unmixed with chartreuse, saving those gardeners intent on cataloging the minute differences among flowers a deal of trouble. The flowers are small, hardly what one would call showy. They are in fact each scarcely an inch across, but against the black-green of the grass-like leaves, they glisten.

Like *L. vernum*, the summer snowflake flourishes in damp, humusy soil, and it will accept and even be grateful for dappled shade. It is therefore best established in the woodland garden among ferns, or perhaps in a hollow bay of the shrubbery, where its quiet, cool beauty will not experience much competition. *Leucojum aestivum* is a little easier to establish than *L. vernum*, but it is still best planted in the green. And since well-established, large clumps always look most beautiful, division should occur only when absolutely necessary. There is a slightly more vigorous, taller form, called *L. a.* 'Gravetye Giant', though only by close comparison is it marginally taller (by three or so inches) than the typical form. Get it if you can, but do not be very disappointed if you cannot.

It is a peculiarity of the genus *Leucojum*, which contains at best only ten species, that the two most common are native to damp European woodlands and almost boggy meadows, while all the others inhabit dry, rocky slopes around the Mediterranean from Spain to North Africa. Almost in compensation for the arid deprivations of their homelands, the remaining leucojums—what might be called the "other" leucojums—are fey and rather fussy, but they all possess a tiny, refined charm that will appeal most to the rock gardener, or to those who grow winter- and spring-flowering bulbs in pans in the cool greenhouse. Once cultivated in either place, they are apt to become addictive.

Most commonly grown in this group is *L. autumnale*, which, as its name suggests, blooms from August to October, at just the opposite end of the seasonal progression from the spring and summer snowflakes. It is an airy, delicate little plant, producing fine, hairlike leaves of a deep black-green scarcely five inches tall. Often, however, the first equally slender flower stems appear before the leaves even emerge, looking pathetically vulnerable until the leaves follow. The flowers are tiny, scarcely one-quarter-inch long and across, typically tinged with pink, though lacking any markings. A delightful form with even tinier growth bears flowers tinted a stronger pink—though still quite pale—which is usually given separate species status, as *L. roseum*. We grew it for years without, we are embarrassed to say, perceiving the difference.

Three other species closely resemble *L. autumnale*, though they are scarcely grown except by specialists in rare bulbs. *Leucojum trichophyllum* bears tiny bells composed of pale pink, pointed and reflexed sepals, and *L. longifolium* produces equally small flowers with pure white, rounded petals. Both are very nice. But particularly to be sought out is *L. nicaense*, which seems the most robust of the tiny leucojums, and also sets copious seed that can achieve flowering age within three years. All three species will begin blooming in late winter and continue through spring.

Though *L. autumnale* and the other species that resemble it are sometimes suggested for the rock garden, their precise cultural requirements really make them best when grown in pots. All are native to arid Mediterranean climates, and so demand both a very free-draining soil and a dry period in summer—what the old gardeners called a "summer baking." In most of North America, these are conditions that can far more easily be achieved in a greenhouse. Their fragile autumn, winter, or early spring beauty also richly repays the closest observation. So they are really at their best when established in shallow bulb pans, which must be kept in the hottest, driest conditions one can find throughout the summer, and moved into cool, frost-free conditions in winter. No need to worry about when to begin watering in autumn, for the bulbs themselves will tell you, by the surprise of a tiny, hairlike leaf or flower stem. You can get out the magnifying glass then, to see the beauty that is there, or you can wait for the more impressive show that is soon to come.

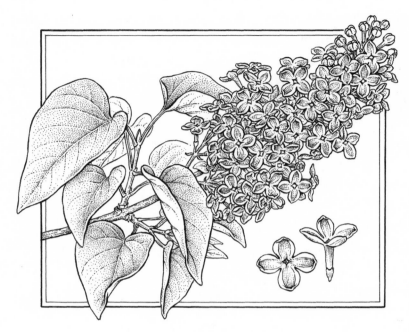

LILACS

PERHAPS EVERY PLACE in the world where plants can grow at all has one that is inextricably bound up with its essential identity. One cannot think of Los Angeles without its improbably gawky Washingtonia palms, towering upward like plants invented by Dr. Seuss. The low-lying areas of Alabama, Mississippi, South Carolina, and Louisiana would be different landscapes entirely without their ancient live oaks hung with Spanish moss. Arizona will always seem to be sprinkled over with saguaro cactus, and Texas will have its interminable stretches of sagebrush.

New England has two emblematic plants. One is of course

the sugar maple. For centuries it has been an economic mainstay, and in any accessible region of New England, specimens exist that will have provided sap for three hundred years or more. They will always be the vastest trees on any property, for though the great pines were cut for flooring, the enormous oaks for furniture, and lesser trees for firewood, maples were always left standing. We have one ourselves, a twin-trunked giant perhaps as much as four hundred years old, "the best sugar tree," we were told when we moved here, "for miles around."

It would surprise many New Englanders that the other plant emblematic of the area, the common lilac, is not native. It has been grown here so widely and for so long that one cannot picture a New England house without at least one, and in fact, arguments might occur over its origins, with stubborn old New Englanders stoutly insisting that it *has* to be native, because the cellar hole of their great-grandmother's house, now fallen in and obscured by weeds, still has a fine old lilac growing in what was once her dooryard. "Stands to reason. How could the pore old lady ever gotten anything fancy?" These are arguments transplanted New Englanders quickly learn to terminate, changing the subject to the weather, or the maggot problem with the sheep.

But the persistence of lilacs for many years, a hundred or more, is not difficult to explain. Longevity has always been prized on New England farms, and like the farmers who planted them, lilacs are hardy, enduring plants. They can resist winter lows of minus 40 degrees and still bloom come spring, and for many years. The Governor Wentworth lilacs in Portsmouth, New Hampshire, were planted in 1750 and are still thriving. The house on the farm in Pepperell, Massachusetts, where we lived when we were young, was built in 1759, and there were lilacs as much as fifteen feet across with gnarled, gray trunks a foot or more wide. One of them stood near a stone commemorating Adah Hassell, one of the first white children born in the Commonwealth of Massachusetts. Plants that live a very long time—the span at least of three human generations, often more—are intriguing, and though we know that the oldest living thing on earth is most certainly a plant, debate as to which plant that might be continues, as new discoveries appear in the pages of science magazines or *The New York Times*. Lilacs do not hold the longevity prize, of a thousand or more years, though a hundred years for a lilac is no large effort.

What makes lilacs treasured is not the years they can accumulate, however, but the beauty of their flowers, which come just as the last memory of winter and its ice and snow and barrenness are passing away in the May sun. They flower exuberantly then, hundreds of cobs of bloom appearing over gaunt, gray trunks. That conjunction is itself an emblem of the renewal of the year, but we wonder whether without the fragrance peculiar to lilacs they would matter so much. For there are fragrances—of roses certainly, of violets, gardenias, and carnations—that seem to carry the most powerful resonances. None, perhaps, is more powerful than the smell of lilacs.

The genus *Syringa* is not a small one, nor is it occupied merely or even largely by the one that is most familiar to gardeners, the common lilac, *S. vulgaris*. There are in fact twenty-three recognized species, all native to the old worlds, to Europe, India, China, Korea, and Japan. There are good reasons for growing almost every one of the twenty-three, and many do grow here in our garden. But the Balkan *S. vulgaris* has given rise to more than two thousand named cultivars, varying in growth habit and leaf, but most significantly in flower. The species has been a particular passion of the French since 1570, when Elizabeth of Austria brought it with her when she became the wife of Charles IX. Cultivation of lilacs quickly spread to gardens throughout France, and beyond. But the modern history of lilacs really begins in the late nineteenth century, when Victor Lemoine (1823–1911) undertook a celebrated breeding program with *S. vulgaris* that his firm continued until 1950, producing hundreds of magnificent plants, many still unsurpassed for beauty of form and scent. The Lemoine hybrids so dominate the world of lilacs that most lilacs are still known as "French lilacs."

It would be easy to make a garden only of lilacs, for there are so many from which to choose, and we have known someone who did just that. Thirty years ago, when we first began our garden, we visited Al Lumley, the track coach at Amherst and a passionate lover of lilacs. He had assembled a remarkable collection, six acres in Pelham, Massachusetts, that were planted to hundreds of lilacs, all arranged in neat rows and all in bloom the Sunday morning we visited. To anyone interested in plants, a large collection of one species is a very great pleasure, for though you yourself may not want to have so many different forms, it is hugely entertaining to evaluate their differences, to compare this with that, and of course, at the end, to make your selections, which will always be more numerous than you thought when you first decided to visit. On that May morning as we wandered among great old specimens, some blue as the sky, some purple like a bishop's cope, one the palest yellow like very rich cream, and some so heavy with doubled bloom that the flower trusses hung down like bunches of grapes, it was very hard to know what dozen young plants we would carry away from Mr. Lumley's nursery. He particularly praised a nineteenth-century selection called

'Bleuatre', whose small single flowers are as clear a blue as any ever seen in a lilac. Over our many years of looking at lilacs, we have never seen its equal in clarity of tint.

We bought others as well. For years we lost the name of the one that hangs double and thick like grapes, but it has turned out to be 'Victor Lemoine', named by himself for himself. The rich, deep purple 'Stadtgartner Rothpletz' also came from our visit to Mr. Lumley, as did the Wedgewood-blue 'President Lincoln', the Jersey-cream 'Primrose' that is called yellow but really isn't, and the double white 'Miss Ellen Willmott', commemorating a great gardener of the last century who employed seventy-two gardeners and bankrupted her huge fortune. All these plants are still very much a part of our garden, all planted around a little terrace below the south bedroom window where their tops are visible in the long June twilight and their fragrance is good company, all night long.

Our lilac travels began essentially in 1979. We had read of another whole class of lilacs, not from an American writer but from Vita Sackville-West, who before her death had become enamored of the Preston lilacs. They were created in the 1920s at the Morden Experiment Station in Canada by Miss Isabella Preston, who made multiple crosses between *S. villosa* and *S. reflexa*. Indeed, Sackville-West has a memorable portrait of Miss Preston, creeping around at dawn with a rabbit's fur brush, performing marriages. It is a fanciful portrait, for we suspect Miss Preston was a sensible scientist. But her achievements were remarkable, and the Preston lilacs are too little known in gardens.

They are large, muscular plants to perhaps twenty-five feet, with thick, smooth gray elephantine trunks. They form generous clumps, though as with all lilacs, three or four should be selected, and the rest removed, to create a structural plant, rather than one that is simply a wad of many ascending stems. They are prodigious of bloom, with hundreds, possibly thousands of flowers on a single large shrub. Many do not admire their fragrance, which is close to a near relative, the cat-scented common privet. But they bloom a month later than common lilacs, and the richness of their color and the abundance of their bloom offer a magnificent tier of flower above the shrub roses, which will just be coming in then. Preston lilacs are sometimes difficult to locate. But we found a nursery to the north of us, almost huddled up against the Canadian border, and up we drove, since a hard day's journey means little to any gardener who is after good plants.

We brought home three, and really, it would be very hard to claim that any of them was finer than the other two. 'Nocturne' forms an anchor piece at the left edge of the perennial garden and produces huge cobs of violet-black that justify for once a plant's fanciful name. 'James Macfarlane', a soft clear pink, is planted on the lawn edge of the rhododendron garden. But our favorite perhaps is 'Agnes Smith', a rather rangy plant to perhaps thirty feet tall, planted at the head of the rose path just as it transitions into the woods. That plant is not actually the work of Miss Preston herself, but of Owen Rogers and Albert Younger, who took up her work at the University of New Hampshire and made their own crosses. They introduced it in the early 1970s, just before we began our most active phase of garden building, and they called its flowers white. They are not white at all, but a pearly soft pink that one might call "bosomy" if one could do that without a blush.

We make elaborate claims for almost any plant we grow, for if we grow them, we love them. That is until we don't grow them, for some have been discarded as worthless, and some have simply shown a bad disposition. Any one of those discards could return again, for sometimes survival in compost piles has a way of glorifying a plant you thought you hated, and anyway, if gardeners cannot change their minds, what is it all about then? Still, there are a few plants that will always have a place here, and for which we make the most elaborate claims. Some are stately and some are lowly, but all of them possess a quality that extends beyond structure of twig or branch, leaf color or form, or even flower or fragrance. That quality we could only call soul. Lilacs have that, in abundance.

MAGNOLIAS

WHEN WE FIRST DECIDED to move from Boston to Vermont, the catalog of what our friends said we would never be able to grow included almost everything we loved. On their list—which they seemed to elaborate with each commiserating letter or phone call—were hollies, stewartias, paper bark maples, dogwoods, boxwoods, witch hazels, and rhododendrons. Our prospects in hoping to establish a garden here looked very bleak. Had it not been for the social wisdom of the state and the care with which it preserves its natural beauty, we might have felt we had made a very foolish decision. Horticulturally, it seemed we had.

The most dismaying part of this endlessly strung-out list was deciduous magnolias, which, we were assured, would not tolerate routine winters of minus 20 degrees. A few might squeak through, but even those few would probably have their flowers blasted by late spring frost, if winter itself had not already mummified their buds. This was distressing information, since both of us had loved magnolias since we were children. They were features of our grandparents' and parents' gardens, and in spring, their purple richness was up and down the streets we walked to school. They were also a distinguishing feature in the older parts of Boston, especially Back Bay, where we had lived. There they really meant spring, in all its floral abundance, and since we were coming to a thrilling sense of our adult life in so many other ways, their freshness on that old city's air meant gardening to us, another passion among many that we shared.

In the beginning, Weston Nurseries, in Hopkinton, Massachusetts, was our main source of good plants, and of all the magnolias they listed, only one was recommended as possibly able to endure the climate of our brand-new, southern Vermont garden. It was *Magnolia* ×*loebneri* 'Merrill', and we could not have begun our enduring passion for deciduous magnolias more auspiciously. That first tree now stands more than thirty feet tall, with three elephantine trunks ascending from the ground, each dividing into muscular branches that terminate in a mass of twigs. All winter long their tips are decorated with fat, fuzzy gray buds that hold the promise of spring, seeming ready to split their calyxes in any warm spell.

Wisely, they don't, waiting until the real warmth of spring, which here is usually in the last week of April. The flowers consist of about two dozen lax, inch-wide petals (tepals, to be technical), though they hang so thickly on the twigs that they recall the snow recently deep on the ground. The end of April is an unstable season, and so the blooms of 'Merrill' risk being frosted. When our great tree is in bloom and temperatures drop, there are agitated nights, with much checking of the thermometer at the back door. It is an anxiety all gardeners know, for many other tender things have ventured out then. But when, one morning, we realized that the blossoms of our 'Merrill' had withstood a night in which the thermometer dropped to 19 degrees, we essentially quit fretting. Come morning, most of the flowers were a full rich white, and not the brown rags we had feared to see.

Most gardeners, no matter what space they are given to cultivate, are also collectors. We are certainly no exception, and since our first deciduous magnolia was planted, we can now count thirty-eight specimen trees in the garden. But the precise moment we decided magnolias were for us after all was in 1973, when an article written by Dr. David Leach appeared in the newsletter of the American Magnolia Society. It was an account of those magnolias that had survived the dreadful winter of 1963, where, in Dr. Leach's Pennsylvania garden, thermometers reached lows of minus 35 degrees. We set out immediately to search for those that had sustained "no" or "slight" injury. Our printout of that article contains red pencil checks by each, and we located every one.

Magnolia stellata was on the list, and it was easy to obtain, since it was stocked by almost every nursery because it is a good sales item in spring, producing its many-tepaled white flowers while still in a five-gallon nursery can. It has many selected forms, including the pink-tinged cultivar 'Jane Platt', which was not so easy to find, but which we located via mail-order from Gossler Farms, in Eugene, Oregon. (Gossler Farms was—and still is—one of the very best sources for hard-to-find magnolias.) *Magnolia stellata* is one of the two parents of 'Merrill' (the other is *M. kobus*), and another cross between the two species produced the free-flowering 'Leonard Messel', which we tucked at the back door, where it would be sheltered from the west wind. Like 'Merrill', the nine petals of each flower are straplike, but in 'Leonard Messel' they are a fine, bright pink. The tree is now as tall as the house, producing thousands of flowers, even in part shade.

Fond as we became of all these magnolias of stellata parentage, we still thought of a magnolia as possessing the opulent, large-petaled cup of those that grow up and down Boston's Commonwealth Avenue. It was a boon, then, to find one *M. ×soulangeana* on Dr. Leach's list in the "slightly damaged" category, *M. ×soulangeana* 'Alexandrina'. We could live with slight damage, if we could even occasionally see its chalices of bloom, rose pink from a distance but actually creamy white washed with pink up close. We planted it near our stream, thereby accidentally discovering a fact invaluable to the future of our garden, that if any tree can accept percolating water near its roots, it gains at least a zone in hardiness. In fact, over twenty or more years, Alexandrina has never failed to bloom, even after our coldest winters.

Working on that same principle we also planted our first *M. virginiana*, the southern sweet-bay magnolia, actually in the bog formed at that edge of the stream, because we read that it would tolerate waterlogged soil. And so it has, growing into a rather lanky but still beautiful fifteen-foot-tall tree hanging over the plank bridge, and producing its intensely scented two-and-a-half-inch, creamy white, cupped flowers, sometimes at nose level. By now, we had really begun to prove our smug Boston friends wrong, because *M. virginiana* is usually rated to Zone 6 (−10 to 0) and we were clearly in Zone 4 (−30 to −20). So we planted other Virginia magnolias, and now there are six in the garden, all in boggy places along the stream.

In the mid-1980s, just at the peak of greatest expansion of

our garden, the number of magnolias that were hardy to Zone 4 suddenly seemed to explode. As a result of breeding done by David Leach, Phil Savage, and others, there were suddenly more magnolias than we had space to plant. Their hardiness descended from the genes of *M. acuminata*, the native American cucumber tree (so called for its narrow, six-inch-long green seed pods), the natural range of which extends from Georgia to Illinois. When crossed with more tender species, *M. acuminata* also contributed flower pigments that produced blooms of clear yellow, introducing that color to the genus for the first time. Suddenly, there was a flood of gold, beginning with 'Elizabeth', released by the Brooklyn Botanic Garden in 1977, and the largest-flowered of the yellow magnolias, with huge, butter-colored chalices of bloom. The flood still continues, bringing new magnolias into circulation with each spring's catalogs.

When gardeners are confronted with a plethora of new plants in a genus they adore, the only possibility is to contrive some special place for them. That prevents the garden from becoming jittery because forms of a favorite plant are scattered all over the place. So we planted a magnolia walk on either side of the pergola that guides you through the woods to the guest house, the daffodil meadow, and the vegetable garden beyond. We could double or quadruple the choices now, but we selected 'Butterflies', 'Ivory Chalice', 'Miss Honeybee', and 'Yellow Lantern'. ('Elizabeth' had already been planted at the foot of the rock garden, far away, and that was a mistake, because she is exposed to the cruelest spring winds in our garden. But she was too big to move.) We interspersed these selections with four specimens of *M.* ×'Who Knows What', called that because they are seedlings gathered from our garden, and are of indeterminate parentage. Two have pure white flowers and one is the palest pink, indicating to us that 'Merrill' and 'Leonard Messel' had gotten together at some point. The walk ends in a single specimen of *M. tripetala*, the umbrella tree, so called because its vast green leaves are produced in whorls and each measures twenty-four inches long. It is hidden a bit in the woods at the end of the walk, both as a full stop and because its distinctly tropical nature would be unsettling farther down. *Magnolia macrophylla* has even larger leaves, to three feet in length, but in our one attempt with it the leaves got hopelessly shredded by our spring winds.

Lately, there have been other crosses with *M. acuminata*, most notably with the rich, red-purple *M. liliiflora*, which has yielded a whole new color range for hardy magnolias, distinctly weird and haunting, almost but not quite brown, with purple and yellow streakings. It is the blend of colors you'd expect in an orchid, perhaps, but never in a hardy blossoming tree. Of course we are fascinated, and have acquired one of these crosses already, a five-foot-tall specimen called 'Woodsman', which last year produced its first strange-colored chalices of chocolate-rose.

Someday, we suppose we will have to admit that we have planted our last magnolia, but on this cold February day, with the catalogs spread before us, it does not seem likely just yet. Surely we can find room for one more. We have at least one spot in mind, behind the poultry house, against the wall of massive boulders that indicates that boundary of our property. *Magnolia sieboldii* 'Colossus' could fit in there, with its five-inch-wide waxy white petals arranged as a bowl around wine-red stamens. Though usually listed as hardy to Zone 6, like so many other magnolias growing here, we are sure it will be hardy in Zone 4. And like so many other things in gardening, it is a case of "Nothing ventured, nothing gained."

NATIVE GROUNDCOVERS

THE WORD "GROUNDCOVER" has an unpleasant sound to many gardeners, too often bringing to mind seas of boring pachysandra or myrtle. Often, it also suggests a certain lack of seriousness about gardening itself. "Want a low-maintenance landscape? Well...plant groundcovers!" It is certainly true that both pachysandra and vinca have their uses, and though they are not the most thrilling plants in the world, once established, they can eliminate many maintenance problems practically forever. But they are not one's only choices. The native American flora is rich with other plants that can also suppress weeds; require no deadheading, staking, or division; and look great on natural rainfall and reasonably fertile soils. Many are also plants of the first distinction, admired worldwide for their elegance and beauty.

Among any class of plants, one has favorites. Within the group of native plants suitable for groundcover, our own is actually a pachysandra. It is not, however, the one usually seen, *Pachysandra terminalis*, which is a native of Japan. Rather, it is a cogener, the word applied by botanists to any plants that share a genetic heritage but developed in parallel but different ways after the continents divided many eons ago. Popularly known as Allegheny spurge from its natural range, its botanical name is *P. procumbens*, an odd mis-description, for its habit is not at all lax, but rather, stiffly upright. Its matte, mid-green leaves are produced in neat, flattened whorls atop naked stems as much as a foot long, beginning with larger leaves at the edge of the circle and diminishing to quite tiny ones in the center, usually numbering a baker's dozen. In a well-grown patch, each whorl overlaps its neighbors to create a dense cover impenetrable to weeds. It grows best in shade, but sad to say, not dry shade, for it craves moist, humus-rich forest litter. Increase is very slow, new shoots rising near existing ones and over time— sometimes a long time—steadily creating a large colony. But as with all desirable plants that take their own time to increase, a modest stock can best be built up by tearing the clump apart early each spring and replanting the bits at wider-spaced intervals.

Growing in almost the same natural range as *P. procumbens* is *Shortia galacifolia*, though it is an even rarer plant, both in gardens and in the wild. Popularly known as Oconee bells, it takes that name from a Cherokee word meaning "beside the waters." That is where you are apt to find it, growing in moist shade near streams and on the shaded banks of woodland lakes. Its rich green, paddle-shaped leaves are heavily veined, and so shiny, both above and below, that they seem varnished. The plant shingles over the soil in an evergreen mass hardly six inches tall, and with the advent of cold weather the foliage takes on beautiful tints of russet and bronze. And in spring, just as the snow melts, tiny shuttlecock flowers rise above the foliage, little snow-white bells that emerge from burgundy calyxes. They last hardly a week, but during that week, you should hope for English visitors to your garden. For there, it is a holy grail plant, and your horticultural reputation will be assured.

The prettiest flowers shouldn't, perhaps, last a long time, but leaves are a different matter. And so another American plant, again found in the same woodland duff of the south-eastern American mountains, has always been celebrated be-cause its leaves have the extraordinary property of lasting up to three months in a vase of water. The plant is *Galax urceolata*, but as it is the only species in its genus, most people call it simply "galax," or by its pretty other name, "wandflower." A first cousin to shortia (which borrows its own species name, *galacifolia*, from it), the leaves are taller, to about ten inches, and slightly cupped, which intensifies their varnished elegance. Flowers, which occur briefly in early spring, are amazingly dainty little bottle brushes borne high above the leaves, on stems so hairlike that they dance in the slightest spring breeze. The leaves, which at their largest measure not more than four inches, turn a beautiful burnished red in autumn, when they used to be picked and dispersed in huge numbers by the florist trade. In fact, the city of Galax, Virginia, was once the center for such export, though since gathering plants from the wild has become appropriately unpopular, the town has turned to other pursuits.

The plants so far discussed are true perennials, all producing lush leaves from crowns or stolons. But the North American flora also boasts several low woody shrubs that form large, monospecific colonies in the wild, and can serve as useful groundcovers. The absolute aristocrat of that group must be *Cornus canadensis*, which bears the inelegant common name "bunchberry," from its thick clusters of fleshy red seed, but which otherwise is indistinguishable in everything but its height from its cousin, the American dogwood, *C. florida*. The leaves are the same, though borne in whorls atop stems hardly four inches tall. In the center, sometime in mid-spring, the "flowers" appear, really four chalk-white pointed bracts surrounding a cluster of tiny true flowers in the center. And because they are bracts, not petals, they look fresh for a long time. Outside the places it chooses to grow natively, which would extend roughly from Nova Scotia to Virginia, it can be cranky to get started. But it is very useful to know that its pink, questing stolons travel best in well-decomposed leaf mold, or even in rotted bark mulch. If young plants are established in such nutrient-poor organic material, they may clamor across it gleefully.

Among our favorites within the group of woody or semi-woody sub-shrubs is certainly *Paxistima*, sometimes also spelled Pachystima, which gives everybody trouble. Of the two species grown in gardens, *P. canbyi* is the nicer, with tiny, needle-like, shiny green, and finely toothed leaves borne alternately on sprays of wiry stems, but thick enough to discourage all weed competition. It is popularly known by a pretty name, cliff green, attesting to the fact that it prefers moist but well-drained sites, and is happiest growing at the top of a retaining wall or in a rock-strewn woodland. Its other popular name, rat stripper, is a little harder to understand, though we once did see plants in a garden stripped bare of every leaf, leaving only the naked brown twigs. Rats must have done that work, though we cannot think why, perhaps for mere mischief. *Paxistima* has several ways of covering ground, for it forms stolons from the mother plant, but also roots wherever its lax stems touch moist earth. This habit may be encouraged by bending a wiry stem to earth and placing a small stone on top to hold it down. Flowers are not much, greenish white in summer, and most people never see them, though presumably they set seed, and spread that way too.

Scandinavians might object to the claim that another wiry little shrub is "a native American," for *Vaccinium vitis-idaea minus* is their much-loved lingonberry, first cousin to our cranberry, *V. macrocarpon*, both members of the magnificent blueberry clan. But lingonberry occurs just about everywhere on the globe that is cool and moist. It forms dense mats of tiny, boxwood-like leaves on wiry brown stems, spreading over the earth by means of stolons and rooting stem tips as it goes. It is an adaptable little plant, as comfortable growing in Zone 2, where winter temperatures reach a low of minus 50, as in Zone 7, where they only reach zero. We cannot imagine how the Scandinavians can gather so many tiny berries, each twice the size of a BB, to put up in jars, and then use them to glaze their superb roast chickens in winter with lingonberry conserve and heavy cream. In our own garden, we often see their lovely nodding white bells in spring, and even an occasional red berry at Christmastime. But it would be a poor chicken indeed that could be glazed by any lingonberries we could gather. Still, the plant is very pretty, and on a rather barren sunny hillside slope here, it has flourished without care for years.

All these lovely plants are native to the eastern seaboard of

North America, ranging from the White Mountains of New Hampshire, where many vacciniums flourish, down to the Virginias, where sheets of galax may be found. But the West Coast offers treasures too, the best of which perhaps is *V. hexandra*, named for the English explorer George Vancouver. A native of Washington State down to the redwood forests of California, it has proven—as many West Coast natives do—surprisingly adaptable to other climates throughout Zones 4 to 8. Wherever it grows, if it can be given cool shade and moist soil, it will form thick sheets of thumb-sized bright green leaves arranged on wiry stems. It is a first cousin, related to the beautiful Asian epimediums, but it grows lower than any of them, hardly ever reaching more than six inches in height. There are gardeners who have complained that it is rampant and needs controlling every year by spading the outsides of the colony. We could wish you to be that lucky.

No real garden should ever show bare earth, much less a sea of bark mulch, which always represents both an opportunity lost and a failure of horticultural seriousness. A good garden may be recognized in many ways, but one of them is in the richness of its ground-hugging plants. Those gardeners who scorn "mere" groundcovers might seriously rethink the issue.

NERINES

IT TOOK US MANY YEARS to understand the specific needs of
nerines. Thirty, to be precise, because it was that long ago that
we acquired our first one from beside the garbage can of
a friend in Marblehead, Massachusetts. "They are one-shot
deals," he explained, "like paperwhites. You can't make them
bloom again." But they seemed so promising, each one sitting
on top of the soil and looking like a fat daffodil bulb. There
wasn't any foliage, but there was one wizened pink flower on a
long stem that seemed to tug at us. Anyway, bulbs always give
you that feeling of potential life that makes them hard to throw
away, even if they are only sprouted onions in the crisper

drawer. The bulbs were shoulder-to-shoulder, not nicely spaced like you'd plant a pot of tulips for forcing, but joined at the base and pressing against the rim, as if they had multiplied to that extent. And there was also the pot, an old clay one, white-crusted with lime. In any case, at that time we seemed to be running a Shelter for Unloved Plants, rescuing half-frozen ficus trees from city curbs and shrunken, dust-covered African violets from the rubbish room of our apartment building. So we took these nerines. At the least, the pot would be nice to have.

The first thing you feel about anything you rescue is that you should be especially good to it. So we tipped those nerine bulbs out of their pot, divided them carefully, and then repotted them into two pots, the first the one they came in and the other recycled from somewhere else. We used the richest compost we had, and fertilized them carefully all that first winter, during which very healthy, straplike, eight-inch-long leaves appeared. We were really hoping for abundant bloom in autumn—from two pots now—but nothing came. Our plants ripened their leaves and then quietly went to sleep for the winter. This happened for several years, but as they were no trouble and we had hopes that flowers would eventually occur, the two pots just hung around. But still, our friend had been right. They seemed a "one-shot deal." And we hadn't even had the first shot.

Then we had the great privilege of visiting a very old garden in a small village in Normandy that had been tended for over forty years by its owner, the Comtesse d'Andlau. Like many antique French houses, hers presented a blank north face flat on the street, but its south side opened through wide French doors into a large walled garden. When the house was built in the eighteenth century, much of that space would have been a paddock, a small home orchard, a place to tether the family cow or even to raise a pig or two. But it was now planted with remarkable trees and shrubs, some—like the white-berried *Sorbus cashmiriana*—of extraordinary credentials. ("Clementine Churchill gave me seed of that.")

Sadly, our visit was in late October, on a cold gray and drizzly day, and mostly there was little to admire in the garden except bark, berries, and impressive plant labels. But as our little group turned back toward the house, we noticed that the whole of the narrow bed between the old stone terrace and the French doors was vivid with carmine and coral pink, white and purple. We must have given a gasp of surprise, because Mme d'Andlau said, in her richly accented English, "Very fine, do you not think? They are nerines. Of course, you must not be too good to them!" Of course. For there was the mystery solved, in fewer than ten words: *You must not be too good to them.*

Two species of nerine are commonly grown in gardens where they are hardy, and in pots elsewhere. *Nerine sarniensis* was cultivated in France by at least 1630, and in Guernsey by around 1655. It is popularly known as the Guernsey lily because of the supposition that large numbers of bulbs washed ashore from a foundered Dutch merchant ship, took root on the shores of that island, and flourished. This watery survival gives the genus its pretty name, after Nerine, a water nymph, and the species name derives from Sarnia, the ancient Roman name for the Isle of Guernsey. But though *N. sarniensis* thrives in the mild maritime climate Guernsey enjoys, by whatever path it came to be cultivated there, it is magnificent, producing strong bloom stems to as much as eighteen inches tall, topped by an almost spherical umbel of inch-wide, six-petaled flowers. There may be as many as twenty separate flowers in an umbel, from each of which protrude prominent stamens, rather like the whiskers of a cat. The color of the typical species is an extraordinary rich scarlet dusted over with flecks of gold. It is hard to better, though there are beautiful selections that may be pinkish white, strong pink, or orange.

Our nerine—the one that came to us from beside our friend's garbage can years ago—is *N. bowdenii*, first introduced into gardens by Athelstan Bowden-Cornish, a specialist in South African flora, in 1902. In its typical form, it produces bloom stems to about fifteen inches tall, each crowned by a rather ragged umbel of two-inch-long, five-petaled flowers of a warm rich pink, ruffled along their edges and often marked with pencilings of darker pink. That seems to be the form we have had for years, though it is now relatively rare in commerce, having been superceded by hybrids that produce fuller umbels of apricot, coral, peach, pink, grape purple, and even icy white. We have some of those too, but we don't like them all that much better than the form we started with. Or rather, we like them differently. And after we received our clue from Mme d'Andlau, we have not been without nerine flowers in late autumn, ever since.

Actually, she was perhaps only repeating what many good European gardeners know. For Tony Norris, an English nurseryman who accumulated more than eighty thousand nerine bulbs and nine hundred cultivars by the end of his life, observed wild plants of *N. sarniensis* growing lustily north of Cape Town, South Africa, in some of the worst soil on earth. The chosen habitat of that species is gravelly scree or rock crevices where the nitrogen content of the soil is as low as three parts per million. Norris reasoned, then, that the previous assumption that nerines would relish the fat soils preferred by their cousins in the family Amaryllidaceae—the Hippeastrums—was simple error. He suggested a potting medium of three parts acid sand to one part peat, and no fertilizer. Other specialists have suggested other mixes, though it is certain that the best results occur from lean, fast-draining soil that is poor in nitrogen but fairly rich in phosphorus and potassium. Also, it does no harm to lace the potting medium with a bit of the worst soil in one's garden, to supply necessary trace elements. On this lean diet, nerines may flourish for ten years or more in a pot, and they ought to be left alone for just about that time, since "Do Not Disturb" is the motto for them all. They will flower best when they become so crowded that their bulbs touch the edges of the pot, in fact just exactly the way the bulbs in that pot we rescued were, before we mistakenly made them more comfortable.

Mme d'Andlau grew her beautiful nerines on garden soil above a bed of ancient brick rubble and decayed mortar. Anyone who gardens in Zone 9 or 10 could do that as well, but the rest of us must grow our nerines in pots. Bulbs are always expensive because named forms can be reproduced only from offsets of mother bulbs, a slow process at best. However, three bulbs established in a six-inch-wide clay pot, with one-half of each bulb showing above soil level, will multiply to ten or so in five or six years, blooming more profusely each year and representing wealth in many senses. After the foliage has withered, the advice repeated in many books is to turn the pots on their sides and place them in the driest, hottest place available, such as on a shelf at the top of the greenhouse, to ripen them for bloom the following autumn. We've had better luck, however, by treating our nerines more gently, placing them in sunny, protected places over the summer where a little water— but not much—may occasionally reach them.

However they are stored, they generally tell you when they have woken up by producing a slender bloom stem from the neck of each bulb. This sense of timing is a minor horticultural mystery. When the buds first show, the pots must be brought into strong sunlight, watered sparingly at first, and then more frequently as the flower stems extend and the tips of new leaves begin to appear. In a greenhouse or on a sunny windowsill, the flower stems will always bend toward the strongest light, and so pots should be rotated a quarter turn each day. It is a gentle attention and the most that nerines really want from you.

PEA SEASON

No one can say that a gardening life is rich in leisured holidays, but a gardener's rewards are festivals, big and small, though we make little distinction there, for they are all wonderful. There are other activities in which effort and labor are so certainly followed by achievement and celebration, and anyone who takes an active hand in shaping life must know equal causes for joy. We know only our life, which is largely one of gardening. So bulbs planted with raw fingers in October flower in April, their abundance in rewarding proportion to the effort of five months before. A richness of roses comes fast on the heels of the painful pruning and staking, feeding and spraying that roses both require and so abundantly reward. And for all our bruised knees and chapped fingers and sunburnt noses, we feel lucky. For whereas even children have only their birthday and Christmas, Hallowe'en and Easter, and the End of School mostly to anticipate, we can look forward to a host of special events: the season of snowdrops, and then of daffodils, then of magnolias and stewartias, and after that of lilacs and roses, poppies, asters, colchicum, autumn crocus, and snow.

Our years are rich, but though we are generally aware of our wealth, it is the vegetable garden that most makes us clip our coupons and chuckle at our dividends. We start with Egyptian onions, our earliest crop, which may be harvested and sautéed as scallions in early April when the snow is barely gone. Fine spring lettuces and radishes overlap them, and then green garlic and asparagus, and then strawberries and raspberries, blueberries and currants, and then we are at sea with high summer, the great bark of which is corn and tomatoes, all one wants in that season to eat.

A few crops and the festivals that attend their maturity are simply no trouble at all. Squash is like that. You put the seed in the ground, and a few short weeks later, you harvest the young fruits. Tomatoes require more effort, for they must be trained into cordons on bamboo stakes, and suckered and tied in, and the pests that get them in the end—wilts and mosaics and fungus—must be fought constantly with organic sprays, copper sulfate for choice. Cucumber vines must be twiddled up on strings, lest the vines crab along the ground, making the harvest a process of wading through a surf of sticky green leaves. Most vegetable crops are labor-intensive, really, but it is by the sweat of one's brow that one eats, and that is a good thing always to remember.

No crop is more labor-intensive than peas, and perhaps none is more treasured here. Effort may well equal appreciation in many human activities, and we would argue as much. What those who do not garden never seem to understand, however, is that the effort exists in one place (and brings its own pleasures) and the appreciation of its reward is in quite another. Peas are a lot of work, for the ground must be prepared early, heavily enriched with good, well-rotted poultry-yard compost, and made mellow with powdered lime. The work doesn't stop there, for once the peas are sown in mid-April, cages must be constructed above the drills to support the vines. Peas are climbing plants that attach themselves by tendrils to whatever will boost them up into the light. In the wild, any old bush or twig will do, for their interest is entirely in reproducing, and they often form hopeless tangles that matter little to their essential purpose, though it matters greatly to anyone bent on harvesting their edible seeds.

For the support of peas we have two methods, depending on their anticipated height. Tall-growing varieties, such as 'Alderman'—also wonderfully named 'Tall Telephone'—may reach as much as seven feet, taller in fact than the eight-foot bamboo poles we get from A. M. Leonard, a foot of which must be inserted into the ground to make the long, two-sided structures on which the vines are trained. A row of poles is set four feet from one another, and a second row is set exactly opposite the first, at approximately three feet apart, row from row. The poles are then crossed at the top to form an X, and lashed to a ridgepole down the center. A second set of poles is tied along the length of this structure at near ground level, and to both sides we attach lengths of black plastic bird netting. Generally, we plant tall peas in long rows of about twenty feet in length, so a good half of a day's work is involved simply in building the structures, which will then be disassembled after the pea crop is finished and the last over-ripe pods have been gathered for Old Pea Soup. It is a lot of fun, and the great nineteenth-century gardener William Robinson did it for his sweet peas, which yielded nothing for the table, but only beautiful flowers.

Even more entertaining is the construction of supports for lower-growing peas, often called "bush peas," though we have found there is no such thing, since all peas scramble and their wayward habits irritate both gardener and cook, often one and the same. The lower-growing sorts include some of the very best and most flavorful peas one can grow, the famous *petits pois* of France. For them we use a different staking method, one that carries a glimpse of antique gardening the second it is put up.

Many willows grow throughout our garden. Most of them are pollarded in spring, their last year's growth cut into four- or five-foot lengths and carefully bundled up with twine from hay bales fed to the cows all winter long and hung on a forest branch. The willows are really grown for their own beauty, for the vivid egg-yolk yellow of *Salix alba* var. *vitellina*, the orange of 'Chermesina', the scarlet of 'Winter Fire', or the dusty, silver leaves of *S. a.* var. *sericea*. But the prunings are carefully saved as supports for the choicest peas we grow, not our main crop, certainly, for *petits pois* are quite frankly petite, each one hardly the size of a peppercorn. Still, they are worth this trouble, which begins in early April and does not end until they are shelled in July.

Harvested willow twigs are inserted on either side of a rather wide row, with a hand-width trench down its middle, into which the tiny pea seeds have been generously sown about twice their thickness deep, as close almost, as the old gardeners used to say, "as peas in a pod." (Or at least, almost that close, for you can overdo the advice even of the Old Ones.) The twiggy willow stems are then gathered together into little huts or domes spaced about two feet apart and four feet tall, their tops bundled and tied with the same baling twine the twigs came up to the garden in, and the tops clipped off neatly all at the same height. The result is an effect that would have been quite familiar to Marie Antoinette, who cosseted her peas and cooked them herself in a silver saucepan with her own butter.

Beside the trouble of constructing supports—which, as we have tried to indicate, is a pleasure in itself for us—the cultivation of peas has two problems. Just after they have sprouted, peas have a curious way of thrusting themselves out of the ground. There is a wonderful sonnet by Robert Frost that alludes to this fact, called "Putting in the Seed":

> *You come to fetch me from my work tonight*
> *When supper's on the table, and we'll see*
> *If I can leave off burying the white*
> *Soft petals fallen from the apple tree.*
> *(Soft petals, yes, but not so barren quite,*
> *Mingled with these, smooth bean and wrinkled pea;)*
> *And go along with you ere you lose sight*
> *Of what you came for and become like me,*
> *Slave to a springtime passion for the earth.*
> *How love burns through the Putting in the Seed*
> *On through the watching for that early birth*
> *When just as the soil tarnishes with weed,*
> *The sturdy seedling with arched body comes*
> *Shouldering its way and shedding the earth's crumbs.*

Pea seed must therefore be very firmly planted, and perhaps nothing is better than a foot newly naked to the warmth of spring and the feel of the living earth. But a gentler touch is required when the "sturdy seedling with arched body comes," for then a sprinkling of earth from the side of the trench should be gently placed over its head until it can catch root and grow. The other great problem is crows, mischievous heavy-thinking birds that know when a pea shoot is at its most succulent, most ready to be snatched from the ground and gobbled up. But our staking methods foil them, since both methods look as if they could snare a bird, even a very big one.

Peas are beautiful even as tiny shoots, and their beauty increases steadily as they develop into little vines, clinging by tendrils to their supports. Soon mothlike flowers appear, snow white and never very numerous, each producing its tiny pod, which develops into a plumpness the gardener recognizes as ready. Actually, the first ones are eaten straight from the vine, without the grace of even a splash of water, hot or otherwise, but soon there is a flood of peas, throughout July and even into August.

Everyone works for peas. They must be picked just at youthful maturity, when the pods are plump but not bursting at the seams, nicely filled out but still fresh with flavor. If the pods are yellowed or speckled or translucent, the peas inside will be dense with starch and stolid, fit only for soup.

But when they are at their prime, the last joyful work of peas can begin, the shelling of them late in the day, usually at the kitchen table or even before a fire if the evening is cool, as it is in July, usually, in Vermont. As green as anything on earth, the fresh peas are shelled into bowls and the pods tossed into baskets on the floor, a prize for the pigs, who fortunately do not discriminate between pea and pod.

It is interesting that all the great cookbooks we know have very few recipes for peas, and many lament the fact that there are never enough peas to do much with. That is, as it happens, not our problem, though we still cannot improve on the simplest of all recipes for peas, which is to plunge them into briskly boiling water for two or three minutes, drain them, and toss them with an appropriate amount of fresh butter. You could skip the butter. For that matter, you could skip the boiling water.

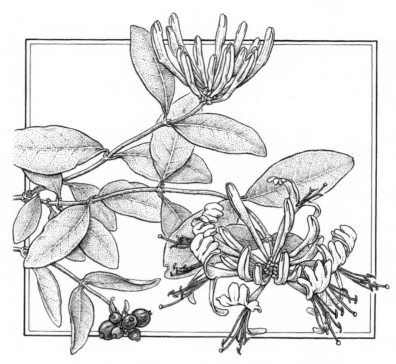

THE PERGOLA WALK

SOMETIMES THINGS WE DO in the garden work out so well that we wonder why it took us so long to get to them. The pergola walk is the best of many examples. It was put up about eight years ago, and is therefore the most recent major addition to the garden. But because its craggy locust logs have weathered quickly, and also because it is half smothered in vines, it seems as old as the very oldest parts of the garden. Older, maybe, because pergolas almost always carry the resonance of antiquity, for they are direct descendants of the *pergula* that was an essential part of ancient Roman gardens. Garden features that have been around for a long time are not always worth emulating, but at the least, they should receive careful consideration.

It was in Italy that we ourselves fell in love with pergolas, on a vacation on the Amalfi Coast one winter to escape the snows and frigid winds of home. We don't usually favor picture-book vacations, far preferring the confusion and the artistic richness of major cities. But Ravello is very close to the ancient ruins of Pompeii and not too far from Naples, where the great Borghese marbles are housed. So we had two quiet, sunny afternoons to walk the ancient streets of Pompeii almost alone, and peer into houses, taverns, and even latrines that would have been teeming with humanity two thousand years ago. We drove through Naples, an experience that makes driving in New York or even Athens seem like a ramble in the country, to see the great marble statues that Queen Christina of Sweden restored when they lived with her in the Borghese Palace in Rome. Standing below them—for they are huge—they seemed magnificent in just about every way.

But we also visited the Villa Cimbrone, a Renaissance gentleman's residence perhaps best known because Greta Garbo and Leopold Stokowski fled there briefly in a futile attempt to avoid the world's eyes. There's a small bronze plaque on the gate recording that fact. Though we saw not a soul about, we believe the house is still rented, but the grounds are open to the public for a small fee, and they are extraordinarily well kept. In early February, no flowers were apparent. Italian gardens aren't generally given to flowers anyway, and that makes them disappointing to people who think that floral color is everything there is to see in a garden. But in an old Italian garden, the walls, terraces, balustrades, paths, and most especially its segmentation into separate experiences, are always worth careful study. At Villa Cimbrone—as in most Italian gardens—

there were also trellises, arbors, pergolas, and even freestanding screens on which shrubby or climbing plants had been trained. We left there convinced that we had done far too little with vines, and that once we got home to Vermont, we would fix that, though we were not quite sure how.

People travel for all kinds of reasons, and wherever they go they find stimulation for what most absorbs them. Ideas about what to do in the garden, like other ideas about making things more beautiful—interior decoration, for example, or your wardrobe, if you care about that—come from many directions and sometimes also from simple need. Even before we made this visit to Italy, we knew that Gertrude Jekyll, perhaps the most influential garden-maker of the last hundred and fifty years, almost never made a garden without including a pergola in it. Marshall Olbrich had also told us early on that a beautiful garden was made as much from what lay above as below, from spaces and volumes in the air. We have found that out for ourselves. Even in the vegetable garden, for example, the construction of a bamboo pea trellis or a frame to support tomatoes or cucumbers always transforms the horizontality of mere rows into something far more interesting.

So a pergola—or at least what one might call the basic theory of a pergola—was already in our mind, and that trip to Italy confirmed it. But the final decision to build one came quite simply from the fact that we were unhappy when we moved through part of our garden. Above the stream the garden is split into two parts, separated by a wide grass path. That path ends in a rustic wooden gate, and for a long time, the only access to the guest house, daffodil meadow, vegetable garden, and poultry house—all important places we go to every day—was simply a dirt path through the woods. A connection seemed lacking, and a pergola seemed the solution. The day the structure was finished, it had an inevitability that made it seem it had been there forever. That is always the surest way to know you have done a good thing in the garden.

Our pergola is made of locust, which, as old Vermonters say, "lasts exactly one year less than a stone in the ground." It is improbable that we will ever test that theory, at least until we join those stones and locust posts ourselves. But it does seem certain that they will not need to be replaced during our actual lifetime. The pergola consists of eleven bays made of upright posts connected one to the other by stringers, with smaller posts placed horizontally across those to make a sort of open roof. Vines have been planted on each post—sometimes two to a post—and trained across the top. There are four honeysuckles, four climbing roses, and three wisterias, two blues and a white. They are selections of the native *Wisteria macrostachya* (once *kentuckiense*), which may lack the glamour of its oriental cousins, *W. sinensis* and *W. floribunda*, but which always blooms reliably in Vermont and is quite pretty in its way. There are also two mock oranges, which we learned can be turned into something like vines if they are tied to posts. On all these sturdy plants we have trained clematis for additional bloom, and also others, like the quite improbable climbing aconite, *Aconitum episcopale*, with hooded blue flowers late in the year, usually in mid-October. All these would be enough to make a garden, but as rich open woodland lies on either side, obviously we have added other plants, making a broad garden that melts into the surrounding woods.

And that has been the greatest pleasure of the pergola walk, since we could concentrate there on growing the rarest woodland plants we could find. Dan Hinkley has helped immeasurably in that effort, for three years after any of his amazing treks to the Himalayas or eastern China or the high mountains of Chile, some plant he collected there from seed will be growing on our pergola walk. At present, its most remarkable plants are two specimens of *Syneilesis*, *S. palmata* and *S. aconitifolia*, both members of the vast daisy clan, the first with broad, eight-inch circles of leaf cut into points at their margins, and the second with fernier, more finely cut leaves that look like those of some geraniums. There are two large clumps of *Podophyllum pleianthum*, its leathery, star-shaped pads of leaf each about a foot across, looking like no other plant that we grow here except water lilies. *Glaucidium palmatum*, the rare wood poppy, thrives both in the ethereal lavender form and in the equally beautiful white. Ferns are plentiful, none of them particularly rare, though the ostrich fern, *Matteuccia struthiopteris*, grows to an alarming seven feet tall, and native maidenhair ferns are becoming almost weeds. Certainly, though, the stars of the pergola are orchids, of which *Cypripedium kentuckiense* has proven the most vigorous, two separate clumps of it providing perhaps thirty blossoms each. We have not yet tried the most beautiful of the hardy lady's slipper, *C. reginae*, which occurs natively in the woods around here and much farther north, even to Zone 2. Stock of it is scarce, and one simply does not dig from the wild, wherever it has settled down to grow. But we will find it someday as a nursery-propagated plant, and we are sure that it will thrive on our pergola walk.

The segmentation of a garden into separate experiences is an essential part of its beauty. Usually, these separate parts are metaphorically called "rooms," and great care must be taken to be sure that each has its own identity and offers its own particular delight. But equally important is the way those rooms are connected by hallways, stairways, or corridors that link one part to another. They are the vital filament on which the beads are strung. There is great pleasure in simply getting from here to there. The connecting functions of a garden are also usually linear spaces. You walk down, up, or through them, surrounded by the garden rather than simply standing in front of it. That is why access is such an important concern of a garden designer.

Our pergola, for all the wonderful plants we can grow along it, takes its primary value simply because it connects place to place, guiding you firmly up to the daffodil meadow and the vegetable garden, which you really ought to see. So we imagine that Pliny the Younger might stroll down it in sandals, toga flapping in the cool spring breezes of Vermont, and say, "What took you so long?" So might his uncle, Pliny the Elder, though he was so fat that he simply leaned against a tree when Pompeii was engulfed, and died. He probably couldn't make it up to our vegetable garden. But he would like the pergola, which we got in large part from the place where he lived.

POPPIES

NOT ALL POPPIES look like poppies. Bloodroot is a poppy, but it looks like a daisy unless it is the rare double form, when it looks like a gardenia. *Macleaya cordata* is called the "plume poppy," but it is hard to see the poppy part in a flower that hasn't any petals at all, and waves its bronze plume on a stalk eight feet tall. What most of us call a poppy is characterized above all else by petals, most typically a double row of four to six, in a color so clear that it has a name among painters, "poppy red." It is the flower sprinkled over the elegant green and gray landscapes of Camille Corot, and its paper facsimile is given out on Veterans Day, as proof of a contribution.

There are more than seventy species of poppy, most of which are herbaceous—either annual or perennial—but some are woody, including two California natives that are among the most beautiful in the genus. *Romneya coulteri* bears spectacular, five-inch white blossoms surrounding a thick boss of golden stamens. We have flowered it here, beautifully but briefly, for it resents a confined life in a flowerpot. In fact, its questing roots can break through asphalt driveways, as we once saw in a friend's garden in Los Angeles. With *Dendromecon rigida* we had better luck. It happily settled into life in our little winter garden off the kitchen, blooming as early as March, with rich yellow, sweetly fragrant four-petaled poppies against leathery gray, arrowhead-shaped leaves. But like so many California native plants we tried to grow here, it resented the abundant summer water its neighboring camellias and tender rhododendrons required. It languished, and after three or four years, it died. So luminous and beautiful are its early spring flowers that we might try it again, but next time in a pot.

Happily, another California native poppy, *Eschscholzia californica*, has gladly accepted life here in Vermont, not in the protected climate of the winter garden but out in the open, where it seeds about exuberantly and returns faithfully from year to year. Though technically a short-lived perennial, it develops rapidly from seed the first season, flowering in a huge range of color from the brassy but beautiful orange most often seen in the wild, through red, bronze, pink, apricot, cream, and white. Double forms also exist. The one absolute requirement of California poppies is for excellent drainage, for they are native to arid soils, and so ours grow in a freestanding planted wall about four feet high that extends the length of our lower greenhouse and shop. In early summer, tufts of filmy

183

gray foliage appear from self-sown seed, pretty enough in their own way to provide an effect, but flowering soon begins in June and continues into August. Then the plants begin to grow shabby, so we cut them to within three inches of their base. They quickly send up fresh foliage, and produce flowers that last until hard frost in early October. From that second flowering, enough viable seed usually falls to guarantee a good crop of plants the following year, though for security we sprinkle packaged seed over the bed in early April.

Mixed among them we grow another poppy, *Hunnemannia fumariifolia*, native to the mountains of Mexico. Like the California poppy, it relishes cool nights and requires sharp drainage. It is called the "Mexican tulip poppy" because its four crepe-like petals form a cup around a boss of golden stamens and are perhaps the clearest, purest yellow of any flower we grow. All poppies resent root disturbance and so are best seeded in peat pots or directly in the open ground. Hunnemannia, however, does not merely resent disturbance; it is completely intolerant of it, and so it must be sown where it is wanted.

High above the planted walls at the other end of the garden, among the roses and peonies, opium poppies are in flower by late June. These are known botanically as *Papaver somniferum* from their use since ancient times as a soporific. But their rich, bosomy opulence makes them most unlike their Californian and Mexican cousins. They are sometimes called "lettuce poppies," or even "bread-seed poppies," for that is the most benign of their uses. They are in fact the source of opium and of its refined forms, morphine and heroin, but here, they are grown for the beauty of the flowers. Usually we grow three sorts, our favorite of which is a rich Concord grape single that we originally got from Lauren Springer, and which has traveled the world since as 'Lauren Springer's Grape'. We have fondness, too, for a huge white double with more than sixty petals, ethereally called 'White Cloud' but looking more like an exuberant cheerleader's pompom. Our third is a mysterious double black without a name, the inky petals of which do in fact suggest sinister properties. But two years ago, a loose, blowsy single appeared, of a pale strawberry sherbet color with a dark mauve stain at the base of each petal. We are sure it was sprinkled into our garden by some waggish visitor, as the great Ellen Willmott is said to have done with the silver-leaved *Eryngium giganteum*, which has since always been known as Miss Willmott's ghost. We are not yet sure what we think about that.

Opium poppies are self-fertile, and so we keep some distance between the various types to have them come true from seed. Seed is sown in April in peat pots to minimize root disturbance, and we have strong young plants to set out in May. But self-sown seedlings always also appear, and those develop into the best plants. However, whether transplants or volunteers, opium poppies should not be crowded together, since at maturity well-grown plants can be a foot wide and up to three feet tall. Their broad, celadon-gray leaves are eight inches long and four inches wide, laid one upon another to form a wide rosette, quite beautiful in itself. And the unfolding flower bud is balletic in its grace, first arched like the neck of a swan, and then straightening as the calyx bursts to shake out crinkled petals, much like a butterfly emerging from its cocoon. Though the double forms lack the grace of the singles, they persist twice as long, lasting four or five days before shattering, as opposed to merely two. However, even single forms will last three or even four days, if they are cut early in the morning when they are just opening, the cut ends dipped immediately into boiling water or seared with a candle flame, or, less glamorously, a cigarette lighter.

Dancing all about the garden are the great-great-grandchildren of a poppy we grew from seed at least twenty years ago. It is *Papaver rupifragum*, and it seems as long-lived as a peony. It originated in Spain and therefore is called the "Spanish poppy." It is also an abundant self-seeder, so once you have it, you have it forever. Like all poppies, however, it hates root disturbance, so unwanted seedlings can simply be scuffled out. The flowers are very delicate, always single, each born on a two-foot-tall wiry stem, and of a beautiful clear orange. There are many plants of it in the rock garden, where the first one was planted. But others have appeared between the stones of terraces and paths, and even in pots of tender shrubs that are used to ornament the garden in summer. How reassuring it is on a cold March day to find a little plant of *P. rupifragum* shyly unfolding a flower in a tubbed wisteria or camellia. The Turkish *P. spicatum* is similar to rupifragum in size and in the delicious tangerine color of its flowers, but it is double, and for us at least, not a self-seeder. So we have only one plant of it, though that one has returned faithfully for over fifteen years. We always mean to gather seed and give it company.

One can never have enough poppies of any kind, and so we grow many others, including perhaps the representative of the genus in most people's minds, *P. rhoeas*. It is called the "Veterans Day poppy" because after the dreadful carnage of World War I, the fields of Flanders were ablaze with its scarlet flowers. It comes in many shades and in doubles, but nothing quite equals the purity of the original scarlet red. We are very fond also of *P. commutatum*, called the "lady bird poppy" because each of its four tiny, inch-long scarlet flowers is marked with a black spot at its base. But the signature plant for our garden at

North Hill is yet another poppy, one much rarer in American gardens because it is a lover of the cold. It requires a small story.

When our garden had been just begun, we paid a call one spring afternoon on an (even then) legendary gardener across the river in New Hampshire. Kris Fenderson was not our senior in years—perhaps, indeed, he was a little younger—but he was certainly far ahead of us in making a garden in the colder parts of New England. We were both delighted and encouraged by his collections of conifers and rare deciduous trees and shrubs, and especially by his accumulation of all sorts of primroses, many of which he shared with us that day. But with a true gardener's generosity, just as we were leaving, he took up his trowel and dug six rosettes of the fabled Himalayan blue poppy, *Meconopsis betonicifolia*. We hesitated to accept so rare a gift, but Kris assured us that they would do just fine for us if we simply gave them what they needed—humus-rich moist soil, dappled light, and regular division every two or three years. We have been faithful to his instructions, and the original six crowns became several dozen, blooming here every June, to our great delight and the envious astonishment of many visitors. Even a few miles farther south they can be cranky, and in Boston they are impossible, since they will consent to thrive only where nights are cool, and here, even in July or August, we generally have a fire in the kitchen fireplace.

But it is not mere rarity that justifies growing any flower. Meconopsis are a sort of holy grail among gardeners because of their color, which is the most limpid blue in perhaps the whole flowering world. If grown on acid soil, which they prefer and we have, it can only be called pure sky blue, with no admixture of red or purple. Thick, hairy gray leaves emerge in early April, each one shaped like a rabbit's ear, and as they expand, fat stems and buds appear in the center. The first flowers open in late June. They justify our long life in this place, where so much is denied us. Not just blue-leaved palm trees and tropical creepers, but plants that gardeners in climates only imaginably more temperate than ours take in stride, like crape myrtle and English holly, camellias and osmanthus. Still, for show, we have this bed of utterly improbably blue poppies, and we find in it much compensation.

POTS

MANY GARDENERS are in part historians, concerned with creating garden effects that are redolent of other places, other times. And for them, one of the most precious parts of gardening is the sense of being in their own place while also catching whispers of being somewhere else. It is partly for this reason that gardeners so much value potted plants in the landscape. No one knows for sure how early the realization occurred that plants could be grown in containers, though the skill was well understood in Egypt by 4000 B.C., and certainly had been learned from even more ancient Babylonian and Mesopotamians practice. In our time, growing plants in containers is as obvious as boiling water in a pot, and every kitchen windowsill has at one time been graced (or disfigured) by a potted plant, briefly for show or in permanent residence.

But when you think of it, scooping a plant out of the earth, establishing it in an earthenware jar or stone basin, determining its needs for drainage and extra nutrients and water, finding the right exposure of sun or shadow—those are all earth-shaking discoveries to gardeners, equal practically to the discovery of the wheel. And if it is true (it is at least fancifully true) that our development as individuals recapitulates the development of the species as a whole, then child gardeners begin just where the Mesopotamians and Babylonians did, with the joyful discovery that a plant growing in the earth could also grow in a container. And better, it could also be portable, for carrying things from here to there is very important to a child.

The portability of potted plants has been of inestimable importance to our species as a whole. The discovery of container gardening made possible the transport of plants from far places and actually began the endless exploration of plant hardiness, which really is only a determination of whether something that grows far away can also grow here, in whatever country and place gardening occurs. Some cuttings and bare-rooted plants could endure long transport and still survive. Witness the banana, the best forms of which never set seed, yet were "disseminated" as basal cuttings with a bit of root tissue all throughout the subtropical world long before Columbus made his famous voyages. An important food source, bananas could be transported with very little earth about their roots, and reestablished far from Southeast Asia, which is their original home. In the seventeenth century, when the great importation of plants began, fruit from potted citrus and pineapples graced the Christmas tables of titled and wealthy gardeners from Germany and France through Poland to Russia, grown in stove houses and orangeries that allowed the tubbed trees and plants only a brief summer vacation. Actually, the history of potted plants seems almost as long as the history of human civilization. And the cultivation of plants in pots has a significance that extends through the entire band of human concern from pure sustenance and utility to the highest levels of horticultural embellishment.

There must be strong resonance of all that for anyone who grows a plant in a pot. For committed gardeners, however, it is also an essential act, making possible the cultivation of something rare, something special, in a way that gives it an intimate focus and keeps it under the eye until it is known. Then it might spend its entire life in a pot if it is not hardy, or planted out into the garden if it is. Or perhaps just discarded. For it is a fact about pot culture that it is easier, somehow, to upend a potted plant into the compost than to hoick it out of borders and beds. Plants grown in pots also allow for endless experiment, and for that reason, in our many years as gardeners, we have gone through a huge number. Some, such as our Xanthorrhoea, now over thirty years old, or our bay tree, almost that venerable, seem apt to remain for the rest of our time in this garden, if not even longer. Others we have grown we hardly remember. They are "leptospermums without number . . ."

This we do know, however. The sure mark of a lovingly tended garden, whether it is a great estate or a simple cottage, is a clutter of choice plants in pots and tubs, all in thriving good health. Most will be tender plants, gardenias or citrus, begonias or camellias. And some will reveal surprising histories, originating as cuttings given by great-aunts or far-flung cousins, or inherited from grandmothers, family heirlooms that go back a hundred years in a single trunk and leaves.

There are so many plants, also, that simply will not agree to live where you live, except in a pot. They are too tender for your winters, or they dislike your soil, or—and this is often the case with very small properties, or with gardeners who are reduced to cultivating on a balcony—there just isn't room elsewhere. We are always touched by the shifts and contrivances gardeners exercise to save a precious plant over the winter, or to transport it many miles away to a new home. We've done a lot of that ourselves. And we have known for many years that almost the heart of gardening lies in cultivating plants in containers. Most plants, after all, enter the garden that way, and a good many might also leave it in the same manner.

In the matter of the pots themselves, we are very particular. They must be of clay, as was most anciently the case, and good clay if we can afford it. There is no argument that plastic pots are easier to maintain, for it is simply true. They do not break, and they endure severe weather without punking into slivers. Moisture levels are much easier to maintain because the walls of plastic pots do not constantly transpire moisture as clay ones do. It must even be confessed that some plants actually prefer growing in plastic pots. For these reasons, plastic pots are the nurseryman's darlings, manufactured (and discarded) in countless millions. Burn just one in the fireplace, and you will know the oil-based energy they contain. Now they can even be bought in stylish models that are advertised as looking exactly like good Italian pottery but able to withstand the worst rigors of winter. That may be true until you thump them. For then, instead of the rich ring of a clay pot, you get a hollow plunk sound. Most gardeners don't need to thump, however. Any plastic pot is as unmistakable for what it is as an artificial flower on a tombstone, and no one is really ever fooled. Even common clay pots from the local hardware store are vastly to be preferred, for with one season they take on a wonderful patina, a whitey encrustation that forms over the brick-red surface as salts and lime dissolve and weep through the porous walls. If heavy, thick-walled pots are inherited, or found in junk shops, garage sales, or even town dumps, they are especially to be treasured, for they are sturdier than most modern ware and they already possess the grace of age. Sometimes, one might even find one that broke a century ago, and was patiently put back together with wire brads. That is a great treasure for the care and thrift it shows.

For many years, our clay pots either came from the local farm supply store or were lucky finds we stumbled on in the corner of some old nursery that had shifted to the convenience of plastic or was going out of business. In fashionable antiques shops we occasionally splurged on a fine old English or French pot, and once, in Florence, we bought three Impreneta pots with rolled rims, made in the same way since the Italian Renaissance. We brought them home on the plane in our laps, at a time when you were still allowed to do such things. Then, about fifteen years ago, we met Guy Wolff, and our whole pot habit altered. For he was willing to make hand-thrown clay pots to antique designs, and that is what we wanted. It must be said that the first experiments were not a success, but quickly Guy came to understand this medium, new to him, and the pots grew finer and finer. Now, working from historic fragments, his pots are without compare, and our collection is enriched each year by a new firing.

Among the many models he makes, our favorite perhaps is taken from the portrait of the myopic young Rubens Peale, painted by his brother Rembrandt, in which Rubens lovingly holds an old clay pot with one of the first pelargoniums grown in America. It is a scrawny thing, and Rubens, though charming, is not precisely a handsome man. But the pot is beautiful, and its reincarnations under Guy's hands line our greenhouse benches and when empty are displayed on shelves in our potting shed. We will never have enough of them.

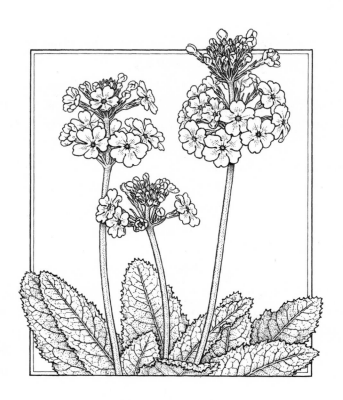

PRIMROSES

'FIFE YELLOW', 'Cowichan Blue', 'Barnhaven Gold', 'Duckyls Red', 'Enchantress', 'Guinevere', 'Granny Graham', 'Broadwell Milkmaid', 'Sailor Boy', 'Prince Charming', 'Satchmo', 'Winter Dreams', 'Hurstwood Midnight', 'Königin der Nacht', 'Parakeet', 'Seraphim', and 'Cherubim' . . . and 'Wanda'.

Even without a picture in a catalog, it is hard to resist ordering plants with such names, for as with roses, their beauty begins there. Add a picture, and the gardener is sunk, the plant budget spent, and the vegetables unordered. There are primroses in every color—canary and butter yellow and cream, indigo, sky blue, purple, maroon, carrot and burnt orange and

Chinese red. Except for close study, however, one seldom looks at a single flower, but at many, one packed next to the other in a tight bouquet, or in whorled tiers arranged like Chinese pagodas.

There are primroses for every site—full sun, full shade, and every exposure in between; for dry ground, moist ground, even boggy ground. They can be had to flower in April, in May, in June and July, and under glass from November to March. That leaves only three months out of the year without primroses, and they are for reading up, ordering, and starting seed.

The first primroses we grew came as pass-alongs, shared with us by a neighbor named Mrs. Oakes, long dead now, who had divided and redivided them in her own garden for fifty years. We in turn have divided ours, both to have more and to share with others. Primroses also come easily from seed, flowering about eighteen months from sowing. And seeds of hundreds of species are available at minimal cost if you join the American Primrose Society. But there are also many named cultivars, for most species show genetic variety, and some intercross freely, both in gardens and in the wild. In the genus *Primula*, there are approximately 425 species, but hybrids and selections are impossible to count. A gardener's whole life is not time enough to grow them all.

And just for that reason (among so many others) primroses endlessly engage us. Each winter, standing at the kitchen counter, we sow half a dozen new species or hybrids. We sow them in lovely old wooden flats which are then watered well, covered with window screen, and set outside to freeze and thaw. Exposure to alternating periods of harsh and mild weather, called stratification, is necessary to break their dormancy, a protective mechanism that prevents them from germinating in autumn and going into winter as helpless seedlings. By mid-spring they have germinated and begun to form tiny leaves; by mid-summer they are large enough to be established in their own individual little pots; and by early autumn they may be transplanted into permanent locations in the garden, where they may be expected to flower in one or two more years. But whereas a young primrose at the nursery will cost eight or ten dollars, one packet of seed, with some labor, will yield a hundred plants. The labor itself is very satisfying, but the resulting drift is more so. For primroses are like daffodils. The more you have, the better they look.

The first primroses of the year are already in bloom when we sow our seeds, and their flowers are before our eyes as we work. In early January, cultivars of *Primula vulgaris* appear for sale in the local supermarket as single plants in three-inch plastic pots, each consisting of a ruff of healthy, dark green quilted leaves surrounding a thick bouquet of flowers in shades of white, yellow, blue, or red, most with a contrasting yellow eye. The price is modest, usually two plants for five dollars, and we suppose that most of the ones sold live very short lives, done in by too little or too much light, or too much heat on someone's kitchen table. As blooming plants, they are too often asked to survive conditions that really only plastic flowers could be expected to endure, with an occasional dusting. But unless they are treated as something that can be enjoyed for a day or two and then thrown in the rubbish can, winter primroses still have their needs. Those are chiefly for well-drained but constantly moist soil, bright light without too much strong winter sun, and temperatures that do not get much warmer than 65 degrees in the daytime, with a drop of perhaps 10 degrees at night.

Ours are stood on the kitchen windowsill that opens out on the winter garden, where conditions seem ideal. The plants are transferred to clay pots about three times the size of the plastic ones they came in, they are watered regularly, their spent flowers are faithfully removed each morning, and they are sprayed with a very dilute liquid plant food while the coffee is brewing. Treated this way, they will remain in bloom from January until April. And still they are not for the compost bin, for they may then be planted out in the garden, where most—not all— will return in springtime for many years. The most likely to persist are the whites and many shades of yellow, which are closest to the natural form of the wild *P. vulgaris*. But it is always worth taking a chance with the blues, purples, and reds. If you like them.

Just when our windowsill primroses pass out of flower, outdoor primulas come awake. *Primula denticulata*—called the "drumstick primrose" because of its congested balls of flower atop straight stems about two feet tall—is always the first to show, the fresh green, lettuce-like rosettes and soon-emerging flowers defiantly proclaiming winter's end, even if a light snow should fall on them, leaving them unscathed. They love moist ground, and in early April their purple, lavender, and sometimes white flowers join the chrome-yellow, satiny blooms of marsh marigolds (*Caltha palustris*). They signal the most joyful days of the gardening year, for there is nothing finished as yet, nothing passed, but only joyful promise of what is to come.

The drumstick primroses are soon joined by the many woodland primroses that carpet the pergola walk and the rhododendron garden. Those are almost all descendants of the much-loved English woodland wildflower, *P. vulgaris*, so called not because it is coarse or common, but because in a fine English spring it is everywhere, blanketing the earth beneath hedgerows and woodland lanes. Ours are scarcely less numerous, especially since the ranks of those with impressive pedigrees have been swelled by generations of winter windowsill plants from the supermarket that all share their descent. Among the earliest is *P. vulgaris* subsp. *sibthorpii*, one of the many gifts to us years ago from Linc Foster, whose great garden, Millstream, enriched so many other gardens we know. Its lavender-pink blooms carry an orange-and-yellow center, striped and pointed toward the little green button of an ovary, probably to guide bees drunk on springtime to its center. In the woods near it will soon be many others, white and yellow and a dozen shades of pink, with some precious doubles, of which our favorite (perhaps) is the pale lavender one called 'Quaker's Bonnet' that we got from Dan Hinkley.

All these will soon be joined by *P. veris*, which the English distinguish by the popular name cowslips. We like cows a lot and we keep several here, essentially as pets and as compost machines, but if you feed one of our cows an apple or a carrot from your hand, you will quickly see that the comparison breaks down. *Primula veris* differs from *P. vulgaris* chiefly in the fact that its nodding flowers are produced in branched umbels about eight inches above the ground-hugging rosettes of quilted leaves. They are mostly various shades of yellow, but we have red ones, mahogany ones, some that are almost brown, and a few that are "laced" with an outline of yellow on a dark reddish ground.

Indispensably lovely as all these primroses are, most primrose fanciers would admit that the jewel in the crown of the genus is *P. auricula*, once considered a genus all its own. Plants were brought to England by Huguenot refugees and grown on deep, cool cottage windowsills and bred to astonishing colors and combinations, of red and black and cream, usually laced with other contrasting colors. They were "florist's flowers," when the word "florist" meant a person fanatically devoted to the cultivation of one special plant, usually for fierce show competitions that were almost blood sports. The tradition survives in England, and so, just about when ours are in bloom, one could go to auricula shows there and see fantastic plants on display, with celadon rosettes of perfect leaves surmounted by almost unreal umbels of flower. In some cases, leaves and flowers might be coated with a dusty meal, called "farina," which gives the plants a curiously remote look. We have none of the jewels you might see there, but we have some very nice auriculas, blooming in early May just at the base of the rock garden, in shades of yellow and cream and brick red. Unlike the other primulas we grow, their clumps form tubers aboveground, and each one can be detached at any point in the plant's active growth—even in full flower—and inserted in moist ground to establish a new plant. It is so easy that we are quickly running out of space for auriculas.

By May's end, the first *P. japonica*s show color. These are streamside plants that love percolating water at their roots. From a rosette of leaves that looks much like romaine lettuce, whorls of flowers appear, sometimes as many as six or seven, arranged pagoda-fashion and opening from the bottom to the top. Generally, the flowers are a rich plush purple, the color so much favored for Victorian upholstery, though in the cultivar 'Postford White' (sometimes simply called 'Alba') the flowers are a pure, rich milk white with a canary-yellow eye. Both forms are lovely, but they deserve places separate from one another, else they muddy each other's effect and even interbreed into a rather dull, bluish pink.

We must have thousands of *P. japonica* along our stream, but we never bought them or were given them or grew them from seed. Years ago, when the garden was new, we bought a potted peony and in it was a small, fresh-looking rosette of leaves of a plant neither of us recognized. It seemed far too attractive to be a mere weed, and so we dug it from the pot and planted it elsewhere. It flowered a year later, and we knew it to be a candelabra primrose. Still, it got forgotten again until the next year, when dozens of little primrose babies appeared along the stream below our solitary findling. The primrose race was on, and twenty-five years later, both banks of the stream are rich with flowers in May, not one of which we planted.

When one grows many plants in a genus, the question sometimes comes from other gardeners, "But which is your favorite?" There's only one answer, really, and that is that we love them all, in their separate ways, like parents respond to children in a large family. Still, we are sometimes pressed for a clearer answer. Perhaps we press ourselves. And we know that among primulas we do have a favorite, and it is *P. ×bulleesiana*. We are not sure from where we got our original plants—probably from the American Primrose Society—though we do remember sowing them, for that was a great year for primrose sowing, and cases and cases of tiny seedlings got pricked out. The resulting plants still enrich our garden.

"Enrich," however, is hardly the word for *P. ×bulleesiana*. "Gild" might be a better one, for at the base of our rock garden, in permanently moist, rather stiff soil, there are perhaps two hundred plants of this cross, which seem as long-lived as peonies. From late May almost to the end of June, they carry many tiered umbels of flower above their fresh, lettuce-green leaves, and the flowers are in many shades that could only be called edible—tangerine and lemon, peach and apricot and melon. That is not the way they started out, however, for in the original seedlings there were other shades, grapish shades of mauve and purple and wine, all, we assume, from the blood of one of their parents, the rose-colored *P. beesiana*. Those were certainly nice enough in their way, and at first—loath to throw any primrose away—we segregated them to a far corner. But they did not survive, and now we are guaranteed the colors we love from 99 percent of our seed, which, perhaps hubristically, we call the "North Hill Strain," and is the only plant in general commerce that carries the name of our garden. All the colors are warm, almost Mediterranean, redolent of the sort of early summer we hope we will have in southern Vermont.

The last top whorls of *P. ×bulleesiana* end our primrose season in early July. But it has been long and rich, and it commences again in November, when the first plants of *P. obconica* appear in florists' windows. It is a species from the warmest parts of China, with large, lobed, and haired leaves above which it bears foot-high umbels of faint-scented flower. They are usually blue or white, but occasionally one sees a plant with flowers of a haunting salmon pink set off by an acid-green eye. If we can find it, one plant of that color will decorate our Thanksgiving table. For like the turkey and the stuffing, we cannot resist it.

PRUNUS ×'HALLY JOLIVETTE'

IN 1976, WHEN OUR FUNNY LITTLE HOUSE had just been completed, we spent the whole first winter staring out the windows. Only the view to the north was beautiful, consisting of old-growth New England woods across a stream. The front of the house looked down on a raw new driveway, below which was a narrow strip of degraded meadow from which the topsoil had been scraped off in the fifties to pay some farmer's mortgage, or perhaps to buy some cows. Out the back door were the corpses of large maples and beeches that sadly had had to be cut to level the ground on which the house stood. But the worst view was to the south, which seemed to be a great sea of raw clay studded with rocks, but which was actually only about two hundred feet from the public road. We had a clear view of it, and whoever passed on it had a clear view of us, thanks to the glass walls of the winter garden we had so much desired. It was a disheartening sight.

It wasn't the raw earth that troubled us so much, for we knew that though it was subsoil, it could be improved with leaf duff that lay thick in the woods, and with manure supplied by neighboring farms, which was then almost free for the hauling. Instead, it was the sheer sense of nakedness, of chilling exposure to the world, that disturbed us. Ours is a friendly town, and if our coming here among settled Vermont folk felt intrusive, we never heard about it. So what unsettled us was not hostile or chilly glances from our new neighbors, but just the sense of being visible at all, in the way that some quiet woodland creature who prefers to go unnoticed might be unnerved by being stared at.

So the first problem we faced in our infant landscape then was the creation of a vegetable shelter, a green wall between us and the road that would not only protect us from view but, more crucially, give us the *sense* that we were protected from view. Privacy is said to be the ultimate luxury. For us it was a necessity, especially because we intended to build a garden here, and gardens are by definition private and enclosed spaces.

It is the law in Vermont—and perhaps in other places—that precisely twenty-one feet from the center of the road is set aside for public use—whoever in fact owns it, it's essentially public land. So the following spring, we began establishing a line of sturdy conifers at just that distance from the road's center. Screens work best when there are several layers, and it is important to start with evergreens, which ensure protection at all seasons, but especially in winter, when other trees and shrubs are bare and they seem to step forward. In front of the evergreens we planted several small trees and a selection of shrubs that would grow thick and tall. Five were planted in an arc to embrace what was to become the front yard, and they consisted of two clumped white lilacs (*Syringa vulgaris* 'Alba'), a multistemmed Sargent crab apple (*Malus sargentii*), a larger, standard crab apple (*M.* 'Snowbank'), and what has proven the most delightful tree of all, the little flowering cherry called 'Hally Jolivette'.

It is a pretty name for a tree, and it originally belonged to the wife of Karl Sax, director of Harvard University's Arnold Arboretum from 1946 to 1954 (who himself is commemorated by the chrome-yellow, free-flowering *Forsythia* ×*intermedia* 'Karl Sax'). During the 1940s he made a series of complex crosses between *Prunus* ×*subhirtella*, the delicate rosebud, or Higan, cherry, and *P.* ×*yedoense*, the Yoshino cherry, most famous from the plantings around the Tidal Basin in Washington, D.C. From the hundreds of seedlings that reached flowering age, he selected one to honor his wife. Anyone who grows it will quickly understand why he chose to single it out in this way.

Both *P.* ×*subhirtella* and *P.* ×*yedoense* are relatively tall trees, quickly reaching a height of about twenty-five feet. But as both are themselves hybrids, something in their remote genetic makeup produced a relatively diminutive offspring: 'Hally Jolivette' seldom exceeds fifteen feet, and is more likely to reach only ten. Left to grow naturally, as ours has been, it produces a dense multistemmed tree. It has other landscape uses, however, for it can be trained to a standard, with a single trunk, in which case it becomes a small tree of great distinction. We have also seen it espaliered in a fan across a high, sunny brick wall, and it is dense and twiggy enough that it might be used as a deciduous hedge, as the Cornelian cherry,

Cornus mas, sometimes is. It could also be tucked into the corner of a small city backyard where two fences meet, or perhaps used as the one tree selected for the square scrap of ground left in front of so many Victorian town houses, a pleasant alternative to the ubiquitous purple saucer magnolia.

The chief glory of 'Hally Jolivette' resides not in its form, however, or the many uses to which it might lend itself, but in its flowers, produced in late spring in such numbers that its willowy, russet-colored twigs are almost obscured. Flower buds are vivid even when they first appear as tight little cones of deep, rich pink, and they are lent extreme beauty by the tender, newly unfurled leaves that are tinted bronze or chestnut brown. When fully opened, each individual flower is about an inch and a quarter across and dangles downward on a slender, threadlike stem as long as an inch. The frilly petals, in a double row, are tinted almost white at their edges, but deepen down through pink to a rich wine-red in the center of the flower. Blossoms are born in clusters of five or more all along mature twigs and even old wood over a period of as many as twenty days in mid- to late May, some in bud and some fully open. This is an extraordinarily long time for a flowering cherry to remain in bloom, for the blossom time of most flowering cherries is generally so brief as to offer a cautionary example of the transitoriness of youth and beauty. But apparently the tree is sterile, never setting fruit, reminding us that Karl Sax and his wife were early and fervent supporters of Planned Parenthood.

When we first planted the deciduous shrubs and trees against the evergreen screen in the front border, it seemed to us that we had plenty of space. So we allowed our 'Hally Jolivette' to form a dense, twigged mass of stems to perhaps twelve feet tall, really more a shrub than a small tree. At one point we thought we might have done better to restrict our plant to three or five ascending trunks, in order to make more room for the hostas and other shade-loving perennials that grow at its feet and face down that border along the lawn edge. But the quichee of growth that has resulted has had one happy benefit: as old trunks have become moribund, we have been able to remove them, counting on a stock of youthful ones just ascending. In this, 'Hally Jolivette' is also unusual among flowering cherries in that it forms stools, or thickets, of many trunks, much in the manner of the shorter-growing flowering quinces, selections of *Chaenoemeles*.

Though *P.* × 'Hally Jolivette' is sometimes still listed as hardy only to Zone 6, it is a favorite small tree all across North America, and has grown happily here for twenty-five years. It seems indifferent to the quality of soil, provided it is open and well drained, for as with all cherries, heavy, poorly drained clay soils will almost always result in root rot. The results are heartbreaking, consisting of abundant flower and some twig growth for a time, and then suddenly abundant flower and death. Our soil is open and friable, and so we have not had to struggle with that problem, but soils that are heavy by nature should be lightened by incorporating generous amounts of peat, sand, and compost, and the young tree might be planted on a slight mound. Artificial fertilizers should be avoided, as growth is quick in any case, and too much may produce weak wood and encourage diseases.

Fortunately, they are few, the worst being an anthracnose-like fungus that attacks the delicate, inch-long leaves in unusually wet springs, causing them to shrivel and blacken. Generally, plants throw off the disease and refoliate as soon as sunny, settled weather arrives, though a severe infection might merit the single application of a fungicide spray.

Like so many things we planted in the early years of our garden, 'Hally Jolivette' strikes us as a piece of pure luck. We knew very little about it beyond a rather dry description in *Wyman's Gardening Encyclopedia*. We had not even seen a picture, either of its mature form or its unforgettably beautiful flowers—at that time the age of glossy picture books, illustrated garden encyclopedias, and the Internet still lay before us. Now, if we were to set out to choose a flowering cherry, even one hardy to our zone, we would be presented with a bewildering number of choices, among which we would be hardpressed to choose the one we liked best. 'Hally Jolivette' makes us glad we started out without those resources, in simple happy ignorance.

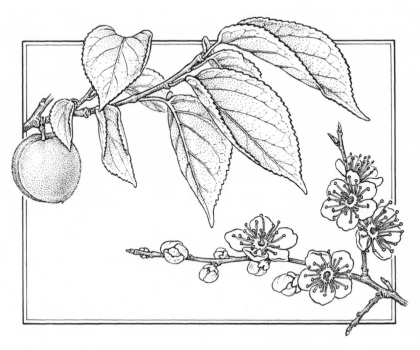

PRUNUS MUME

AMONG THE MANY PLEASURES of our early years as schoolteachers were the vacations—summer of course, and February, and best of all, Christmas. Just as the days grew achingly
short, the cold intense, and the snows deep, we were sprung
from stuffy classrooms, free to play in the snow, huddle by the
fire, or best of all, go someplace else. Colleagues would travel
to warm places, Florida, the Islands, or Mexico. But we would
go to San Francisco, always San Francisco, year after year. We
went for all the generally understood reasons—the beauty of
the city, its restaurants, its opera and ballet, the Castro, and—
for us, just beginning to make a garden—the plants. We would

wander in Strybing Arboretum on foggy early mornings, marveling at so much already in flower: the great *Magnolia campbellii* with its huge down-hanging cups of pink or white; camellias in every shade from scarlet red to tender pink, cream, and white; even the earliest tender rhododendrons, one of which, a sturdy bush, bore huge trusses that were the most intense blood red we had ever seen in a flower.

We also visited nurseries, first in San Francisco and Berkeley, and then by rented car others in Marin and Sonoma and Palo Alto. But every visit ended with a drive up to Occidental, ninety miles north of the city, to visit Lester Hawkins and Marshall Olbrich's Western Hills Rare Plant Nursery. We went to visit them, but also to buy plants, some of which we knew would be hardy in our newly developing Vermont garden, and some we knew would not be. Still, they would say, "Take it and try." Often, the tenderest ones were in flower at that season, and so we bought them in the expectation that they would grow in our little greenhouse off the kitchen. We thought of that greenhouse as a tiny San Francisco backyard garden, and what bloomed in it made us miss the real thing less when we had to come home.

Late one December when we visited Western Hills, Lester was striking cuttings of the iconic little Japanese apricot, *Prunus mume*, then in full flower in many West Coast gardens. It is perhaps the most universally recognized of all Japanese flowers, appearing as it does so often on porcelain and in paintings, its beautiful cup-shaped blooms held tight against angled bare green stems. Because it is among the first flowers of earliest spring, it has come to signify longevity to the Japanese and is much treasured by them. In the garden—a warm Zone 7 garden at least—it makes a small tree seldom taller than twenty feet and as wide. But it takes well to pot culture.

Because we had admired Lester's bundle of blossoming twigs, later that day he thrust a rooted plant into our hands, already a miniature tree three feet tall with a straight trunk and little round head of twigs, a few of which were even decorated with a flower or two. "Take one," he said. "It'll do for you." He meant outside, in the garden, for Lester had only the vaguest sense of the cold we gardened in, since he and Marshall had never gardened anywhere but in Occidental. If a plant had survived their worst freak winter, they thought it was bound to do well in Vermont. We stayed silent and accepted his gift. For in our little imitation San Francisco backyard, we thought it would do fine.

And so it has, now for almost thirty years. The trunk has thickened—though not as much as one might suppose over that many years—and the head has grown dense with twigs, which are encouraged to multiply by hard pruning just after flowering and the cutting back of long soft growth by half in mid-summer. The pot is larger too, a good clay one about fifteen inches high and ten inches across. That is as big a pot as our little tree will ever occupy, because a larger one would be out of proportion to its height and the greater root run would encourage it to grow larger. So we have recourse to the same root-pruning technique used by Japanese bonsai masters. Every two years we remove the root mass from the pot in late spring after the first growth has hardened, and scrape away the compost with a chopstick until we can trim off about two inches of dangling white root all the way around and as much off the bottom. Then the tree is repotted with fresh compost, well watered, and stood in the shade for a week or so until fresh roots have formed and top growth has resumed.

Lester's gift was the English cultivar 'Peggy Clark', with two rows of petals of the clearest shell pink cupped around numerous yellow stamens that give each flower a slight gilded appearance. The fragrance is of almonds on any sunny day, and bees are grateful for so early and plentiful a source of pollen. The consequence is an abundance of fruit. But since our tree bloomed under glass in the depths of a Vermont winter, we saw little fruit, only what a passing draft had caused to form. The fruits are charming, fuzzy little oblong yellow apricots hardly more than twice the size of a thumb. When they are ripe, the taste is rather acrid, yet pleasant, if you stop to think about it before spitting it out. So this year we took the trouble to brush each flower painstakingly with the bristles of a small artist's brush, several times, because the flowers open successively over a month or more. We hope we have supplanted the absent bees and actually secured the formation of a good crop.

We have gone to this trouble because we want to make umeboshi, the marvelous pickled plums that are often served at the conclusion of a Japanese meal. They cleanse the palate, are thought to aid in digestion, and are very good, once you have acquired the taste. We have, both in Japan, where we have had two apiece, served side-by-side in exquisite little bowls, and in New York, where the chef Nao Sugiyama serves them, each suspended in a perfect cube of shimmering clear aspic. We have the pickling recipe, taken from Shizuo Tsuji's authoritative *Japanese Cooking: A Simple Art*. If we succeed, we may even try his recipe for rice balls, with an umeboshi at the center of each. But as Mr. Shizuo Tsuji comments, "There are as many variations in making umeboshi as there are villages in Japan." So apparently, we have leave to experiment in creating the North Hill version.

RAMPANT PLANTS

A COUPLE OF YEARS AGO, on a day our garden was open for the benefit of the Southern Vermont AIDS Project, we were down in the lower greenhouse when a woman stormed in. The day was beautiful, and visitors had been most appreciative and generous to the cause. Everyone else was beaming, and so we had to wonder what had upset her so much.

"Are you the owners? I have a bone to pick with you!" (That expression itself is terrifying, like "I want to pick your brain . . .") "Your garden is *full* of invasive plants!"

"Oh, well . . . Yes . . . some . . . I guess . . ." one of us stammered out. For though a seven-acre garden has a lot of plants in it, "full" seemed a bit of an overstatement.

"Yes," she insisted, "full of them! How can you have so little concern for the planet?"

We sat there, selling lemonade and chocolate chip cookies made by the volunteers, and we wondered how to answer. Ours is a carefully worked garden, where few things are ever allowed to get out of hand. Besides, over thirty years, we have learned tricks and devices for controlling all plants, whatever their proclivities. And the foothills of Vermont are very cold, after all, exercising an almost inevitable restraint on just about anything exotic we might wish to grow. We offered up all these reasons for our choices of plants, but they were clearly not convincing. She drove off with a very sour face in her new SUV. When we asked at the contribution table, no one remembered her, and so we did not know how generous a donation she had deposited in the jar when she entered.

But the challenge of this visitor has left a question in our minds, since home gardeners are clearly more sensitive than many other people to the well-being of the earth. They are keenly aware of the alarming climatic changes we are experiencing, the balmy days in December that are more reminiscent of San Diego than of Vermont. But though we may be thrilled by the fact that the sweet, tiny *Cyclamen hederifolium* now persists under the crab apple tree from year to year, greeting us each autumn with its inside-out flowers of strong or pale pink and pinkish white, it really ought not to survive here, in what used to be a cold Zone 4. Glorying as we do in its survival, we can experience no joy in the conditions that make that survival possible.

We recycle our garbage with the stringent conscience of Catholic schoolchildren, but exploiting the chance to grow plants previously forbidden to us—a chance afforded by conditions quite beyond our individual control—is quite different from willfully introducing a plant, however beautiful, that might escape from domestic gardens to threaten native habitats. So we have made an inventory, a sort of roll call, of the most sinister plants, those most likely to pose an insult to the planet. Or at least to our part of it, a corner of southern Vermont.

There is one clear offender, and if there is a Circle of Hell reserved for people who willfully introduce invasive plants, we might find ourselves occupying it. That plant is *Impatiens glandulifera*, a native of the foothills of the Himalayas. It is by anyone's measure both beautiful and satisfying to grow. From seed that over-winters and sprouts when frost is barely out of the ground, it quickly ascends to a height of as much as eight feet, each branch clothed in handsome, four-inch-long lance-shaped leaves of dark, watery green, marked by a prominent tan rib. Flowers are borne in loose panicles at the tops and the tips of side branches. Each flower possesses the complex structure of an orchid, with a flared upper and lower lip, and a nectar-rich pouch that is irresistible to bumblebees. There may be as many as fifteen or twenty flowers in a panicle, colored fully opened and as tight buds, and the colors are sumptuous, sometimes a pale pink shaded with white, sometimes peach, and sometimes a deep old rose. A rare and less vigorous variety, 'Pallida', produces flowers of so pale a pink that they appear to be white. The plant is bold and stately, and it can make a fine annual hedge along the damp side of a barn or at the edge of the garden. And finally, on certain days, mature plants emit a strong fragrance of ripe apricots.

The trouble comes with the seed, for each flower will produce a narrow, ribbed, pointed seed pod that when ripe will explode at the lightest touch with something that feels like an electric shock, propelling the seed many feet from the parent. Most species of impatiens can do this trick, from which they get their popular name, touch-me-not. But none perform the trick with such gusto as *I. glandulifera,* making it at once the delight of children and a genuine threat to the environment. A single mature plant may produce a thousand peppercorn-sized seeds, and though most will sprout near the parent plant in a congested thicket, some will be propelled a farther distance, and will in turn propel some of their seed even farther. It is a very prolific plant.

Defenders of *I. glandulifera* will point out that it is site-specific, thriving only in rich, permanently moist soils in semi-shaded conditions near the edges of woods. But of course, loosestrife (*Lythrum salicaria*) is also quite site-specific and gloriously empurples miles and miles of wetland in late summer, to the exclusion of all native vegetation. *Impatiens glandulifera* might well prove its successor, though in a different growing environment. It is a plant to be feared, and each spring we attempt to eliminate as much of it as we spot here. That may be closing the barn door after the horse has escaped. But we have seen stands of the plant as far away as Chatham, New York, certainly not progeny of ours, and though it does our consciences little good, we are clearly not the first offenders. Still, for all its undeniable beauty, its cultivation here was a mistake.

We'd not say the same, however, for the gentle Japanese primrose, *Primula japonica*, which came here twenty-five years ago as a rosette of green in the pot of a peony from Weston Nurseries, in Hopkinton, Massachusetts. It was both attractive enough and unfamiliar enough to arouse our curiosity, and so we transplanted it near our stream. The following spring, it produced a whorl of leaves that looked like a romaine lettuce, from the center of which emerged our first candelabra primrose, five tiers of cherry-red flowers with wine-dark centers opening successively from the bottom to the top. We cannot guess how many plants have descended from that first flowering and the poppy-seed-sized grains of seed that followed, though now they occur in patches all up and down our little stream, and many young plants have been shared with other gardeners who admired them.

Like all streams, our own continues its life long after it leaves us, disappearing into a beaver swamp below our property and reemerging across the road, where it empties into larger streams that in their turn empty into the Deerfield River, which itself contributes its waters to the great Connecticut River, which flows into the ocean. We have heard from people who live farther down our stream that beautiful flowers have appeared growing out of leaves that look like lettuce. They are our primulas, clearly offspring of that first plant. To them we have added a pure white variety with a honey-gold center, sometimes called 'Postford White', and we hope people downstream may get some of that, for it is very wonderful. But though robust, *P. japonica* is like all primulas, gentle in its ways, long-lived where it is happy but fragile if conditions do not suit it. We cannot believe that it could ever become a pernicious weed.

Several bamboos we grow might be a different matter, especially as what we recognize unmistakably as global warming continues to advance. Bamboos divide into two categories—clumpers and runners. The clumpers, chiefly members of the genus *Fargesia*, are no real problem, for they form congested colonies that widen annually, but always in delightful and nonthreatening ways. Running bamboos, on the other hand, produce long-noded, straw-colored underground shoots, each terminating in a sharp tip that can penetrate through the soil (and indeed, even through asphalt), sometimes surprising distances from the mother plant. Bamboos are thrifty plants, surviving well on little, and where conditions suit them, they can create whole forests, devoid of any other vegetation. For some beautiful creatures, such as the giant pandas, this is fortunate, since 99 percent of their diet consists of bamboo leaves. But we have had to go to such trouble to grow bamboos in our cold garden that we do not much fear their escape, and sadly, we cannot anticipate the appearance of a giant panda, much less the capacity to satisfy its hunger.

Even in our climate, however, running bamboos can be wayward, appearing in places they were not planted and are not wanted. We therefore employ several tricks to contain their growth, the chief of which is to site them very carefully so that some barrier, such as a path or mown lawn, restrains their progress. Also, the more cold-hardy running bamboos will grow toward sunlight rather than toward shade, and if a planting is backed by some shade-producing shrub, a rhododendron perhaps or a crescent of mountain laurel, it will not spread in that direction. Where none of these tricks are possible, we have also employed underground barriers or buried containers made of marine plywood, causing the bamboo essentially to grow around and around itself as if in a large pot.

Our first experiment with bamboo was *Phyllostachys aureosulcata*, the yellow-groove bamboo, which we planted at the outside corner of our glassed-in winter garden. We reasoned that the inevitable heat loss from its foundation would increase hardiness, since we knew that the species itself was reliably hardy only to Zone 7. Still, as an extra precaution, each year we bent the culms to the ground and covered them with evergreen boughs. In this way, we managed a vigorous clump with canes reaching eight to ten feet.

Various other bamboos have followed, some for ground-covering purposes, such as the golden-leaved *Pleioblastus auri-*

comus (*Arundinaria viridistriata*), or the silver-leaved *P. variega-tus*, or the most elegant *Sasa veitchii*, with green leaves that develop straw-colored margins in winter. We particularly treasure *S. palmata*, not for groundcover but for its broad, dark green leaves borne on slender canes that reach four feet before the heavy foliage bends them gracefully into arcs. Though climate changes probably mean they could all survive without protection, we take no chances and still cover them with evergreen boughs for winter.

The only other plant we grow that might qualify as a danger to the planet is the giant Japanese butterbur, *Petasites japonicus* var. *giganteus*. It is gigantic indeed, with single, rounded, grass-green leaves as much as thirty-one inches wide, each on a stem as much as five feet tall. When crushed, the stems emit a pleasant celerylike fragrance, and they are in fact a vegetable in Japan, where the plant is called *fuki*. We are culinarily adventurous, and so we have tried preparing it in every imaginable way and found it consistently nasty, though there may be a technique we do not know. Its leaves, however, are a treasure, offering a startlingly tropical look to a northern garden, though in fact the plant is hardy to Zone 4. In early spring, just as the ground has thawed, it produces beautiful yellowish-green flowers, tightly packed in a cob and surrounded by a neat little rosette of pleated, yellow-green leaves. It is the first perennial to bloom here and provides early forage for bees. Probably no other plant in the garden attracts more admiration, or—in the case of our challenging visitor—more scorn.

Certainly it is not a plant to establish without the most careful thought. It travels vigorously underground by thick, quick-growing fleshy white stolons that spread outward on all sides of an established plant. In the wrong place, such as in a wetland or beside a large lake, it could quickly cover acres. It has in fact completely colonized a boggy, rocky area about fifty feet wide each way at the top of our garden, where nothing else will grow. But we watch it very carefully, and two or three times in a summer, we yank it back to the area it is meant to occupy. We have seen it grown in other gardens confined by underground barriers such as those used for running bamboos, or surrounded by grass where wayward plants may be mown down. It might also be sited in a moist, semishaded place surrounded by dry ground, for it will not travel into dry soils. It is superb in a large pot or planter that shows off its architectural magnificence. And, so long as one confines oneself to plants originating from a single source, there is no fear of seed, for petasites is dioecious, each plant and all the plants it vegetatively produces being either male or female. Obviously, it takes one of each to produce viable seed.

Beyond all the precautions we take, we probably have no defense for a few of the plants we grow. They are a tiny fraction of the hundreds of genera and species that flourish here, including many endangered natives, such as the beautiful lady's slipper orchids, *Cypripedium* in several species, and many rare ferns. But in a larger sense, gardening, like agriculture itself, has always depended on the dissemination of desirable plants. Though the flora of North America is rich, all our gardens would be poor things without the contributions of the great plant explorers of the last three hundred years, whose primary interest was in contributing to human pleasure the beauty of the plants they saw in faraway places. A wonderful side effect of that concern has been to ensure the survival of species that were on the edge of extinction and have never since been seen in the wild. Still, there are sins on their heads too. We could wish that theirs—and ours—were the greatest of humanity's many insults to the planet.

THE ROCK GARDEN
AND PLANTED WALLS

Seventeen years after we built our house, we decided to build a greenhouse and potting shed at the bottom of the garden—more like a conservatory—that would provide winter storage for all the tender potted plants we had accumulated and at the same time put a full stop to that end of the garden, just as the poultry house and pig house had at the top. But to construct that building, we needed flat land. And as no land in southern Vermont is flat except when it is made so, a gentle slope had to be cut into a much sharper one to steal the earth on which the new building would sit. The result was an ugly precipitous gash that oozed water. In any housing development, such a slope would have called for elaborate drainage and the establishment of "lawn." But we had read enough on alpine gardening to know that instead of the eyesore it seemed, our slope was a treasure. A natural scree.

In that way, a rock garden was given to us by a necessary alteration of the land. It only required the setting in of huge lichen-encrusted granite boulders, laid down in natural-seeming ridges, each half or two-thirds buried in the ground as if they had been exposed by centuries of erosion. We laid a fieldstone path that wandered through this brand-new out-cropping, and at the bottom created a natural bog. That, too, was an unexpected gift, as were the frogs and dragonflies that soon showed up there. In our bog we planted candelabra prim-roses (*Primula* ✕*bulleesiana* and *P. japonica*), irises, rushes, and other bog plants, all as if they had come of themselves.

While we were creating the rock garden, the greenhouse was constructed, and from the first day that it was completed, it was wonderfully rich with possibilities that would increase the scope of our garden life. Though the land all around was wounded and raw, from experience we knew that we could fix that. The building is a long rectangle measuring approximately fifty feet by twenty, and a little more than half of it is greenhouse. The rest is a utility building, which first was used to store things for which we could find no other place. It then had a brief history as extra plant space lit by a horrible halogen grow-light we hated and feared, the sort used by people who grow marijuana indoors. Finally, it has come to be a simple but satisfying place to serve lunch or dinner for larger groups than the house can accommodate. It has a beautiful old brick floor; a view into the greenhouse where thick bunches of muscat grapes hang in summer, the produce of a single old vine in a huge clay pot; and even a snug bedroom tucked into the eaves, where little windows open to night breezes and a view of the rock garden, just opposite. From the house far above, the sun glinting off its shingled roof was just what we had hoped to see, perhaps for a longer time than we had realized, or even had occupied this land. Visitors who are new to the garden often say, "Who lives down there?" We do, much of the time.

But some sort of serpent waits in every Eden, and in the case of our magical little building, it was this: The siding was pressure-treated, but we ran short of funds at the end, and the last section to be sided was the front, below the windows of the shop and the barn-sash windows of the greenhouse. They were sided with bits and ends left over from the back and two eave sides, short lengths that initially looked just fine, especially when the rather sick green of the pressure-treated pine was covered by a charcoal-gray stain. But the little sections lacked enough length to hold them firm, and they began to warp, to the point that between them one could actually see inside. This is not a desirable thing in any greenhouse, and certainly not in Vermont in a howling winter blizzard. The obvious solution—had we had the money—would have been to rip off the bits of siding and use proper lengths, restrained from buckling by nails all along their extent.

We didn't have the money, and therefore—as so many times before in the making of this garden—we had to consider the problem as an invitation to creativity. Ingenuity is not always a good solution to a lack of funds, and in certain dire necessities, it does not serve at all. But in gardens, we have often been surprised by how frequently ingenuity can come to the rescue, sometimes offering solutions far better than could have been bought for ready money. A perception crystallized that, like most of the lessons one learns in life, was simply the realization of what we had known for a long time. At the risk of sounding pretentiously like the great Frank Lloyd Wright, we could even put it in a maxim: The best of all garden effects are made out of difficulties that initially seem impossible to surmount. It may be true that economical contrivance meant to solve a problem in the garden results in some of its greatest charm. In the case of our faulty greenhouse siding, it was so.

Our solution was to cover the faulty siding with sheets of marine plywood to just below the windows, flashing the top with copper to make it look dressy. Against the plywood we built planted walls, all across the long south face and west gable end. The east gable end that faced up the garden and toward the house was sided early on, with proper lengths, and so did not need this treatment. That, as it happens, was a lucky thing, because no view of the planted walls is offered from above. They come as a complete surprise, visible only when one has descended the rock garden path and come around to the face of the greenhouse.

The construction of a planted wall differs from that of a free-standing dry wall, for the wall itself is a veneer over a core of earth, or to be more accurate, of sandy, reddish clay and coarse pebbles called "bank fill." It is ugly stuff, normally used only in road construction. No gardener would want it except for this purpose, since the species established in a planted wall are not greedy feeders, and in any case should not be treated too kindly, lest they grow rank and coarse and die out.

The process is easy, though it requires thought and some physical strength. A first course is laid about six inches below grade, as level as possible, and bank fill is packed inside and under it. Then a second course is laid, taking care to jump the joints of the first, so that no two layers of stone abut each other in the same place to create a fault line or seam. For stability, it is also good to lay a "deadman," sacrificing the fine distance one might get from a handsome long rectangular stone by placing it perpendicularly to the wall rather than horizontal with its face.

The second course is then packed solid with bank fill, but at this point, little plants can be inserted between the stones. The root mass is flattened out gently so it becomes a sort of filling between a sandwich of stone, and good, fibrous loam is added to connect the root mass to the bank fill, into which the roots will eventually penetrate. You continue to plant as you build upward, course by course, until the wall is capped off at whatever height you want, using the finest, flattest stones for the last course. Six or so inches of good soil is laid over the bank fill and level with the capstones, resulting in a raised bed that is then planted like a little landscape, with handsome craggy rocks protruding like miniature mountains. The whole top surface is mulched with attractive gravel and random-sized pebbles, watered well, and the planted wall is done.

The effect is almost immediately one of settled age, even of significant antiquity. And that effect increases as gray lichens come, and the plants spread out across the face of the wall, working their way into crevices where they were never planted. Sometimes amiable weeds also appear, ferns and columbines and filmy, yellow-flowered *Corydalis lutea*, which, once it is growing anywhere nearby will always find any wall that contains earth enough for it to sprout in. Unless the wall falls down because of some construction flaw, its beauty increases each year for a very long time, requiring neither fertilizer nor weeding nor even watering except in very dry periods. For stone acts as a sponge, storing water and then releasing it when soil dries out. In any case, one does not want plants in a planted wall to flourish too much, swamping their neighbors. You think you cannot have too much of *Campanula poscharskyana*, especially when its starry bells of light blue are borne in profusion in mid-summer. But you can, when it has completely overwhelmed some precious rarity.

Planted walls are a curious bypath of horticulture, one that is seldom practiced deliberately. The effect is more often the result of accident, when the decayed mortar of ancient masonry allows pretty plants to seed themselves among stones or bricks, their roots in cool moisture while their crowns bask in the hot sun among sleeping lizards. Actually, a large number of beautiful plants find such a situation a wonderful place to grow. Most common are the valerians, armerias, aubrietas, dianthus, drabas, saxifrages, mossy phloxes, sedums, and rock campanulas. Sempervivums, sometimes called "hens-and-chicks" or "houseleeks," are always happy in such conditions, and of them alone there are enough species and varieties to furnish an ample planted wall. But to all these one could also add rarer ones—dryas and moltkias and even rock daphne—and in shaded old walls, little ferns and mosses, rare corydalis, and the much-coveted *Ramonda myconi*, which looks like an African violet and will grow only in north-facing rock crevices, but is hardy to Zone 5. Any walk through the streets of an old town or long-settled rural landscape will offer examples.

It has been said that before the restoration began on the Coliseum in Rome in the nineteenth century, botanists cataloged more than ninety species that grew among its stones, most or all of which must have come there with animal fodder from the far-flung edges of the ancient Roman Empire. But always, wherever plants find a home among the rocks of constructed works, there is the magic of ruins, of nature reclaiming the works of humanity. Such a sense of antiquity makes one shiver with delight. It is to be sought in making a garden—much sought—and this effect was exactly what we hoped to accomplish, against a building that for all its satisfactions presented the one woeful defect that made it useless for the purposes it was built to serve. So again, the sow's ear was turned into a gardener's silk purse or, to move the perception from homely wisdom to the sublime by quoting *King Lear*, "Our mere defects become our commodities."

ROSES

WE HAVE A FRIEND in Los Angeles who is a collector. Her house is crammed with beautiful things, not as single objects, but in rows and heaps, groups and gaggles. There are rare porcelains, Tiffany vases, tiny Chinese figurines, a whole wall of ironstone platters hung like paintings, and even a tabletop scattered with exquisite ivory back scratchers. We asked her once how she decided what she would collect, and the answer was quick and sure: "It is easy. I begin whenever I have two of anything." Gardeners are like that too. Or at least we are, for once we come to know a genus, it is hard to keep from trying to acquire every species within it. When a genus is small, tidy, and beautiful, and one species has done well in the garden, it is impossible not to prick up our ears when another is mentioned—or stretch out our fingers.

We vividly remember seeing a geranium garden years ago at Wakehurst Place in England, containing hundreds of species and varieties of true border geraniums. It offered just the pleasure we find in collections, which consists in noting the similarities and differences among closely related plants. To our delight and amusement, it even included *Geranium robertianum*, the lowly biennial that springs up wherever gardening occurs. It is popularly called "herb Robert," with two-inch, lacy, wine-colored leaves and minute pink flowers, and it grew in the Wakehurst Place garden for comparison, we suppose, but also in appreciation of its modest charm, for no geranium could ever be ugly. We always leave it to grow here wherever we can, and we have read that there is a rare white form, which we mean someday to have. Should there be a golden-leaved form, we'd have that too, though most gardeners consider it a weed.

In a garden history that seems long, at least to us, and that has occurred largely in one place, we have built dozens of collections over the years, many of which, like hellebores, geraniums, epimediums, or snowdrops, have become great passions. But we never collected roses, or thought of them even as a plant to collect at all. From the first, they have simply been elemental to our sense of what a garden should contain, as important in their special way as tall screening conifers or the yews and boxwoods that cannot be passed over in defining and weighing down internal garden spaces. A very old Italian lady once toured our garden, and when she noted that we grew culinary sage (*Salvia officinalis*) as ornamental plants commented, "Ah! Sal-vi-a! *Un giardino senza salvia non e neanche*

228

un giardino!" which we believe translates as "A garden without sage is no kind of garden at all." We'd say the same for roses.

And we are certainly not the first to ask why. For roses are not easy plants to grow. They are subject to a host of ills, including mildew in high summer that turns them a disturbing powdery gray; black spot that shows first as vivid orange dots and then causes complete defoliation, leaving naked stems behind; aphids that curl and deform leaves and flowers; and Japanese beetles, which chew their flowers and leaves and, for added insult, fornicate in their blossoms. Roses are, in fact, the darlings of the pesticide industry, for of all plants commonly grown in gardens, only lawn grass produces greater annual sales of chemicals. And there is the mysterious "rose replant disease," which for reasons quite unclear causes a rose planted where a rose has recently grown to pine away and die. That does not always happen. It mostly happens. So to any gardener, William Blake's great poem that begins "O Rose, thou art sick!" makes perfect sense.

Any other group of plants with such difficulties would be banned from the gardens of sensible people, and for all these ills, by such people roses often are. But there is something about a rose . . . Its history as a garden plant stretches back thousands of years, to the ancient Persians and Medes as early as the twelfth century B.C., for whom the typical five-petaled flower borne by many wild species was a significant religious emblem. From then until the present, roses have enjoyed uninterrupted cultivation, even in the Dark Ages, when roses were nurtured in monastery gardens for their medicinal properties, particularly as a salve for skin diseases and to encourage the healing of wounds. Though the genus is not particularly large, comprising between one hundred fifty and two hundred species, all of them cross freely among themselves, producing an incalculable number of hybrids, to the extent that the modern rosarian Peter Schneider has remarked, "Someone has estimated that crossing any modern rose with any other modern rose will produce one of seventeen million possible results."

Few of those crosses would actually be of great interest here, for most would fit into the ever-blurring classes of hybrid teas and floribundas, the roses most people imagine when roses are mentioned, the staples of the florist's trade for holidays, for reconciliations and all other romantic occasions, for proms and funerals. We might grow them if we could grow them well, for a flourishing old tea rose, well pruned to a height of perhaps five feet, thick of cane with healthy, glossy, burgundy-tinted leaves, and rich with buds and flowers—a 'Mister Lincoln', perhaps, a 'Queen Elizabeth', or a 'Peace'—has to be admired. And when we see one, we do, and there is an undeniable tug at the heart. But we do not live where such things are possible, in California or Texas or the middle South. We live in Vermont, and we are realistic about that. Somewhat, anyway. For we confess that in our early days here we grew those three and others in pots, as we had seen done in Roman courtyards, and we even once buried our plants in trenches in the vegetable garden, only to find, come spring, that we had given a fine winter's sustenance to whole families of mice. We have never believed that going to a great deal of trouble was any argument against growing a wonderful plant. Quite the reverse. But the effort does have to pay dividends. And all our experiments with tea and floribunda roses have ended in few. Or none.

Fortunately, however, the world of roses is so vast and varied that we have never lacked for them, and each year we add a few more. They are all shrub roses, either antique or modern hybrids. The antiques are chiefly in the four important groups designated as alba, gallica, centifolia, or rugosa, once thought to be species though now considered to be complex crosses themselves. For example, we have grown the tall, vigorous, and quite hardy rose called 'Tour de Malakoff' almost from the beginning of our garden here. It was bred in 1856 and has been popular ever since because of its good health and its rich, smoky deep purple flowers. And it has always been classed as a centifolia, though modern analysis has indicated that it possesses genetic material of *Rosa gallica*, *R. moschata, R. canina*, and *R. ×damascena*. Modern shrub roses may also be a complex blend of almost anything, though they are apt to have a strong tincture of American native species in them, particularly carolina, or the sturdiest and most cold-resistant Asian species, such as rugosa and multiflora, to guarantee their hardiness. But fuzzy as the genetics are, all the ones we grow here are within the classifications of antique and modern shrub roses. There are perhaps a hundred, though we have not counted. If there are that many, we do know there will be a hundred and five, come spring. For that is what we have ordered this year.

Of course, with very few exceptions these roses bloom only once, and people who want "a rose for every month," as the old catalogs used to hype about teas and floribundas, hold that strongly against them. Actually, it has been a complaint since Virgil extolled the "rose of Paestum," an autumn damask that grew in abundance around the famous temples at Paestum, three of which are still standing. It was later celebrated in France as "quatre saisons" (an exaggeration) because it bloomed once in spring and later in autumn. And in 1817 a random hedgerow mating occurred on the Isle de Bourbon (now Réunion) in the Indian Ocean, between the autumn damask and *R. chinensis* 'Old Blush'. That produced the repeat-flowering

'Rose Edouard', and the promise of monthly flowers was almost within grasp.

It is impossible to overestimate the significance of this first Bourbon rose. Many roses offered in recent catalogs trace their most important characteristic, which is perpetual flowering, back to this improbable ancestor. They are called "carefree roses" or "landscape roses," and contain the hugely popular 'Knockout' series. They promise both disease resistance and perpetual bloom from late spring until frost. The latter they certainly deliver, in abundance, for months and months. Their degree of disease resistance depends on where you garden and how much care you give them and the kind of summer it is, though certainly they are more "carefree" than many of the antique and modern shrub roses, and assuredly more than any hybrid tea. If carefree and perpetual bloom are for you, then rosewise, they are your best bet.

But we have thoughts about nonstop bloom in anything, just as we have thoughts about plastic and paper flowers. It isn't just that the roses marketed that way lack soul, for that is obvious to anyone who knows Empress Josephine's rich pink 'Souvenir de la Malmaison', or the superb white 'Madame Hardy' with its haunting green eye, raised by her gardener there and named after his wife, or the bawdily named 'Cuisse de Nymphe' (nymph's thigh) that the English prudishly renamed 'Great Maiden's Blush'. Of course, "A rose by any other name would smell as sweet," but the modern landscape roses don't smell either. To date, beyond their undeniably healthy constitution, they also offer the promise of boring you to death.

Gardens are made up of festivals, great or small, and like any other holidays we celebrate, they require advance preparation—the getting of the tree, the boiling of eggs to paint or dye, the putting together of costumes for Hallowe'en, the buying of birthday presents and the trick candles and the baking of the cake, the gifts exchanged on anniversaries. When the roses bloom here, one of the great celebrations of our garden has come round. It also is not without its elaborate preparation, of laying down the more tender plants and covering them first with Remay and then with evergreen boughs; of uncovering them in spring, propping them up, and trimming out winter-damaged wood; of fertilizing and spraying and watching closely for bugs and diseases, of which there are some, though fortunately not many.

It is tedious work. Gardening often is. But in June, the most glorious month of our gardening year (if one had to choose just one), the roses bloom. Most are concentrated on either side of a long path that leads first through an eight-foot-tall yew hedge to the perennial garden, and then back out and beyond, to a shaded woodland walk and across the stream. Christopher Lloyd, on one of his many visits here, christened it the Rose Alley, and the name has stuck. But there are other roses, clustered against terraces and trained on the pergola or wherever a rose might grow.

From the beginning of our garden, it has been our custom during Rose Season to pick one from each bush and arrange them in bowls in the house, for their fragrance and to study their differences, maybe even to identify them individually, though alas, we have forgotten many of their names. Now there are so many roses in the garden that they will not fit into a single bowl, and so several are required, on the dining table, on the coffee table, and by each of our bedsides. Their fragrance is a haunt, all day long and well into our dreams. But it is the garden outside that draws us incessantly, many times in the day and from whatever task we have in hand. It is like a birthday. And who wouldn't want a birthday every month of the year?

SEMPERVIVUMS

FOR SEVERAL YEARS, summer and winter, a pair of boots stood by the doorstep of a house in our village. Well-worn and down at heel, they were nevertheless Sorels, the sturdy boots with leather uppers and rubber treads that are almost as famil-iar a symbol of Vermont as a can of maple syrup. These boots, which belonged to the retired owner of the local sawmill, had clearly seen hard wear. But before being discarded (little is completely "wuthless" in Vermont), they had found a second use. Their rigid interiors were filled with earth, and from the top, from the laces, and even from the split toes, sempervivums spilled out. We are not sure this is the very best use we ever saw for such wonderful plants, but certainly it brought home the truth about them. They are both adorable in themselves and endlessly adaptable.

We doubt that our neighbor had ever heard the word "sempervivum." If he had, he might have thought it referred to some sort of horticultural anthem and not what was growing in his boots. It is, however, the most reassuring of all plant names, made up of two Latin words signifying "always living." And indeed, only two things can kill sempervivums outright— shade and poor drainage. Given a very little soil and a great deal of sun, colonies will continue their slow but steady increase as happily after the Zone 4 winters of Vermont as in the all-year mildness of San Diego (Zone 10). Wherever they grow, they make compact rosettes in tight colonies, the smallest species being little gray buttons scarcely half an inch wide, and the giants seldom achieving a diameter of five inches. They are native to high elevations through central and southern Europe into Asia Minor, and they are essentially rock plants, growing in thin deposits of gravelly scree or finding a toehold in fissures of granite cliffs. But as rock plants, they are unusual—even perhaps unique—in that their cultivation is child's play (sometimes literally), but their charm is hardly lost on the most sophisticated members of the American Rock Garden Society.

Sempervivums have a long and distinguished history in western gardens. Pliny the Younger is the first to mention them by that name, recording the belief that plants growing on roofs deflected lightning and prevented fires. To the Middle Ages, apt even more than Pliny to blur the practical and the fanciful, this belief made entire sense. Why else would sempervivums choose to grow in such unlikely places? So, in the ninth century, Charlemagne, ever concerned with the well-being of his subjects, issued an edict that sempervivums were to be established on every house roof. It naturally followed that any plant possessed of unusual capacities must be medicinally valuable, and so medieval physicians prescribed teas of sempervivums to cure sores of the mouth, irritated throats, and bronchitis, all diseases of "heat" or fever, and the mucilaginous tissue of the inner leaves was believed to soothe burns and bee stings, as perhaps, like aloes, it does.

The two principal common names for sempervivums—hens-and-chicks and houseleeks—equally endear them to gardeners and nongardeners alike. Hens-and-chicks describes the growth habit of the plants, where every mature individual produces miniature versions of itself, either growing close beside its perfectly crafted rosette of leaves, or on corky, threadlike stolons an inch or two long, suggesting either a mother hen with her chicks tucked close about her or one whose chicks have strayed a bit. Houseleek is of less clear application, for no species even remotely resembles that garden vegetable. It is true that the succulent leaves have been gathered for salads, but the name, which descends from medieval English, more probably refers to the bloomy, gray-green color that some sempervivums share with the common leek, *Allium porrum*. In a time when spelling was more inspiration than science, houseleek was also a pun, since the most decayed roofs of houses both supported the plants best and could be presumed to leak.

Though universally pleasing to gardeners, sempervivums are cause for serious indigestion among botanists, for the genus is completely confused. It consists of about forty species, though for three reasons, no one can really be sure. First, all species show variants in the wild. Second, plants of the same species will differ markedly in appearance according to the conditions under which they are grown. And finally, all are dreadfully promiscuous, freely intercrossing among themselves and with their parents. Possibilities are therefore almost infinite. Even a bit of vegetable crusting isolated high on a Swiss mountainside might actually consist of two species and a swarm of offspring, each resembling one or the other parent, or each other, or nobody at all. And there are hybrids occurring naturally in gardens or by deliberate intervention, a welter that caused T. H. Everett, in his great garden encyclopedia, to cut through the Gordian knot of nomenclature by remarking bluntly, "The wise gardener will pick the sorts that he likes and use them in his garden for what they are, and not for what they are called . . ."

Inevitably, however, this very plethora of variations, so frustrating to the botanist, is a joy to us, who seem born to collect one of this and one of that and one of the other, wherever we can. Once you own two forms of sempervivums (or "semps," as they are called), you'll soon acquire a third, and then perhaps a dozen, submitting happily to the disease someone has called "sempervivuphilia." After all, propagation is easy, cultural requirements are clear and undemanding, and plants will . . . well . . . live forever. It is hard to know how many chance encounters with sempervivums on visits to other gardens have caused us to beg a chick or two, bringing them home safely in our pockets. They have all survived.

Across nomenclatural confusion, a convenient broad distinction can be made between two clear species of sempervivums. Most plants on the market belong either to *Sempervivum tectorum*, the true houseleek—"tectorum" means "growing on roofs"—or to *S. arachnoideum*—from the Latin *arachne*, a "spider"—the cobwebby houseleek, so called because its tiny rosettes are netted over with threads of silver. Though the two species are closely related, they differ significantly in appearance. Houseleeks tend to be larger, sometimes to as much as six inches across, fleshier, and more open in their construction. Even when they seem colored a characteristic uniform, dull olive green, there will be a shading of bronze toward the tips of the leaves, or even deep metallic or rusty colors diffused throughout. By contrast, the cobwebby sorts are generally smaller, sometimes mere buttons a half-inch across, more rounded or ball-like in shape, typically celadon green, though their characteristic webbing gives them a silvery appearance. To these two dominant species may be added a third, *S. calcareum*, which repeats the fleshy, open rosettes of *S. tectorum*, but, in selections and hybrids, possesses some of the most subtle colorations in the genus, of plum and bronze. But throughout the three species there is such variety that you can simply buy or beg—never of course steal—what you like best.

The culture of sempervivums is simplicity itself. Their only requirements are a gritty, perfectly drained soil and baking sun. Indeed, their preferred mountain habitats, where soil is thin and summer sun abundant, give the vital clues to their needs. It also suggests their most exciting uses in gardens, for they require only a little soil, even so little as a cupful, settled in the hollow of a rock.

They relish stonework of all kinds, making glorious the faces of old decayed walls and even giving to new ones a look of settled age with surprising rapidity. (For that, they are often also called "stonecrops.") Our largest collection grows happily across the face of the planted walls of the lower greenhouse. But because we find sempervivums irresistible, we have poked others into the low retaining walls of the perennial garden, though there we have concentrated mostly bloomy purple forms of *S. calcareum* and *S. tectorum*.

No other plant is as easy to establish in a wall, for a narrow crevice can be packed with fibrous loam or decomposed sod and a nursery-grown plant freed of its four-inch pot and squeezed gently in. No harm will be done by teasing away much of the earth from the roots of the plant so that its rosettes will be even with the faces of the stone. Even a single rosette can be inserted in a fissure with a little soil behind. It will soon occupy the space it has, and then colonize the adjoining stones.

Though sempervivums and walls seem made for one another, almost any shallow container will support a colony, or even a collection, provided it is perfectly drained. For all-year effects in cold gardens such as ours, and for chilly urban roof gardens, semps are perfect, for their gelatinous leaves seem to possess natural antifreeze, preventing them from bursting apart or turning to mush even after subzero winter lows. They are one of a very few plants that may be expected both to live and to be attractive in urns and pots in gardens that experience very cold winters. They may glorify an old chipped dishpan, a flat rock with the barest hollow, a terra cotta chimney tile, or a weathered cinder block. They'll even do in an old pair of boots, if you happen to have one.

SNOWDROPS

EARLY EACH SPRING, we wonder whether we would love snowdrops if they bloomed in June, rather than at the end of a long, cold winter. Certainly they are beautiful enough to love at any time of the year: silken pearls in bud and winged when open to the warmth of an early spring day. They dangle on delicate, threadlike pedicels, dancing in the slightest breeze. They are the very definition of whiteness, the more for the icy, ethereal green that marks them all. But our passion for them (passion it is, for we love them more than any other flower) stems as much from our great need as from their great beauty. That need is for light, change, and life after the still of winter. Somehow, they seem possessed of magical properties, breaking a curse of darkness. For when they choose to appear, winter cannot come again. Or if it does, it cannot stay.

Though it is possible for a person almost completely indifferent to flowers to conjure up the image of a snowdrop, there are in fact many snowdrops in the world. Nineteen species are recorded, and perhaps as many as five hundred cultivars. From one to another they look very much alike, especially when their tiny, modest flowers are viewed from high above. Always they are white, with three outer and three inner tepals. The outer tepals flare outward, and the three inner ones are gathered together to form a tiny cup. There is usually a green mark on the tip of each inner tepal, though sometimes—very rarely—that mark is yellow, offering a cause for great celebration. And there may be marks on the outer tepals as well, of the same haunting green. Sometimes the whole flower may go quite mad, with three to five outer tepals and as many as fifteen inner ones, bunched all together like a tiny rose. In the just over one hundred years that snowdrops have been closely observed in gardens (as opposed to merely cultivated, however lovingly), every smallest variation has been noted, named, and multiplied. An entire tribe of obsessed gardeners exists called "galanthophiles," who vie with one another to amass the largest number of different forms, especially those that most rarely occur. Even variations in scent are noted, for most snowdrops possess a faint but delicate lemony fragrance. Not all, however, for *Galanthus koenenianus* is said to smell of urine and *G.* 'William Thomson' of soured laundry. (We do pity Mr. William Thomson, whoever he might have been, because of his snowdrop namesake. But we long to have him—it—in our collection.)

Our own membership in the galanthophiles was pretty

much assured about eighteen years ago when a friend in Philadelphia offered us a single bulb, just twice the size of a garden pea, of one of the rarer species, *G. reginae-olgae*. It was collected on Mount Taygetus in 1876 and named for Queen Olga of Greece. Her snowdrop has the very curious (one might almost say perverse) determination to bloom in autumn with the falling leaves, and not in spring when a snowdrop should. It is otherwise nearly indistinguishable from the far more common *G. nivalis*. Unfortunately, my friend was unable to share with me the even rarer *G. reginae-olgae* subsp. *vernalis*, which blooms in spring alongside any common snowdrop, there for only the very learned to recognize (or take on trust). That one is still a lack here.

Otherwise, we really cannot be said, snowdropwise, to suffer, largely due to the offerings of Mr. Hitch Lyman, proprietor of the Temple Nursery in Trumansburg, New York. He is the only purveyor in this country of snowdrops "in the green," a term that must be carefully explained to anyone seeking the rarer snowdrops. Most spring-flowering bulbs—daffodils or tulips, for example—are usually planted in autumn when they are dormant and may be conveniently shipped, usually from Holland. Snowdrops are shipped this way too, though they do not like it, and only the sturdiest forms will survive such treatment. They are all best acquired just after they have flowered and while still in active growth. This makes them a completely undesirable commodity to the large growers, who are geared to supplying dormant bulbs in autumn like supermarket onions. That leaves a niche, however, for the Temple Nursery, which offers the rarest and most beautiful (and sometimes culturally the crankiest) snowdrops in the green, within days of their flowering, each wrapped carefully in a damp paper towel and accurately labeled. So from Mr. Lyman we have bought dozens of bulbs, almost all of which have settled into the garden without a backward glance toward home.

The most common snowdrop—here and everywhere—is *G. nivalis* ("nivalis" means "like snow"), but it is not to be scorned, for sheets and sheets of it blooming happily in shaded places make for joy, a different kind of snow. It is native to central Europe but has naturalized wherever people have gardened, to the extent that it often marks the cellar holes of deserted farmsteads now deep in the reclaiming woods. It is easy to grow, asking only a humus-rich, woodsy soil and part shade. In our Vermont garden it grows beneath old sugar maples mostly along our front walk, flowering over bare ground that will later be occupied by hostas and ferns. It is unusually prolific, and so it is the one that grows most readily if you must buy dried bulbs and plant them in the autumn. One cannot have too much of it, under trees, beneath the bare shanks of shrubs, or wherever it can be planted.

Here, among the masses of *G. nivalis*, grow rarer forms of that species and others. 'Flore Pleno' is easy to recognize, for though it has three outer tepals, at least a dozen green-tipped inner ones form a heart-shaped bundle within. Though it hardly possesses the grace of the plain common snowdrop, there is an old-fashioned charm to its puffed-out hoop petticoat shape. Being a double, in which the fertile parts of the flower have been modified into extra "petals," it sets no seed, though for that same reason it lasts a very long time in flower. It can be divided quite easily, and it freely produces offsets from each bulb. Another vigorous and much-treasured nivalis cultivar is *G. n.* 'Viridapice', which has, in addition to green tips on the inner tepals, hairline brushstrokes of green on the outer tepals as well. While some snowdrops need to be looked at carefully to discern their particular distinctions, 'Viridapice' catches the eye easily. But within the group of single snow-drops heavily marked with green, the most subtle and wonder-ful is perhaps *G. nivalis* 'Virescens', which originated at the Vienna Botanical Garden in the late nineteenth century. The outer tepals appear to be completely washed over with the palest green, though very close observation reveals thin, dark green stripes expanding outward into a sort of green fog.

Galanthus nivalis 'Sandersii', which is elusive because it is so difficult to grow, displays a queer yellow wash both on its in-ner and outer tepals and on the ovary, the rounded structure like a tiny pea that tops all blooms of galanthus. 'Sandersii' is said to flourish best in soils that are acid, though all snowdrops seem to thrive in the somewhat acidic woodland soils of our garden, 'Sandersii' among them. However, it has been very slow to increase, and we never see more than two or three strangely yellow nodding bells from our original single-bulb purchase some years ago.

Doubling in any flower, but especially in something so naïvely elegant as a snowdrop, always requires a stretch of ac-ceptance. Still, in this case we value the double snowdrops be-cause they make a difference in the display at a time when there is little difference to be noted elsewhere in the garden. Among the doubles the most engaging is *G. nivalis* 'Blewbury Tart'. The spelling makes clear that it has nothing whatsoever to do with blueberries, it having been discovered in the churchyard of Blewbury, Oxfordshire. Nor has it anything to do with pas-try, the tart part referring to its extraordinary habit of lifting its outer tepals upward like an immodestly raised skirt. It is imp-ish and adorable, with all its parts shaded by dark green stripes so close together that they seem a solid field of color. Perhaps all snowdrops should really be looked at with a magnifying glass, but this one especially so.

Of all the snowdrops we grow, however, *G.* 'S. Arnott' is the star, both for beauty (even at a distance) and for reliability. A very robust cultivar, it is tall (up to eight inches) and substantial. It is also almost the first snowdrop to open. It pushes out of a bed of myrtle, *Vinca minor*, with which it has seemed to have no trouble competing for many years, just outside the living room windows, always the first sure sign of spring. Its large, opalescent pearls open to expose a deep green heart-shaped stain on the inner tepals. We have seen a foot of snow weigh down the fully opened flowers, and still they stand proudly upright when the snow melts away.

If snowdrops were roses, the small differences that make them special would be obvious and appreciated by all. But they are very little flowers, and that is no small part of their charm to those of us who preserve the fascination with tiny things that all children have. You need to get close to them—an easier thing perhaps for children, who are nearer to the earth than we are. But for adults, a tiny arrangement of snowdrops on a desk or dining table might be the best way, where then the various shapes and forms and the minute gradations of green or chartreuse or yellow can be more easily appreciated.

SORBUS ALNIFOLIA

Though ours is a large garden, many of our favorite things are planted near to hand. Lilacs and roses cluster beneath one bedroom window, and our oldest stewartia grows beneath the other. Our one precious *Ilex opaca* crowds against the foundation of the living room below one window, sheltered both by the winter shade thrown by the house and the warmth of the basement wall. The bright yellow culms of *Phyllostachys aureosulcata* 'Spectabilis' enjoy a similar protection and brush against each other, creating what the Japanese call "the sound of silence." The beautiful soft pink hybrid magnolia called 'Leonard Messel' overhangs the kitchen door. And across the face of the house are three deciduous hollies, *I. verticillata*, which are as old as it is and have grown into muscular shapes like small trees.

Because our house is small, that leaves only one aspect, out the upstairs bathroom window, and it is dominated by one of our most treasured small trees, important enough to share a place in our affections even with the stewartia or the magnolia. The tree is *Sorbus alnifolia*, the alder-leaved or Korean mountain ash, and we see it every hour of the day, every day of the year. Best of all, we look into its crown, close to its leaves and flowers and fruit and somber winter bark, not as if the tree stood out in the garden but almost as if part of the room we are in.

We were in pursuit of *S. alnifolia* from our first year here. We had read Donald Wyman's enthusiastic description of it in his *Trees for American Gardens*. In those days, we had room to plant trees and we intended to plant a great many. We then found a living specimen at Harvard University's Arnold Arboretum in Jamaica Plain, Massachusetts, and our enthusiasm was fixed. *Sorbus alnifolia* was definitely on our list.

But despite Wyman's praise, the tree was little known then and rare in nurseries. Even Weston Nurseries in Hopkinton, Massachusetts, which supplied us so many wonderful trees and shrubs in the beginning, did not list it. That seemed odd, for there was little question of its hardiness (as, for example, there was about *Stewartia pseudocamellia*, on which we took a chance anyway). *Sorbus alnifolia* originates in a very cold part of Korea and is rated as hardy all the way to Zone 3. Eventually, however, we found the tree offered by Wayside Gardens in South Carolina, which made a specialty of the rare and unusual, always at a hefty price. We bought the tree from them, of course, though years would pass before the wisdom of that purchase became clear. What arrived that spring at the post office was just a little sapling barely two feet tall and as thin as a pencil. However, its very smallness was a piece of luck because of where we intended to plant it.

Our garden was taking shape in the shadow of an old New England hardwood forest. Many of the trees, mostly ash, beech, yellow birch, and maple, were perhaps a hundred years old or more, but because they had grown close together for all their lives, they rose straight and tall, with no lower branches anywhere closer to the ground than thirty or forty feet. The woods needed to be brought to the ground, needed the under-story that is often lacking in old woods this far north. But their interlacing root zones made it impossible to establish well-grown small trees with large root masses of their own. A sapling, however, could be tucked in easily among those roots, and so we planted our sorbus almost at the foot of a great sugar maple that towered above the ash's puny self. We really do not remember giving it any special care those first years, either because memory has failed us or—more likely—because it didn't need much and grew quickly. Now, and for a long time, it seems always to have been a stately tree perhaps thirty feet tall, with a trunk measuring thirteen inches in diameter and a wide-spreading crown still comfortably below its much older companion.

The two have existed in perfect harmony, but they never seem so suited to each other as in October, when both are dressed in autumnal blaze. Against the scarlet orange of the maple, the ash's simple, toothed leaves turn from darkest green to butter yellow and then to orange, then a tawny brown. A spectacular display of fruit accompanies this steady change of foliage as October advances. Each of thousands of pretty white flowers arranged in puffs that covered the tree in May will have formed into corymbs of coral fruit shadowed red beneath a powdery, dusty bloom. In most years, the fruit is not with us for long, since a host of birds—jays, robins, cardinals, and chickadees—descend on the tree, making its crown even more alive with color. If the flight path of the robins lies directly over us, they can strip it bare in a week. But if not, the much less voracious birds find something for themselves all winter long, even in the shriveled, dark brown raisins of fruit that may cling almost until spring. And even in winter the tree is beautiful, and somehow noble, its thick trunk supporting a crown of secondary branches. Both the trunk and older branches are smooth and gray but dotted over with straw-colored lenticels, forming a pattern like the skin of a snake.

Over the years, so much in a garden happens by accident, or with a vague hope that somehow things will fill the expectation formed only in the mind. But in any older garden, there may be successes so striking that the gardener himself cannot imagine having foreseen them and can take no credit for what seems essentially an unexpected gift, a happy accident that occurred beyond his best-laid plans and wishes. Our *S. alnifolia* seems that to us now.

STEWARTIAS

THE STEWARTIAS ARE IN FLOWER as they always are here in July, but this year they are more full of bloom than ever before. Each tree—there are six in the garden—is weighted down with flowers, four-inch-wide, six-petaled blossoms of silken white crepe cupped around a center of golden stamens. The slender branches are so burdened, in fact, that they bend at unaccustomed but still graceful angles away from the trunks and spent blossoms, complete and not shattered into single petals, fall every few minutes while marble-round buds are still swelling. The littlest tree, planted on the bank of the stream, is the least floriferous of all. It has been there for only three years, though it flowered shyly at four feet, and now, as a gangly adolescent of perhaps eight, it is still sparing of its flowers. But the four trees that give structure to the lower hillside, two on each side of the winding fieldstone path down the center, have hundreds of flowers apiece. And the oldest, which grows behind the barn and just below the bedroom windows, may have thousands, more, it seems, than any twenty-foot tree could bear. When we look down on it at dawn and at twilight, we can count a hundred on one branch. In the depths of the summer night, the spent blossoms can be seen to drop silently from shadowy black-green leaves like falling stars. Most particularly then, silhouetted against the gray wood shingles of the barn roof, each open white flower glowing in the dark, it seems like a tree in dreams. But in the morning, clearing away the spent blossoms is reality.

So little is really known about stewartias. But in our experience at least, as trees grow older they blossom more abundantly. Our oldest tree was planted five years before the barn was built in 1983, and moved the year after, when we were able to extend the garden in that direction to create a quiet courtyard on two levels. It grew before that in a little bed beside the kitchen door, where many treasured plants began their lives, but now occupied by a wonderful and weirdly contorted *Magnolia* ×'Leonard Messel', which came finally to stay.

Our first stewartia was small when we planted it out of a nursery can and still hardly six feet tall when we moved it to its present home. It accepted relocation with barely a whisper of complaint and has since grown on from strength to strength. Now one can catch glimpses of it over the barn, even from beyond the front yard. In its almost thirty years of life here, even the severest winter has not harmed it, and it has never failed to flower in July, each year more than the year before. We love it, for that and for many other reasons, not the least of which was the prediction we received in the beginning from many well-meaning friends with great gardening sophistication, that no stewartia could possibly live in the cold hills of Vermont. It seems they were wrong.

Stewartia pseudocamellia in fact comes from the colder regions of western China, and has been grown in European gardens since the late nineteenth century. Wherever it has thrived, it has always been recognized as a great aristocrat. So it is curious that when we first began to garden here, it was still a rarity, not so often grown by home gardeners, and certainly not written about. But we ourselves had seen the magnificent old trees at Arnold Arboretum with their man-thick trunks of mottled cream, beige, and dull orange. In the beginning, we did not see them in flower. Flower is not always the reason for growing something. The stature of those trees and their mysterious beauty were enough to cause us to try one here. But as young gardeners we were cautious, or perhaps cautious in a different way from the way we are now. So we looked into books.

We found no mention of the tree in our bibles of that time, Josephine Nuese's *The Country Garden* or Thalassa Cruso's *Making Things Grow Outdoors*. Other bedside companions—Elizabeth Lawrence and Vita Sackville-West—had nothing to say, though Donald Wyman did, for the tree has been at the Arnold for a century, and as its director, he had much praise for it in his *Wyman's Garden Encyclopedia*. Like so much else in *Wyman's*, however, *S. pseudocamellia* was listed as hardy to Zone 5. That is where the Arnold Arboretum is, and so many beautiful shrubs and trees were tested there and subsequently designated as "hardy to Zone 5." Still, we were willing to take risks, and over the years that have inevitably followed, we have found that hardiness ratings are always to be questioned. Or at least tested. Often, they are hobgoblins to unadventurous gardeners. But our oldest stewartia gave us courage early on to stretch the hardiness ratings generally listed for all woody plants grown in American gardens. Our stewartias appear to be as happy here as in their native land, and in fact bring that land here, since almost nothing we can imagine except the place itself (which we have never seen) looks quite so much like western China as our old stewartia in full bloom against our weathered barn, here in southern Vermont.

But wherever stewartias can be grown, they are beautiful in all their parts and at all seasons. The flowers really are like camellias, fragile, two-inch-wide blooms of the clearest silver and gold, though each lasts only a day or two and then litters the ground like summer drifts of snow. Bloom here begins almost always on the last day of June and extends for the month of July, the last flowers opening even into early August on shaded branches where they develop slowest. Then, in autumn, there is no tree more brilliant in leaf color, starting a deep burgundy red in branches exposed to sun and shading from there to scarlet, pumpkin, and yellow, all the colors of autumn borne together, and always later than the great trees of the surrounding woodland—the maples, beeches, ashes, and birches. When the leaves have fallen, there are the trunks, always part of the general beauty, but then so prominent and muscular, mottled over with warm taupe and buff and cream, smooth to the stroke of the hand, irresistible in winter, in snow.

A tree must be loved by any gardener. Trees are something for all seasons—in bud, flower, leaf, twig, bark, and trunk. Trees are companions, and one can even hug them, if need and desire and their presence through a significant extent of time justify that demonstration of affection. But in any garden, some trees are visitors and some are guests. Stewartias are true love, and anyone who can should therefore plant one. In the early years, their presence in the garden should be thought of as a courtship, not a settled romance. For they are not for all places, soils, and cultural conditions. We have had good luck here in southern Vermont, where, though winters are cold, our soils are deep, slightly acid woodland loam, and moisture is abundant. But even for us, and as with any other potential love affair, a certain amount of courage was required.

SUMMER-BLOOMING BULBS

IMAGINE THE POSSIBILITY of eating one meal that would cure you of hunger for life. Or a room that was decorated once and for all, never needing rearranging or freshening with a new pillow or a bouquet of flowers. Then try to imagine the possibility of a garden that once planted, grew and bloomed without any further attention from you. If you can even imagine these things, then the culture of summer-blooming bulbs will not be of much interest. For most are tender in all but the warmest parts of North America, requiring either to be bought fresh each season, or, if you are very thrifty and can contrive the right conditions, to be lifted in autumn and stored through winter. They are all a deal of work for a flowering season that is hardly a month. Or less.

But summer-blooming bulbs (which include corms, tubers, rhizomes, and other underground storage mechanisms) have become the source of great enthusiasm among gardeners. If their culture is often fairly labor-intensive, it is at least usually not difficult. The bulbs themselves are often absurdly cheap. They are dramatically beautiful in flower, and that flower comes in the dullest parts of late summer when both the garden and the gardener need a lift. Finally, summer-blooming bulbs offer a complexity of form that no other summer flowers can claim. They are, quite simply, interesting. And gardens ought above all things to be interesting, especially in summer, when one is most in them.

Within the surprisingly vast world of summer-blooming bulbs, gladiolus have always been popular with gardeners. But the question is, with *which* gardeners? Mostly, they have been treasured by those whose sense of growing flowers was close to their sense of growing vegetables. (If you visited your great-uncle Otto in the summer and you admired his glads, in neat rows, you had to take home a sheaf along with some beans and zucchini.) But all that has changed now, for as part of the general reevaluation of "common" garden flowers, the florist's glad has received its share of attention. It is true that the colors of many cultivars are brash, their forms uncompromising, and the size of their flower scapes makes them difficult to combine tactfully with summer-blooming perennials in the border. Still, even the most outrageous of them have their uses in summer gardens. They can provide an emphatic flash of scarlet magenta or lime green that can lift a banal garden composition into something interesting. And they need not be planted singly as rigid exclamation points (or, as many gardeners feel, as insulting fingers), poking up through gentle border geraniums and veronicas. A clump of five, or even seven, planted so the corms almost touch, can look more natural. And staking, which will be necessary for so heavy a fan of leaves and flower, is much easier to achieve. A peony hoop will serve.

Nor need gladiolus seem so redolent of hotel lobby arrangements or a funeral parlor sheaf atop a coffin. For among the butterfly glads are many graceful, delicate forms, of which the best is perhaps a clear scarlet with widely spaced florets. Nice too are the so-called hardy gladiolus, often offered as *Gladiolus nanus*, though that is not the proper botanical name for them. For like the larger florist's glads, they are correctly grouped under a catchall botanical category, *G. ×hortulanus*, that reflects the crossing and recrossing of many species. They have been selected, however, for an appearance more pleasing to many gardeners. At full maturity, they stand slightly more than a foot tall, and their flowers are borne in rather spontaneous ranks, never in the carefully regimented rows of florist's glads. Catalogs always seem to offer them in mixed colors— of cherry red, rich or pale pink, cream or white, and often splotched with deeper shades. Get them in single colors if you can, though the mixes generally combine beautifully. As for the promise of hardiness, they are no more hardy than the larger glads, surviving winters not much farther north than Zone 7. Still, for their delicate beauty, patches of them are worth planting anew each spring.

Beyond the familiar gladiolus there are also many pure species, delicately wild and wonderful in form and color, that any gardener should search out who likes to go back to the original sources of things. Most commonly offered—and it is very commonly offered once one knows to look for it—is acidanthera, called the "Abyssinian glad" or "Peacock orchid." Its correct botanical name—at present—is *G. callianthus* 'Murielae', after E. H. Wilson's daughter, Muriel, who is commemorated in many plants. It has been in gardens for a long time, having been brought from its native Ethiopia to England in the mid-nineteenth century, where it was almost immediately popular. Generally, gladiolus are plants one can take or leave, but acidanthera is practically indispensable. From corms hardly the size of a quarter, surprisingly large plants develop, first with a handsome fan of pleated, dark green leaves, and then with a graceful, arching inflorescence of many slightly pendulous clear white flowers, each marked in the center by a blotch of maroon. At twilight, fully opened flowers release a fresh, strong fragrance, rather like that of vernal primroses. And best of all, spent flowers hang in graceful fringes, never looking depressing and never requiring deadheading.

Acidanthera is very easy to grow. Five or six corms can be planted in a quart plastic pot in early June, and grown in an unobtrusive place, behind a shed or garage or anywhere, provided there is full sun. By mid-July, handsome clumps of foliage will have developed, ready to be slipped into any bare section of the perennial garden. In August, there will be magnificent flowers in a place that otherwise would be dull and homely. Only paperwhite narcissus in the dead of winter are easier.

Even after acidanthera one is not quite finished with the gladiolus family, however, for within it still are many wonderful summer-blooming plants, not least of which is crocosmia. It is a plant with mixed reviews, depending in part on where one lives and in part on one's tolerance for hot colors, in this case usually a vibrant, fire-flame orange. Where it is happily perennial and self-seeds (which is to say Zone 8 and warmer), it is as common as *Hemerocallis fulva* is along New England roadsides, and like that plant it is scorned, though both surely give a lift to the heart when seen from a car window. Where it must be cosseted a bit, its thick fountains of grass-green leaves to three feet tall and its arching inflorescences of fifty or more burning scarlet flowers give it its own special value. Of the many cultivars available, 'Lucifer' is still the most vigorous and the hardiest, surviving with good winter drainage well into Zone 5. Those gardeners who grow faint at violent colors might seek out 'Solfitare', with soft, amber flowers the color of a Lorna Doone cookie.

It is a very interesting fact that many plants considered until recently fairly tacky by sophisticated gardeners have experienced a surprising reevaluation and even a sort of vogue. Cannas are a case in point. Each year, along with the old standards like 'Le roi Humbert' (pronounced by some *Leeroy Umbert*), catalogs offer forms that are softer in color and finer in form, and as one catalog puts it, "self-cleaning," which means that spent flowers drop off tactfully to make way for fresher ones. Great excitement has been occasioned too by the elegant cultivar 'Stuttgart', with cool green leaves liberally splashed with clear white, and gentle, coral flowers. For a canna, it is a cranky plant, since in the full sun that most cannas enjoy it will quickly burn to a crisp. But in cool part shade, however, and liberally watered—or even with its roots standing in water, for it is semiaquatic—it adds great elegance to a group of plants that seems to have gained increasing refinement in the last few years. Still, the fine old forms, including 'Le roi', with its purple leaves that catch the light so beautifully, are not to be superceded. Viewed rightly, they still have great value in gardens.

One waits for similar progress with dahlias. It is of course true that the gardeners who like them have always liked them, for their outrageous, late summer flowers the size sometimes of dinner plates, and for their generally Carol Channing forthrightness, in orange, scarlet, flame, magenta, purple, or any of those colors brushed one over another. One can easily have a fondness, frank or sneaking, for all of them. But great tact is required in combining them with other flowers in order to prevent that "Look at me!" quality they often have. It is odd, then, that the most stylish and serviceable dahlia is in some ways the brashest of them all. It is 'Bishop of Llandaff', a very old cultivar with bronze leaves that stands about three feet tall, surmounted by blood-red semi-double flowers. This is the dahlia used in substantial masses by Lawrence Johnson in the famous red border at Hidcote, though until recently it was difficult to find in any U.S. catalog. Gardeners who wanted it had to beg it from other gardeners, though that has always been the way with many old-fashioned summer-blooming bulbs. Now it is more easily acquired, and the suavity of its burgundy leaves and its scarlet flowers makes it a valuable component in gardens that might suffer too much from misty-mauvey good taste.

Though a certain boldness of form and flower may be the salvation of many a dull late summer border, not all summer-blooming bulbs are dramatic full stops. A large handful of them offer a gentler beauty, making them easier to blend into the garden. *Galtonia candicans*, the "summer hyacinth" of old southern gardens, is at the head of that list. Its scapes of bloom are more finely crafted than any hyacinth, standing about eighteen inches tall and furnished with many delicate down-hanging bells of greenish white. Though they are fragrant, it is their grace that recommends them, for they can be planted beneath more stolid perennials to rise above them in airy minarets. Galtonias originated in South Africa, but they are surprisingly hardy, reappearing in Zone 6 gardens. Still, for insurance, new bulbs should always be planted in early spring wherever one expects things to look dull in late August and early September.

Another confusion with a familiar spring blooming bulb occurs in the common name of hymenocallis, an elegant South American native often inexplicably called the "Peruvian daffodil." Though its flowers have the cup-shaped perianth most daffodils possess, it looks nothing like a daffodil, except perhaps to the myopic and from a very great distance. But certainly it looks good enough, for from a sturdy clump of amaryllis-like foliage two-foot-tall flower scapes emerge, each topped by five or so three-inch-long flowers consisting of a central cup surrounded by filamented spiderlike petals. Their plump bulbs can be expected to flower about six weeks from planting, and three or more bulbs should always be planted in one hole, to make a natural-seeming clump. In the most familiar form, the hybrid *Hymenocallis* ×*festalis*, the flower is white and very fragrant. Another hybrid, 'Sulphur Queen', is a clear primrose yellow. Close to frost, they should be lifted and stored over the winter as one does amaryllis, to be replanted in late spring or early summer. They are superb as cut flowers and delicately lily-scented.

For fragrance, however, nothing among summer bulbs can top tuberoses, *Polianthes tuberosa*. Their heady perfume might seem morbid to some, for as Mexican natives, they are the *flores para los muertos*, funeral flowers. One can think that way if one must, but otherwise, they are divinely fragrant, with a power equal only to *Magnolia grandiflora* and gardenias. It is good that they smell so wonderful, for tuberoses are not among the most graceful of garden flowers. Their towering spikes of bloom, white in the single and pale pink in the double cultivar 'The Pearl', are nice enough, rising up to three feet or more in height. But by the time the blooms open at the tops, the onion-like leaves have withered away, and the general effect is of something beautiful atop something that is very shabby. Many of the larger spring blooming alliums have the same problem, and so one must simply anticipate it by planting tuberoses in and among other plants that will clothe their bare shanks. It does not generally do, however, to plant them in the bare ground in early spring, for they are slow to develop, and in colder gardens, flowers will not occur before frosts. They should therefore be started indoors in warm conditions in early spring, grown in pots, and eased into the garden as soon as the weather is settled.

Though many summer-blooming bulbs have their greatest value in the ground as enrichments to borders, others are pre-eminent for pot culture. There are tuberous begonias, much loved for the beautiful camellia-sized flowers in any color from snowy white to soft and deeper yellow through orange, scarlet, and true red. Those splendid flowers look so sad when drag-gled in the mud, and so beautiful hanging heavily off the edges of a clay pot. There are also oxalis, pot cultured where they are not hardy, forming soft mounds of green or burgundy clover leaves in which the flowers nestle, white or ivory or pink ac-cording to species. Delicate achimenes are a pleasant alterna-tive to impatiens in shade, their arching, eight-inch-long stems crowded with long-lasting, flat-faced flowers in many shades of rose, pink, purple, and white. Do not be startled at being of-fered twenty-five or so rhizomes for eight dollars, as it will take that many to furnish a ten-inch pot. A well-grown pot of caladiums is also always refreshing in the shaded corner of a terrace, particularly if they are the old white and green form, called 'Candidum', a sort of vegetable ice cube on a hot day. An emphatically tropical effect can also be had from *Colocasia esculenta*, called "elephant ears," planted in a really large pot. Do not buy it from bulb catalogs, but go to Asian or Chinese grocery stores, where it is sold by the pound as a vegetable. Finally, a tub of calla lilies is always rich in leaf, beautiful in flower, and for a potted plant, certainly convenient. Most species are semiaquatic, growing natively in ditches and in shallow, stagnant water. They grow best in pots stood in water, into which a little water-soluble plant food can be put for even lusher leaves and flowers.

The world of summer-blooming bulbs has opened for gardeners like a vast new country. Catalogs have quickly caught this interest and are encouraging it, reminding gardeners of old plants they knew as children and of new ones they have never heard of. Among their pages are gladiolus, cannas, and dahlias, all meriting a fresh look. But there is also the delicate, allium-flowered *Triteleia laxa*, best in the cobalt-blue form 'Queen Fabiola'. *Ornithogalum saundersiae*, the 'Star of Good Hope', bears three-foot-tall umbels of white, each star-shaped flower marked with a jet-black center. The deep crimson Jacobean lily, *Sprekelia formosissima*, meaning "most beautiful," is as easy to grow as any Christmas gift amaryllis. There are Chinese lantern lilies, *Sandersonia aurantiaca*, which produce odd goldfish-shaped flowers along winding, two-foot stems, and *Gloriosa superba* 'Rothschildiana', a taller vine to three feet, with lily-like flowers of orange and yellow. Pineapple lilies, species of *Eucomis*, are impossible not to study when they produce their cobs of greenish, sweet-scented waxy flowers each surmounted with a topknot of leaves. Finally, there is the improbable mating of two completely separate genera, *Amaryllis belladonna* and *Crinum moorei*, which produced the bigeneric hybrid amarcrinum, a sturdy bulb the size of a grapefruit with rich blades of leaf three feet long and an intensely fragrant scape of candy-pink, amaryllis-like flowers in early September. In the face of all this unfamiliar experience, one feels like Columbus.

TENDER RHODODENDRONS

So MUCH of what we've grown over the years has been the result of what we have gone to bed with. When our garden was only a hope and a dream and we were living in a rented house, we ended each day with a thick reference book on some aspect of gardening. We did not look things up or skip about, but rather, worked our way systematically from front to back. Though our method might sound to others a little like reading the dictionary, there was nothing that was not of interest to us. So in that way, we plowed through *Wyman's Garden Encyclopedia*, T. H. Everett's *New Illustrated Encyclopedia of Gardening*, and *The Royal Horticultural Society's Color Dictionary of Flow-*

ering Plants. Our reading resulted in a serial involvement with all sorts of plants previously unknown to us—cytisus, fremontodendron, ceanothus, carpenteria, even the magnificent *Myosotidium hortensia*, the rare and cranky Chatham Islands forget-me-not. It was an endless list, and it still seems to be continuing. (Now, of course, we would have twin volumes of the *American Horticultural Society A–Z Encyclopedia of Garden Plants* and start with that.)

One of the largest, heaviest, and most scholarly of these books encouraged the most enduring of all these youthful enthusiasms. When it was published in 1961, David Leach's *Rhododendrons of the World* was simply the definitive work on that large genus. It probably still is, though when we acquired our copy in 1974 it was already out of print. We could understand why, because it is a huge book, oversized, densely single-spaced, and with not a single photograph in all its 544 pages. But it enabled us to see for the first time a whole world of plants we had no knowledge of at all, and we eagerly absorbed the wealth of information it offered, covering distribution, care, diseases, propagation, and so on. As we read, however, we realized that of the thousands of species and hybrids that make up this enormous genus, very few would consent to life in a Zone 4 garden. Of David Leach's hundreds of recommendations, a bare dozen would be for us, and those—with a few remarkable exceptions—were not among the showiest of even the hardier rhododendrons.

Of course, no one knew this better than David Leach himself. For he spent a lifetime creating beautiful hardy rhododendrons, producing one magnificent hybrid after another in the coldest part of Pennsylvania, a place almost as cold as where we had chosen to live. In addition to increasing hardiness, Leach also enormously increased the range of colors available, extending the predominately pink and white and purple forms into peach and clear yellow and even green.

But in 1975, the new possibilities David Leach had created still lay in our future. We had begun to plan the house we would build the following year, and we knew that it would contain a greenhouse. No passionate gardener can survive Vermont winters otherwise. And since there was to be a greenhouse, we thought it should be attached to the house, open to the living earth, and treated as a real garden. It would be a winter garden in fact, no matter how small it had to be, and in it we would grow a whole range of winter and early-spring blooming plants forbidden to us outdoors. So we read with enormous interest Leach's brief, seven-page chapter called "Rhododendrons for the Cool Greenhouse," which contained these words: "the most impressive of all Rhododendrons . . . under glass produce sumptuous flowers of luxuriant proportion and delicious fragrance." For what we had in mind, that sounded perfect.

None of the rhododendrons Leach especially recommended for greenhouse culture were grown on the East Coast. The plants were hardy outdoors only around the San Francisco Bay area, and so for us, that was one more reason to take our school vacations there. The classified ads in the back pages of *Pacific Horticulture* listed several growers of rare species rhododendrons, and we were confident that at least some of the fifty-seven forms particularly recommended in *Rhododendrons of the World* could be found among them.

One of the deepest pleasures gardening offers is the enthusiastic welcome gardeners extend to other gardeners who share their interest. The first nursery on our list, in Oakland, was quite small, perhaps a quarter of an acre in extent, and given over entirely to rare azaleas and rhododendrons. The young man who greeted us was startled that someone would have driven thirty-five hundred miles in pursuit of just what his nursery offered. He insisted on phoning his elderly father, now retired, to come from his home a few blocks away and meet us. For as he said, the plants before us were his father's greatest joy, and he would relish telling us about them and helping with our selection. Mr. Lopez arrived shortly thereafter, intent, we soon realized, on sending us away with the whole nursery. But we had only a borrowed station wagon, and we had already made the resolution to buy only small plants, the more to bring home. But Mr. Lopez offered us a splendid *Rhododendron fosterianum*, the only one he had, which was a large plant already four feet tall, with smooth, reddish-brown bark like a manzanita. It barely fit into the car, and everything else we were to acquire on our trip would have to be packed around it. It was evident, however, that old Mr. Lopez took great delight in the idea of his plant blooming against the snow of a Vermont March, so far from its previous home. And besides encouraging him in his evident pleasure, we simply wanted it, so we cheerfully paid the absurdly small amount of money he asked. It flowered abundantly early in our first spring at North Hill, producing large, loose trusses of white, funneled flowers, each ruffled at its end and strongly scented of cinnamon and nutmeg. That scent, we soon found, was the hallmark of rhododendrons in the Maddenii group, the various members of which originate in India and Bhutan on the lower slopes of the Himalayas between 5,000 and 9,000 feet.

We took one other plant that day, not a rhododendron but a late-flowering azalea of a strain bred in Japan. Called "Satsuki," meaning "fifth month," these plants typically bloom in May. What makes them remarkable, however, is that many varieties produce distinct variations of color when in bloom, all on the same plant. 'Huru-Gusimi' had blooms of orchid pink, though some flowers were marked with rose-purple stripes, and some had white centers. This, too, was the first of a group of plants that would be added to over the years.

We took away two other important things that day, but neither was a plant. We were told to visit Nuccio's Nursery in Altadena for the best collection of azaleas and camellias in the United States, many of which its founder, Guillio Nuccio, had bred. We were also given the name of a backyard breeder of Maddenii rhododendrons in Fort Bragg, at the very northern end of California. Since our quest was primarily for tender rhododendrons, we decided Nuccio's could wait, and we headed north.

The small house we found among the redwoods at Fort Bragg was the home of a true enthusiast, the sort of nursery we have delighted in finding all our gardening lives. Its owner, Marge Drucker, grew everything on David Leach's list, and she enthusiastically filled out his dry, scholarly descriptions with glowing praise of her own. Of the dozen plants we took away, our favorite has been 'Countess of Haddington', though not for its plant form, which is ungraceful, lank, and rangy. But in the winter garden in early April, each terminal growth produces a large, lax truss of tubular three-inch-long flowers that begins suffused in wine red and opens to a pristine white with pink stains, as if a fine Burgundy had been spilled on a snow-white damask tablecloth. And we could not do without 'Else Frye', much smaller in stature and more compact, with tidier trusses of white, fragrant flower, or 'Fragrantissimum', though it seemed in bloom no more fragrant than the others, since all three produce the same rich lily-like scent with strong nutmeg overtones.

Plants grow, of course, and our rhododendrons grew remarkably. Fosterianum increased the most rapidly and was a larger plant to start with. After four years with us, it reached the top of the greenhouse glass and so we gave it to the botany department of nearby Marlboro College. We miss it still. 'Fragrantissimum' gave its place to a rapidly increasing and very beautiful single Higo camellia, 'Yamato-Nishiki', with rose-striped white flowers, and 'Else Frye' succumbed quite suddenly, we think from mice tunneling at her roots. 'Countess of Haddington' is with us still. But one Maddenii rhododendron is hardly enough, and so we have just ordered a new 'Else Frye' from Roger Gossler at Gossler Farms Nursery in Oregon. We miss her snow-white, open-funneled flowers produced in great abundance just a little after 'Countess of Haddington'. We miss 'Fragrantissimum' too, and probably someday soon we will locate it again as well. For though other passions and enthusiasms have come to us in the thirty years since that trip to California, we seem always to return to our first loves.

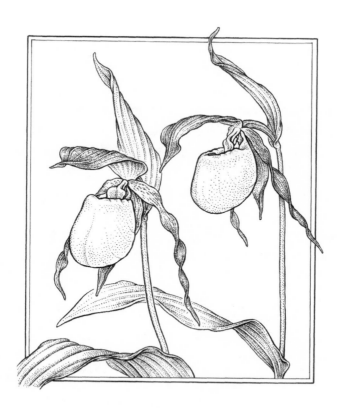

TIME

IN 1976 A GOOD FRIEND took us to visit a garden in Prides Crossing, Massachusetts. The property was large, at least for a community where any inch of land is gold. It consisted of perhaps ten acres, and every bit of it had been developed over more than forty years of constant care. The passage of so many years—years of devising and elaborating, of planting, pruning, and shaping—were obvious everywhere. 'Old Dexter' hybrid rhododendrons lined the long gravel drive and created a tunnel leading up to the front of the house, a generously proportioned Federal mansion from about 1780. At the back of the property was a somber theater of clipped hemlock, complete with exit wings, backdrops, green curtains, and a stone-coped elevated grass stage. Each quaint, weathered little outbuilding had its own mossed-over terrace. Salvage was everywhere; there were wooden balustrades from some old house, free-standing Grecian revival porch columns, an authentic marble Renaissance wellhead, and even—or so we seem to remember—a statue of Bette Davis as a garden nymph, carved when she was a teenaged artist's model thereabouts. The whole effect could have been called "Colonial Palladian," but its whimsy, ingenuity, and beauty completely avoided pretension. It was also just slightly mad. We think that was the first old garden we ever saw, or at least the first we studied with any care. Our own garden had just been started, and we were searching for lessons wherever we could find them.

The property was in the process of being sold to an energetic young couple bent on making improvements. The house and garden had simply become too much for its owner, now old and frail, and he had decided to retreat into an assisted-living facility. So everywhere there was the eerie feeling that this garden was about to become a ghost and fade from memory forever. A great veil of *Forsythia suspensa* lay across the lawn in dishevelment while fresh shingles were being nailed on. "I doubt they'll put it back. It always was a bother. Birds' nests, rats, and bats, you know." We could only marvel at a shrub that had been patiently and laboriously trained up two stories of an antique house front for over forty years and now was doomed for its "bother." A splendid specimen of climbing hydrangea (*H. anomala* subsp. *petiolaris*) had reached the top of a stately beech and then layered its blooming stems outward, a many-tiered pagoda. It was also to be removed, because some consulting arborist had told the young couple it was damaging the beech. "How old is it?" one of us asked. "Oh, thirty years,

I guess." Our hearts sank a bit. We were barely that old ourselves.

When you enter our garden today, there is a large sugar maple just at the point where the path enters the front lawn. The tree was here when we came and so it must now be well over a century old. In the second year of the garden's life, we planted a climbing hydrangea at its base, remembering the one we had seen at Prides Crossing and hoping someday our plant might inherit a shadow of its beauty. Now, visitors invariably ask, "How old is that?" and their faces sag a little when we say, "More than thirty years." Nobody ever guesses at the years ahead, until they have already passed.

We can, however, offer some comforts to young gardeners—or to gardeners of any age who are just starting a garden—and they are not comforts that were extended to us when we first began. The chief of them is that a major part of the pleasure of gardening is in the act of gardening itself. It's no good to say, "I will never see this tree or shrub or vine in its mature beauty." For simply to plant that tree or shrub or vine and see it gradually take hold, getting larger each year, finally surprising you by its size, even though you knew it first as a tiny thing in a black plastic nursery pot, this is where the real pleasure of gardening lies. Katherine White and Vita Sackville-West both oversaw the planting of large numbers of daffodils in their gardens in autumn, when they both knew they were dying. E. B. White remembered his wife, sitting in damp Ferragamo shoes on a lawn chair, pointing out locations. And Sackville-West wrote to Harold Nicolson the autumn before she died, saying she knew they had a policy of both agreeing on things, but in the case of these bulbs, she just couldn't help herself.

And when we had the pleasure of touring Kerdalo, Prince Peter Wolkonsky's magnificent garden in Brittany, he—then ninety-three years old—gestured expansively at a whole hill-top planted with various yellow magnolias, none taller than three feet. "Isn't this going to be magnificent!" We hope we can claim that sort of courage for ourselves.

Many of the effects that are most impressive in a garden have probably been that way for some time. Though a gardener tells you that the yew hedge you admire is forty years old, it has probably been a successful part of the garden for at least thirty. The yew hedges in Christopher Lloyd's garden in England, Great Dixter, are at least a century old, having been planted by his father, Nathaniel Lloyd, before Christo was born. But the job they do, of segmenting the garden into so many wonderful and surprising experiences, is one they have been doing for at least ninety years. Our own yew hedge, which divides the perennial garden from the back lawn, was set out as two-foot-tall bushes twenty-eight years ago, our first mark on raw dirt that organized all the rest. Simply to make that mark was a satisfaction, and greater satisfaction came when the bushes had grown together and formed a real hedge. And when that hedge got to the point that one couldn't quite see over it, which was about five years after its planting, it had done the job it was planted to do.

When we remember the planting of so many things in the early years of the garden, we are led to a hard truth. You may extravagantly admire a mature garden, even your own, and love the specimens in it for the feeling of settled age they convey. But, though few tourists may be attracted, it is the expanding garden that offers the most satisfaction. To clear out an area of brambles or congested saplings, to seed down a new path or lay the stones for it, to have plenty of space to arrange plants just acquired for the garden but coveted elsewhere, to see them catch and thrive and increase . . . all these joys of gardening seem to us in many ways much more intense than the pleasures of strolling paths overshaded by rhododendrons, stewartias, or magnolias. And those gardeners who do visit a raw young garden can share in the gardener's hopes and enthusiasms, just as we did in Prince Wolkonsky's infant magnolia orchard, though below it lay the assured beauty of over sixty years of cultivation.

We don't mean to minimize the pleasures of the mature garden, for if we were prone to do so, we'd obviously move on. Blankets of myrtle and drifts of hostas are wonderful in themselves and also free us from so much of the tedious weeding we used to have to do. Bulbs are everywhere, an abundance of bulbs being one of the great joys of a mature garden. We congratulate ourselves often and rather smugly on the multiplication of costly plants, even though we well know that gardening is the least thrifty of all the domestic arts. But still, when the colchicum are in bloom, perhaps five thousand bulbs in one long sweep against the conifer border, we cannot help but remember the original twenty-five, inordinately expensive (for a bulb), with which we started, patiently dividing and redividing thereafter. The initial price of the Kentucky lady's slipper orchid, *Cypripedium kentuckiense*, almost knocked the breath out of us, though we knew we were going to have it, no matter what. Now, one pip has become two clumps of twenty-five each, and when its curious brown and yellow pouched blossoms open over pleated two-foot-tall leaves, we stand over it and calculate our wealth. After all, people who own real estate, or stocks and bonds, or troves of gold coins, do the same. Why shouldn't gardeners?

We also enjoy the pleasure of harvesting, which comes when we open a bit of bare ground and need to fill it up with a good plant, and have one—an epimedium or hosta or fern—

that we can split and reestablish. When shrubs have become congested and some specimen requires a new location, it is pleasant to wander through the garden, always looking for the place it can be shifted to greater effect. Mostly, however, we love to share with other gardening friends who come for lunch. We always admonish them to bring cardboard boxes. Then, a walk through the garden becomes a vital sharing. "Take some of this. It is wonderful." Gardeners with new gardens cannot afford to do that. But it was said of Ellen Willmott's garden, Warley, now vanished except for a mile of self-seeded *Crocus tommasinianus* along the highway, that "the very weed buckets were full of treasures." We would rather put ours in the cardboard boxes brought by visitors. And we can.

But really, many of the joys of an old garden lie in the remaking of it. For when you have reached either the boundaries of your plot, or more probably the limit of your own capacities to maintain what you have, you have to go backward. That is, you have to look with a critical eye at the borders you have already developed that have given you pleasure for years and ask whether they still pass muster. In evaluating the health and beauty of the mature garden, shade is the creeping menace, for it is true, as someone has said, that "as gardeners grow older, their gardens grow shadier." A shade garden can be a beautiful thing. But damp Stygian gloom under a spreading magnolia isn't ever attractive. In any garden, space also shrinks as specimens mature, resulting in the loss of just that much in which you might grow something else. After all, who ever starts a garden hoping to end up with only trees and mulch?

Mastering the art of elimination may be the hardest part of gardening. But it is necessary. And really, when that aging unattractive specimen is cut down, however rare it is, the light floods in and many new possibilities occur. One goes back again to the catalogs or looks about the garden for good plants to divide, and a certain vigor returns, both to garden and gardener. In the sense of Wordsworth's lines in "Ode: Intimations of Immortality" ("O joy! that in our embers / Is something that doth live, / That nature yet remembers / What was so fugitive!"), it isn't a bad trade-off for the pleasures of making a new garden. Besides, eventually it is what we are given and have to garden with.

In the end, you cannot separate a mature garden from mortality, for on even the most casual stroll through it you are reminded of your own, in a tree grown to maturity or even a patch of snowdrops multiplied from one bulb into a hundred. One can learn to accept the fact that one's own demise and the demise of one's garden may be approximately simultaneous. Actually, that is our greatest hope, for it won't be at all pleasant to see the garden go before we are ready to. But great gardeners we have known have told us that you can get used even to that idea. We are working on it.

VEGETABLE GARDENS

WE ARE ALWAYS SURPRISED when we visit a garden that does not have some section set aside for vegetables and fruits. If the owner is someone we know well enough, we are apt to be a little challenging on the subject, even maybe a little aggressive. Almost always we get the same excuse, offered with the assumption that it is completely convincing. "Why would I go to all that trouble, when I can buy anything I want at the supermarket?" (Or co-op, or weekend farmers' market, or local farm stand.)

Well, can you? Do you find puntarelle there in early autumn, for example, the stems of which you can slit and soak in ice water until they curl, and then dress with olive oil, garlic, balsamic vinegar, and lots of mashed anchovies? Will there be bunches of barba di frate, the famous salicorne of medieval cookery (so perverse because it seems to thrive only on dreadful soil), to sauté with butter and a little lemon? Can you find infant greens there, hardly out of the seed, such as you might serve as a salad topped with a perfect poached egg? Or golden celery, the smell of which is the perfect celestial idea of celery? Will there perhaps be a little bundle of multicolored carrots, some white, some gold, some red, and some orange, none longer than your finger? Tomatoes? Are they vine-ripened, and do they smell of the dust and warmth of the field and that divine odor we can only call "tomatoey"? Will there be white ones and yellow ones in all sizes, big and little, pear-shaped and round, and are some yellow-and-scarlet streaked, or as green as a grape, or flat-out ugly in their folds and bumps, the best of all for taste? Are there purple Brussels sprouts in autumn, each hardly larger than a marble, black and glistening when lightly boiled and dressed with good olive oil? And near Thanksgiving, will you see pumpkins and squash in fantastic variety, pleated and warted, biscuit brown or scarlet, dull green, celadon blue, fit for Cinderella's coach or as long as a baseball bat?

Perhaps you can find all these things. If you are lucky enough to live in San Diego and can get to Chino's, the legendary farmstead that has been in the same Japanese family for three generations—through war and out of it—you certainly will. Or you could live near Walker Farm, in East Dummerston, Vermont, as we do (another family enterprise, in the case of Jack and Karen Manix, the present stewards, extending through six generations), to see what is fresh and choice, and in the process, pick up some cut flowers, a tray of rare annuals, or a loaf of really good bread. There are many other such places, we are sure, since more and more Americans are interested in fresh, organically grown vegetables and fruits, and have learned that a head of lettuce is not just a head of (iceberg) lettuce, and a carrot is not automatically all a carrot aspires to be.

Somewhere also, in every sizeable city, there are open-air markets or gourmet food shops that cater to a really discriminating taste in vegetables, generally referred to as "fresh produce." (What other kind is there, though we certainly do know its opposite, "stale produce.") In New York, for example, there must be such a place, for the appetite is certainly there, and the cash to spend is also, and opportunities for brisk sales generally appear like mushrooms when appetite and cash conjoin. But we are almost half New Yorkers at this point in our life, and we don't know where it is. There is the famous Union Square Market, to be sure, which can, on a lovely summer or autumn weekend, be wonderfully lighthearted, with attractive young people circulating among the open-air stalls, accumulating their week's vegetables and fruits in sensible, ecologically correct canvas bags that are tucked around Baby in its high-tech carriage.

Even, however, if we admit that really great organic farm stands do offer superb produce, picked fresh that day and in the most exquisite sizes and varieties, our argument for a home vegetable garden would still not be silenced. If you are in the mood for an outing, a trip anywhere can be nice, even, if you have cabin fever, to the local supermarket, where rounding the aisle into frozen foods might be distinctly depressing, not just because people apparently eat that sort of thing, but because the experience of being out and about is almost over. However, a trip to a really great farm stand is a lift to the heart, and one might begin smiling half a mile away. But an amble to your own vegetable garden is really quite a different thing. Better too, we'd argue, not just because it is the work of your own hands, but also because you can do it so often and still do it again. We often go to ours four or five times a day, for harvest, to work, for a handful of parsley, or just to go up and stare at the beauty that is there. We would not want to get into a car so often to travel to the best farm stand on earth.

Of course our main argument is a spiritual one, and neither has reference to practicality nor can be overturned by any practical considerations whatsoever. Vegetable gardening—assuming one does it right, and if not right, why at all?—is a lot of work. Also, the work both starts and ends in the least pleasant parts of the year, in early spring when rows must be turned, compost and lime bucketed in, and the first seeds sown of peas and spinach and lettuce, and in the chilly twilights of autumn, when frost threatens and all the crops that are sensitive to cold must be gathered in, tomatoes both ripe and green, eggplants, peppers, squash, and pumpkins. Covers must be thrown over celery, celeriac, and perhaps artichokes, if we have not already taken them all. Sometimes, with aching muscles not yet awake to spring, or with numbing fingers in the desperate early twilight of the first black-frost night, we are near to tears. So what? When were the deepest satisfactions available to humanity ever bought without labor and suffering?

There's more to it than that, of course, and though committed vegetable gardeners might seem to the rest of humanity rather like mad folk, there are good, bright, sunny times, when the work of the garden—sowing, cultivating, weeding, harvesting—is all done under warm skies and seems as effortless as breathing. We know gardeners who approach their vegetable plots in just that spirit, always getting their crops in when the spring sunshine is warm (too late, in our opinion) and cheerfully abandoning their last tender crops to frost, the very thought of which makes them turn more comfortably into their warm pillows. They probably have the best of it, and in the eyes of nongardeners, their attitudes make sense. For such fair-weather gardeners, we have a sort of admiration, though it perhaps barely veils our contempt. To us, and put most simply, work is itself a joy. We do not know what we would do, otherwise.

In gardening, design is seldom a function of labor, but in vegetable gardening, it is. There is a lucidity about its design that makes a vegetable garden a very satisfying place to work and to be. Except for the odd patch of chervil, say, or dill, it is mostly a regular affair, of rows and squares and rectangles. We have seen vegetable gardens attempted with curving rows and swirls and other ingenious free-form patterns. We appreciate the whimsy of the people who made them and their fine, early spring Mad Hatter ingenuity. But those gardens simply never seem to work. Or be workable, for with almost any vegetable gardening chore you can name, there is something soothing about the rhythm of up one row and down the other. It is as indisputable a logic as the feet of cows, which always make paths over fields in a way that is at once most sensible and elegant.

So the paths in a vegetable garden—and there must be some, to get among the crops for cultivation, to fertilize and harvest and spray, and maybe simply to stroll about on a quiet summer evening—must be regular also, and in straight lines. Since we have a country garden attached to no grand house, we far prefer paths of common hay—spoiled and therefore cheap if we can find it—laid over very thick layers of newspaper, or the winter's accumulation of catalogs containing things we cannot afford and would not want if we could. Still, we welcome every one for path making, come early spring. Then they are laid on the earth, and hay conceals them. Since all paper and inks are now soy-based, nontoxic, and rich with nourishment for earthworms and other beneficial soil creatures, we consider each catalog a gift. Even in triplicate.

When all our gardening efforts must be curtailed, the last to go will be the vegetable garden. For it alone, among all the many parts of our garden, reflects that high ideal which motivated both Washington and Jefferson as garden-makers, the marriage of Use and Beauty. And when, from age or other causes, we must give it up, we will still be growing lettuce in a window box.

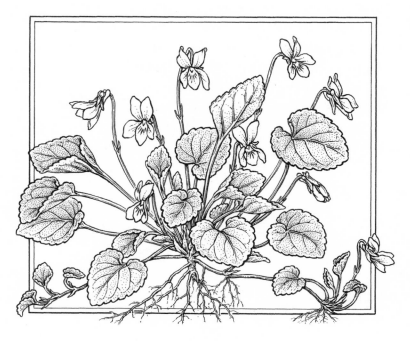

VIOLETS

WE KNOW we have bought violets from time to time, for we remember bringing them home from some nursery or another. Certainly we have also been given violets, since violets are prolific, and anyone who grows them has them to give away. But violets predate our own brief tenancy on our land by eons. Thirty years is nothing to that history, but when we first saw this land that long ago on a mild late-April day, April 30 to be specific, *Viola rotundifolia* was spreading new flowers on every wooded bank above the stream. They were of modest beauty, hardly half an inch across, though of a rich, buttercup yellow that glowed against their few, rounded, laurel-green leaves.

They have been faithful to the anniversary of our first acquaintance, blooming always by the last of April and seldom before, despite the global warming that has altered the calendars of so many of our favorite flowers. They prefer the drier woodland spots, often flourishing best around old maples that have thrust the soil upward with their soaring trunks. We have never chosen to transplant them, liking so much the places they choose to be, and the memory of our first encounter with them there.

Memory, however, accounts for many fewer violets than we seem to have in the garden, and where they all came from is often a puzzle. They are unassuming plants, usually choosing quiet, almost secret places to flourish. They make patches under the shade of deciduous shrubs, beneath the hedges, or even in the lawns. Any fertile spot that is far from weeding hands will suit them, and they seem particularly to favor the spiny thickets of antique and shrub roses, where they obviously feel safest. They have a curious way of reproducing, for the flowers one loves are usually (though not always) sterile. Underneath the sheltering leaves, and later in the year, the reproductive parts are produced, fat green pods that fertilize themselves. Botanists call this mechanism "cleistogamy," from the ancient Greek *cleisto*, meaning "closed or secret," and *gamy*, meaning "marriage." Once a violet is introduced into the garden, perfect clones will reappear, even though the original plant was lost or forgotten many years ago. So from April to early summer, our garden is full of violets, noticed then and forgotten at almost any other time. Often it is a chance encounter with long-lost friends.

One great exception, however, is *V. labradorica*, which we notice as much—more perhaps—for its fine summer foliage as for its May bloom. Though widely distributed through Greenland and the colder parts of eastern North America, our own plants were certainly nursery-bought, though we cannot remember where or when. Like so many plants that persist in any garden over many years, *V. labradorica* seems to have found its own habitat here, flourishing in the narrow cracks of a small planted terrace beside the glassed-in winter garden. There, it produces four-inch-tall tuffets of heart-shaped leaves, studded in late spring with half-inch-wide flowers of rich violet purple and buds of the same color. The remarkable thing about *V. labradorica*, however, is that the leaves are also a deep, purple-flushed green with purple undersides, and though the flowers are magnificent against that backdrop, the handsome leaves remain all season and well into winter, justifying the prominent spot the plant occupies. You need only one plant in such a habitat in order to have dozens, cramming into the narrowest crevices and even into crannies of old mortared walls. They may also happily settle around fine old potted specimens of bay or box or gardenia, where they are equally pretty, and a dreadful pest, stealing their food and smothering their roots. From there, at least, they must be eradicated summarily.

If *V. labradorica* is prominent for most of the year, *V. rosea* catches us always by surprise. It is a shy little thing, blooming in late April among the thick litter of last autumn's leaves caught around the bare shanks of the roses. The flowers are small, hardly the size of an English pea, and somehow shrunken or malformed, with a complexion of strong pink made washy by paler blotches. We'd hardly go looking for it, so we smell it in bloom before we see it. Every year we marvel that so small a thing can be so insistently fragrant, stronger on the air than our best old roses in their season. The original plant came to us from our near neighbor in the next state, the landscape designer Kris Fenderson. We've had it over twenty years, always close to but never where it was planted. Still, it always returns to remind us that though it has moved a few yards, it continues to be with us. We'd miss it sorely any year it did not beckon us to come closer.

But *V. rosea* is hardly the only violet that has an odd way of turning up. A curious case of this "now you see me, now you don't" quality that so many violets seem to possess is reflected in our experience with *V.* 'Sulfurea'. More than fifteen years ago, we had a compost pile in an area that seemed remote to us then but now is at the heart of the garden. The compost has long since been carted away, and the branches of the mature conifers and rhododendrons that now sweep across that space give us little reason to peer among them except to yank away the occasional seedling ash or maple. Three springs ago, in late April, we were desultorily doing that, using up a scrap of time before lunch, when one of us noticed a patch of dull green leaves about a foot wide, studded with small violets of a curious blend of cream, buff, and apricot, with improbably violet centers. They were very beautiful, those chance flowers, and we resolved to dig the plants up patiently, separate out the wisps of fescue and woodland aster entangled with them, and establish them under closer eye in a prominent part of the garden.

We meant to do that, but spring is full of similar good resolutions, and we didn't. The following year, we meant to do it too, for the violets were still there, still shining, still holding their own against the weeds. Maybe we'll do it next year. For we see that a quite beautiful selection of *V.* 'Sulfurea' is being offered by Canyon Creek Nursery under the cultivar name 'Irish Elegance'. It does not seem more elegant than ours, which must have been thrown out, years ago, in a flat of failed seed. Such is the way of violets. They always win out in the end.

We are sure that *V. sororia* and all the selections of it we have planted in the garden over the last thirty years will win out the strongest. We transplanted the first ones into the garden from a five-acre meadow far in the back of our property, where they flourished in sheets before we had cows to graze them and we had the time and patience to pick bouquets of hundreds of blooms. Both in the picking and in transplanting, we took both the violet and the white, really a washy gray, giving it the popular name Confederate violet, from the sadly worn uniforms of the Confederate soldiers in the Civil War. We still have a nice mix of both occurring vigorously along the Rose Alley, where they were first established in 1978. We distinguish among the colors only when they are in bloom, however, or when a nice mix of their delicious young leaves and flowers is needed for a spring salad. Otherwise, they are ruthlessly weeded in spring, for summer annuals, for perennials, and, in spring, for more daffodils, with which those that are left amiably conspire. More are sure to reappear.

"Shy" is no word to apply to our native *V. sororia*, which carries the Latin word for "sisterly," seemingly because it will grow into a gaggle of its kind, often smothering out any plant that cannot get the upper hand with it. Thwack it out as we must, come late spring, we cannot always leave some purple and some white to have each. But we do try to leave behind some choicer cultivars, especially 'Freckles'. It is aptly named, for each half-inch-wide flower is so copiously dotted over with violet spots on a white ground that the whole seems a pale, grayish mauve from above. (It is the particular delight of children, who are closer to seeing things than we are, and therefore discern its spots.)

'Freckles' has been widely circulated and can be gotten from many nurseries, or as a friendly gift from fellow gardeners who grow it. We remember perfectly where we got it ourselves. We were young gardeners at the time and depended heavily for our latest treasures on Johnny Laughton, an elderly retired postman who ran an extraordinary "open-field" nursery in West Brattleboro, Vermont. The nursery consisted of his little house and, behind, really an open field parceled out into perhaps a hundred narrow rectangular beds, each occupied by a single plant, and all divided by grassed paths a mower's width wide, so one sweep could keep them tidy. The idea was that you could—during business hours, though there was no fence to keep you out otherwise—stroll up and down the paths, buying what you liked, in flower or out. We mostly bought "in flower," and Johnny would pull out the plant, shake off every particle of earth, cut off the pretty flowers and leaves (you could take them home, for a vase, if you wanted to), and wrap the roots in damp newspaper. He had a thick bracelet of rubber bands on his right wrist for the purpose, and if you watched carefully (for he was shrewd), a bit of root and stem would always be left on the grass to restock the hole your purchase made. You "totaled up at the house," and everyone was satisfied.

Satisfied later, too, for though Johnny's methods were rough, they were those that any generous gardener practices when he gives plants. For plants taken vigorously alive from the open ground always do best, and if that were not so, old country gardens would be poor things, and we'd all have no heirloom plants. It is the old country way. And if you looked doubtfully at Johnny while he shook off the dirt from a clump of daylily or iris or astilbe, he would say bluntly, "I sell plants, not dirt." A surprising number of his plants have flourished here over a quarter of a century. He has been dead for most of that time, and his nursery is now a "multiple dwelling" with asphalt parking lots where the beds once were. But if

V. sororia 'Freckles' does not survive there (it well might, given the ways of violets), it does here and probably will for many years to come. Above all others, it is for that reason that violets are valuable and valued by the many gardeners who grow them.

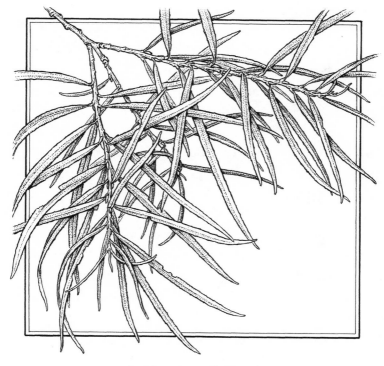

WILLOWS

AT FIRST, willows would not seem to be plants to get excited about, much less to collect. None has flowers that are showy, certainly not like a magnolia or a dogwood. They are not characterized by brilliant autumn foliage like a maple or stewartia. With the exception possibly of the weeping willows, few are as noble in stature as oaks or beeches or ashes. Generally they are short-lived, weak-wooded, and messy. Still, our garden is rich with willows, each of which possesses some modest charm that far outweighs any defect.

The genus *Salix* is a relatively large one, with more than four hundred species and as many as two hundred hybrids. (Of that latter number no one is really certain, for many hybrids occur unrecorded in the wild.) In growth, species can range from one hundred feet to alpines that rise barely two inches above the ground. There are willows grown for the charm of their flowers, which, though modest, appear at the first turn toward spring and are the earliest harbinger of its arrival. There are also willows with beautiful foliage, and willows with brilliant twig color, especially in the depths of winter, when any spark of color is precious. And of course there are weeping willows, a miracle of sturdy upright grace and down-hanging twigs, however banal their use might seem as obligatory plantings next to ponds.

Among the many willows we grow, it would be hard to select favorites, for all of them give us great pleasure in their season. But the ones with brilliantly colored twigs do that first, starting off the willow year in the dead of winter, so we should begin there. Several forms of the protean *Salix alba* grow along the steepest banks of our stream, a conscious imitation of the "willow ditch" in Margery Fish's famous English garden, East Lambrook Manor, about which we read years ago. Like hers, all of ours are pollarded, which is to say that they are cut back each spring within two inches of the previous year's growth so that they form dense heads above their brown-gray trunks. Pollarding is an ancient technique, familiar to Roman gardeners and still prominently practiced along the edges of fields and drainage ditches in northern Italy, France, and the Netherlands. Originally it was an agricultural practice, for the process produces long willow wands that could be woven into baskets and wicket fences, or split into wythies to bind things together. But it also resulted in great beauty, producing richly colored twigs from December until March, intensifying with the advancing year until spring, when they were harvested to produce another year's crop.

We always regret this harvest but treasure the bundles of supple twigs that will later be used to stake perennials and line the rows of bush peas in the vegetable garden. Among the most vividly colored selections of *S. alba* we grow, *S. a.* var. *vitellina* is a brilliant, varnished yellow and called "the egg-yolk willow" for that reason. *Salix a.* 'Chermesina' is yellow with a fine orange overlay, and *S. a.* 'Britzensis' is a rich, cinnabar red. Just when the witch hazels bloom, on the edge of winter and the cusp of spring, these willows are at their most beautiful. We'd regret cutting them except that it is precisely that time of year when the willows valued for flower begin to appear.

The first to bloom here is always *S. alba* var. *caerulea*, the cricket bat willow, a twelve-foot-high shrub that grows at the edge of the bog below the rock garden. After many years, it has produced trunks thick enough to suggest that it could possibly be fashioned into plausible cricket bats, though we would still be sorry for the player who had to resort to ours. Its value here is that its tiny, silvery blue-gray buds begin opening on any mild day in January and remain attractive for almost four months until April gives us other flowers to cut for indoors.

We have a special fondness for *S. chaenomeloides*, which is perhaps the largest-flowered willow we grow, or at least the largest-budded, for it is the unopened furry flower catkins that are valued. Even before they appear, each is covered with a prominent pink-purple bud scale, varnished rather like something that might be done to nails in a fancy salon. They split apart in February, to reveal catkins more than half an inch long, of a beautiful silvery white. If we were marketing this willow in an exclusive mail-order catalog, we would christen it *S. chaenomeloides* 'White Kittens', for that is the effect it suggests. It is a large shrub, ten feet across and as tall, which means that it offers plenty of cuttings for vases indoors, from February into early April.

Of the willows we grow for flower, however, the most dramatic is not silver, or mouse gray, or white, but black. *Salix gracilistyla* 'Melanostachys' is in fact the blackest flower we know. Most black flowers are really deep purple, including the famous black hollyhock and the brilliantly named Louisiana iris, 'Black Gamecock'. Why one should even want a black flower is a bit of a mystery, but if one does, then this willow is as close as you get. Close, at least, in the beginning of its flowering, which starts in late February when its catkins first emerge and a spangle of black is vivid against lime-green twigs. When warm weather finally arrives toward the beginning of April, each catkin becomes gilded over with gold, beautiful also in its way. Like many willows grown for flower, the black pussy willow is not a particularly graceful plant. Ours is about eight feet tall and very stiff of habit. Still, it is one of the treasures of our garden, hard to pass by without staring when it is in flower, and beautiful in a vase, particularly when combined with the tawny-brown witch hazels that bloom about the same time.

The last of our willows to flower is a weeping form of the common goat willow, *S. caprea* 'Pendula'. A whole swarm of these appear to be in commerce, usually marketed as the Kilmarnock willow from the place in Scotland where it was first found. It is a male willow, with gray catkins that quickly produce pollen-laden golden anthers in spring. For some reason, it is usually grafted on other willow stock at a height of about five feet. All of this group would creep upon the ground as abject shrubs, but if a central leader is chosen and staked upward, grafting is unnecessary, and a fountain of growth can be achieved just by training the plant. That is the way we have treated the female counterpart of the Kilmarnock willow, nicely named 'Weeping Sally', which is now a cascade of thick, congested growth that bears silver catkins each April. Like all wil-

lows it is easy to root. So we have also used it as a free-form espalier against a section of our stockyard fence and even as a
sort of vine on one of the supports of our pergola. Its pendulous
habit of growth makes it interesting anywhere and lends it to
many uses.

One does not think of willows being grown for their
leaves, but several produce very beautiful foliage that is unlike
any other shrub or tree one can grow in northern gardens. The
finest of them all is *S. alba* var. *sericea* (sometimes *argentea*), the
silver willow that grows as a rangy, messy tree to as much as
forty feet in swamps and wetlands from Zones 4 to 8. But if it
is brought into the garden, and pollarded as a multibranched
specimen at about ten feet, it is distinguished at all seasons.
Treated this way, it never develops a large trunk. Our oldest
tree, given us by Marshall Olbrich at Western Hills Nursery
over twenty years ago, has a trunk circumference of only twenty-
three inches, but it branches at shoulder level into a craggy
candelabra of thick limbs, each of which terminates in a fist of
dense, twiggy growth. In early summer, its fine, silver leaves
offer beautiful contrast to the soft pink and white antique roses
that grow beneath it, and in winter, after the previous year's
growth has been cut to within two inches of its thick, knobby
knuckles, it offers a picturesque effect common enough along
the streets of Mediterranean cities, but rare in New England
gardens. In fact, visitors to the garden mistake it for an olive tree,
for the resemblance to the "olives of endless age" in Greece and
Crete is strong. We have thought often of creating a mock
olive grove in Vermont, and if we had the land to do it, we
would. Nothing would be easier, as pencil-thick stems always
root when they are stuck into moist ground in early spring.

One other willow is treasured here for its leaves and also
because it is fancifully assumed to look like something else. It
is the rosemary willow, *S. elaeagnos*, which could as well have

been called the "lamb willow," from its Latin name and the gentle effect it has on the landscape. We have only one tree of it, given us as a cutting by Linc Foster shortly before both his death and the death of his beautiful garden, Millstream, in Falls Village, Connecticut. Ours grows in swampy ground just at the base of the rhododendron garden. It has produced a thick-trunked, slender-branched shrub to about eight feet, though it leans over the terrace there, and seems inclined to lean more, to the extent that this year we have had a Japanese tree brace fashioned, a crutch to prop it up in its old age. Willows do age quickly. We hope that someone will give us similar attention, when it is time.

We have never counted the species and varieties in our collection of willows. There are alpines in the rock garden, none of which tops two feet. Our favorite is certainly *S. lindleyana*, which has no common name, but which we would call the "thyme willow" if we had the power to coin common names. It is a creeping thing—we guess not more than an inch in height—though it has coated the top of the large boulder over which it grows with many stems, mahogany red when they are bare, but covered with brick-red catkins in spring and glossy half-inch leaves in summer.

We do not know whether our plant of *S. lindleyana* is a male or a female, though we do know that the difference is determined by the precise color of the catkins, which are reddish in the male, and more silvery in the female. In willows—as in kittens—it might somehow be important to get that straight. But generally, and with any willow, there are no disappointments. All of them quickly become dear to you, whatever their sexual identity.

WISTERIA

LIKE SO MANY THINGS in our garden, our oldest wisteria was an accident. About fifteen years ago, we were planting a garden for a new client in the Soho section of New York. It was a beautiful, quiet neighborhood then, not the circus of thronged tourists mad to purchase anything and the gaggle of shops that cater gleefully to that desire. Our client had renovated the upper two floors of a five-story building, previously some sort of small factory, and the top floor had a glorious, sun-drenched terrace. Across about half of it, a pergola had been built to provide some shady sitting space, and on that pergola we were asked to plant vines. A four-foot-deep planter ran the length of the terrace on three sides, the building wall enclosing the fourth, through which French doors gave entrance from the master bedroom. We thought the root containment the container provided would be perfect to get the most bloom out of a wisteria, which we could see—in our minds' eyes—glorious in new spring sunshine, dripping with fragrant flower. A wisteria would also provide the desired shade quickly, maybe in as little as a single season, and so that is what we proposed. White, we thought, would also be more sophisticated than the usual purple or lavender.

Our suggestion was accepted, and we located a *Wisteria floribunda* 'Alba' that had already spent some years in a nursery pot, giving it an interesting gnarled and muscular structure that we thought beautiful. Much more important, it had *already* begun flowering in the nursery. In fact, it was blooming when we bought it. But our new client (she never had the chance to become simply "our client") changed her mind suddenly and wanted climbing roses instead. We thought climbing roses might be difficult in that situation, with the frequent sprays against black spot and aphids and other diseases dripping all over her pretty, chintz-cushioned white wicker furniture. We also pointed out that she had *bought* the wisteria—or at least we had with her deposit money—and we didn't think the nursery would take it back, it now being after Mother's Day and all. Still, she was adamant in her demand for roses.

"And the wisteria?"

"Oh, throw it away! Put it on the street. Someone will take it. I think it is ugly anyway."

This helped us accept the idea of planting roses, which we did. And we brought the wisteria home to Vermont. It was essentially free for the hauling, and besides, we reasoned, it had been insulted and needed someone to love it.

Fifteen years ago, we knew a great deal less about the climate in which our garden is located than we do now. We certainly also now believe that the world has gotten warmer in just about that space of years, from causes almost too painful to consider. But at the time, we believed the books and climate maps, which assured us we were in Zone 4. So did our more experienced friends who gardened in warmer places and who seemed to need to say, "You won't be able to grow *anything* but Christmas trees and some moss!" We couldn't yet shut them up by mentioning meconopsis, the fabled Himalayan blue poppies that we grow to perfection. Those were still in our future, as were a host of other "tender" things rated to Zone 5, 6, or even 7 that now grow here. We had read that *W. floribunda*, though perhaps slightly hardier than its Chinese relative, *W. sinensis*, still tolerated winter cold only to a warm Zone 5. We knew we had occasional bouts of minus 30 degrees because we had already endured a few. So perhaps when we brought it home we did not do such a kindness to this wisteria, after all.

At that time, we were avid readers of the White Flower Farm catalog, which came then only once a year, around Christmas, and seemed to us the positive cutting edge of horticultural sophistication. It was touting its standard wisterias then (at a price), and it may be still. They were all straight of trunk and mop-headed, but with tops naked of leaves, positive fountains of spring flower. They were even recommended . . . for pots. Of course, ours, the one we bagged, was not straight of trunk, but leaned a bit to the side. But we liked its giant bonsai look, for though it stood about six feet tall, it still conveyed the sense of age and experience and hard-won grace the best bonsai possess. We even knew at the time that wisteria was a choice subject for dwarfing in Japan, for we had pored over those books too and had learned that though the structure of trees could fully develop as miniatures, the flowers and fruit would be of normal size. We saw pictures of eighteen-inch wisterias on polished wooden pedestals with flowers almost as long. So there were other and even more interesting possibilities than planting our wisteria next to a sugar maple or beech and hoping for the best.

Early that autumn, we splurged on a clay pot, actually a heavy-walled square tank about sixteen inches across and as high. It cost a mint and weighed a ton, and the end of that autumn began one of our many close-down rituals in preparation for winter. We have no memory whatsoever of where both pot and plant—or tree, for that is what it is—were stored in the beginning. After the lower greenhouse was built, the wisteria could be lifted onto a dolly, rolled through the garden to the drive, loaded on the pickup, and driven down to spend a winter in the "shop," then little more than a glorified attic on ground level, cement-floored and full of garden clutter. But even at the 45 degrees maintained there, it would bloom sometime in early March, encouraged by the increasing warmth of early spring days and even, perhaps, by its own internal clock. For spring is the time wisterias are supposed to bloom, and it stubbornly adhered to that belief, even when we left the doors open a bit on cold days for a proper chill.

We've done better by it, since. For once it rooted in its pot, we found that it could be grasped firmly by its trunk and lifted out, and pot and tree could be moved separately into a corner of the winter garden, now left specially blank for it. As they both weigh about the same—which we calculate to be about eighty pounds—that cuts the total weight pretty much by half, and we can still manage that. The tree now drips its glorious flowers before our eyes in March, just across from the open double kitchen windows above the sink. At that time, washing up after lunch is a privilege to be fought for.

Luxuriant leaves quickly follow, dark green, pinnate, made up of twelve to fifteen oval leaflets and arching out palm-fashion into a dense head that covers the twigs, leaving only the gray trunk exposed. We let it do what it pleases, shortening only the wayward, questing shoots of vine, until the weather settles and it is time to move it out for the summer. We keep it in luxuriant growth by timed applications of water-soluble fertilizer and almost daily watering, for there is now a great deal of tree for relatively little pot. Pruning can be a little more severe in summer, cutting back to a bud or two above last year's flowering growth.

When our wisteria stands in pride on the back terrace all summer long, we think it almost as beautiful as when it blooms in March. The trunk has curved more through the years and thickened to measure about three inches in diameter. Our four cats seem to find it the tree of preference as a scratching post, and though we discourage that, it always happens when our backs are turned. They seem to do it no harm, only striating the handsome gray trunk a little more.

It is well known that wisteria flower most freely under abuse, and the literature recommends violent root pruning and frequent hacking back of top growth to encourage abundant flower. We have no choice in the root-pruning part, for every three years or so we must lift the plant out of its pot and sever about an inch of root all around the sides and two on the bottom, to be replaced with fresh Pro-mix. We find the best way is the Japanese way, picking and scraping at the root mass with a chopstick until white hairs hang all about, and then clipping them neatly with sharp scissors. So far, we have not found a recommendation that encourages the family cat to sharpen her claws.

But everything we have done, most of it either from necessity or by accident, seems to have worked, resulting in what we have come to consider one of the great treasures of our garden. Our wisteria tree is now a longtime occupant here, just as surely as the cats or dogs or geese, with its own needs and its own diurnal requirements.

We cannot say how the roses have flourished in Soho or whether the furniture survived their requirements. Probably both have been replaced a dozen times or more by now. We do not know, for we were terminated just after the roses were planted and the offending wisteria rejected to its own fate. Sometimes, in gardening, the luckiest things happen.

XANTHORRHOEA
QUADRANGULATA

When we taught school years ago, a colleague gave us a large box of old gardening magazines he had found while cleaning out his grandmother's attic. They dated from the 1930s and '40s, and were different from contemporary gardening magazines in almost every way. They were small in format, with few ads and fewer illustrations, all of which were of course in black and white. Their tone was spontaneous, informal, and direct, making them seem more like good garden conversation than publications. A regular feature was a contest in which readers were encouraged to send answers to a gardening question. The question we remember most vividly was

"What is your oldest potted plant?"As relatively young gardeners, we were stunned by many of the answers. One gardener still possessed her great-grandmother's potted camellia, which several Januaries back had survived the collapse of her sunporch roof and had achieved its hundredth year. Another said she had nurtured the same cyclamen for forty years, though she had had to cut off a shoulder of its corm to fit the pot. Plenty of people seemed to have inherited octogenarian Christmas cactus, proving our already-formed conviction that they could live in boring parlors for a very long time, and of course there was the inevitable jade plant with a trunk grown to a remarkable girth. But now, many years later, the very odd thing about having been gardeners for so long ourselves is that we would have our own ready answer to that question.

Most gardeners have pet potted plants, things they have tended for many years because of Grandmother or an impulsive purchase in the supermarket or sometimes just because some plant has hung around for so long. In our case, a chance visit to the Los Angeles County Arboretum saddled us—*endowed* us, we should say—with a great potted ox of a plant that we now consider one of the finest things we grow. It is *Xanthorrhoea quadrangulata*, bought as a wispy seedling of three or four slender, grass-like leaves twenty-seven years ago. Since we knew nothing about the plant at the time, we can't imagine why we picked it out from the meager offerings for sale. Certainly we had no idea about its great potential beauty, its ultimate importance to our gardening life, or its very great rarity.

Xanthorrhoea quadrangulata is native to the southern parts of Australia, and though largely unknown by western gardeners and scarce even in the collections of arboreta in Zones 9 to 10, where it is hardy, it still has a very long history in its relationship with humanity, for to the Aborigine peoples of Australia, who knew it longest and best, it was of great economic value. The thick, resinous yellow gum that gathered around the stout trunks of very old specimens could be collected, melted, and formed into balls for later use as a strong adhesive to fix arrows to shafts, or sharp pebbles to spears. Two of its chaffy dried flower stems (impressive things that can reach six feet in height) could be rubbed together to make fire. Its sharp seed cases could be used as knives or as tools to dig into decaying wood for nourishing grubs and insects. Further, it was miraculous, since it survived grass fires to sprout anew. Its gaunt, child-high stems standing on fire-blackened plains caused the Aborigines to give it the name black boy. That popular name has clung, particularly in England, though most people now prefer grass palm, which offers another sort of description.

As with so many useful plants, utility has meant potential extinction. You will not find many plants listed under "X" in popular plant dictionaries, and you will not usually find Xanthorrhoea. That is because the Australian government has listed the plant as a rare and endangered species under the provisions of CITES (Convention on International Trade in Endangered Species), thereby preventing the export of plants and even, with Xanthorrhoea, the harvesting of seed. In any case, seed is fairly rare, occurring on plants that are generally twenty years old or older, though for a plant that can easily live six hundred years that is mere infancy.

We were luckier than we knew, then, to scoop up that wisp of a seedling from our chance visit to the arboretum. A plant had flowered there the year before and set seed, though only three were viable. We curse ourselves for not having bought them all, but then we must stop to wonder what we might have done with *three* plants five feet tall and as wide, each in a clay pot almost the size of a bushel basket. From that perspective, one plant is certainly plenty, especially when each spring it must be muscled out of the small greenhouse off our kitchen to its summer quarters outdoors, and then each autumn muscled back in to spend the winter, during which, perversely, it grows. It seems never to have realized that the wan light of a snowy Vermont winter isn't quite the same as an Australian spring. We suppose if we ever turned off the heat, which keeps the greenhouse at a winter temperature of around 55 degrees, it might find out soon enough.

As that greenhouse is only twelve feet wide, with a fieldstone path down the middle and large camellias planted on each side, our Xanthorrhoea is a bit crowded. Or rather we are, for it seems to expand happily from year to year. If it were a brittle plant we would have a problem, but its four-foot-long grassy leaves—of which there must be a thousand radiating out from the central trunk—are as flexible as threads of metal, and in fact it is great fun to brush your hand over the whole symmetrical mass, which then trembles and quivers like a metallic toy from the 1950s. Only once did any outside activity damage the plant, and that was when two canaries flying loose in the greenhouse discovered the charm of snapping off its leaves for pure mischief. The canaries went. The Xanthorrhoea has stayed.

Like most gardeners we are generous with plants, knowing that if you give something away and then lose it, you can possibly get it back. Praise something in our garden and if we have enough of it, a start of it is yours. But though our Xanthorrhoea is much admired by visitors to the garden, it is painful to say that plants are very scarce and that ours is not likely to produce any progeny we can share. There are nurseries that specialize in Australian plants, and they occasionally promise *X. quadrangulata*. But they don't seem to come through with seeds or young plants. So we cannot offer any hope to those who want a plant like ours, and that is discouraging to us.

Though not always. For whenever Dan Hinkley, founder of Heronswood and a great plant explorer, stands before our pet and says, "I wish I had that," though we love him dearly, we confess that it gives us some sort of pleasure to say, "Well, Dan, you probably never will . . ." None of us is perfect, after all. And perhaps we might exercise a posthumous generosity and leave it to him in one of our wills.

THE FUTURE

Sooner or later, anyone who cultivates a garden will become concerned for its future. That much is a certainty, though we are unsure of the amount of time required to cause this concern, this tug at the heart. Probably one glorious month at the shore would be enough, where the opening of each scarlet geranium flower is closely observed. Or it could be years—in our case, thirty years—though when half that time had passed, we knew that we had come to love this land, and further, that we had made changes on it that would last for any foreseeable future. We had become "attached to it," and that familiar expression had all the force of its original meaning, of which we would need no thesaurus for synonyms: Glued? Welded? Grafted? Bonded? Stuck? What we knew then, and know with greater force as each year passes, is that we will never live anywhere else but here. Even the lure of a second home—were we that rich—could not tempt us to divide our time. For if we were somewhere else, how could we walk through the garden here to observe even the smallest changes, the first improbable blooms of *Crocus sativus* in October, the adonis and aconites burning yellow through a crust of snow in April, the soft fall of the snow itself, all winter long?

"Foreseeable future" is a comfortable phrase, though any reflective person knows that it is as hollow as a worm-eaten acorn. We move through our days with the comfort of familiarity, waking at the same time each morning and almost always the same way, padding down to punch the button on the coffee pot, to greet the cats and let them test the quality of the day at the open door, to call in the dogs who have spent a hard night of vigilant barking and are ready for a good breakfast and a daylong nap. We assess our day's chores, writing and correspondence and business things, all housework, all prefatory to going out into the garden, which on almost any calendar day requires something from us. Roses might need to be laid down and covered first with Remay and then with boughs, or uncovered and tied in, the Remay folded neatly and the boughs taken to the burn pile. The perennial garden might need composting, a task that should have been done in October, but usually waits until April. Perennials should be divided just when they first show green, and we always have need of more hostas. Rows have to be thrown up in the vegetable garden to receive the drying benefits of hot spring sun, and then the first crops have to be put in, peas and broad beans, which need the longest, coolest spring we can give them, lettuces and other salad greens, which do not, but which are nicest eaten early. Daffodils must be divided and replanted when the last flowers have withered, and by then, here, it is early summer, and a steady rhythm of summer chores begins, of harvesting and staking, deadheading, succession sowing, summer pruning, and the endless watering of pots stood all about the garden, glorious with the choicest annuals and tender plants, and with the sculptural forms of agaves and standard box and bay.

If the management of any garden does not fall into a rhythm of comfortable routines, there will not be a garden at all but only an embarrassment and a reproach. We treasure the routines of our garden, all based on its seasonal demands, to which we pay close attention, not only to assure its health and beauty but to give pattern to our days. It may be that any deep love one has—for a friend, a child, a dog, even a simple canary in a cage—is treasured essentially because it does that. We have come to feel that an ordered movement through days and months and years is essential to happiness, or to our happiness at least, for we do not pontificate. Of all the many joyful obligations of our existence, the garden here has been the most sustaining just in part because it is the most rhythmic, through winter, spring, summer, and fall. It actually has taught us to love every day of our life. One cannot ask more of love for a garden than that.

But of course one might. One could ask that it all go on forever, that it last, as the Countess in Strauss's sublime opera *Capriccio* sings, "*funfmalhunderttausend Jahre.*" There are some fine June mornings when one might wish for this, when all the roses are blooming and the year is new, and the garden's future holds infinite possibility. Such an impulse is usually the product of the moment—only a fool would ask that of any garden. The vagaries of each season are an essential part of the gardener's experience, and the failure and decline of many a lusty specimen or fragile perennial that had done so well, and perhaps for years, teaches much. Gardens by their very nature are fragile beings that live in the two dimensions of time and care. For their very survival they are dependent on weather, on soil conditions, on predators that come silently in the night, on the neglect or inattention of their owners, and even on the very transitoriness of the lives of their owners, for none of us lives forever or particularly wants to. And there, precisely, is the question posed by any intensely experienced life in a garden, however long or short it might have been: What is to happen next? Oh, not next spring or next autumn, for so far as we know, we are able to plan for that. But eventually. In the long run.

There is a scheme in America that attempts to preserve gardens "forever," largely those gardens built by wealthy people or with some special historical significance. The Garden Conservancy is modeled on the British National Trust, which has preserved a large number of gardens in the British Isles, to the advantage and pleasure of gardeners throughout the world. But ours is a simple house, which we built largely to tuck into the garden that surrounds it. The garden is best described as a domestic garden, maybe perhaps even a cottage garden, though that designation has been freighted with meanings of casualness we would not recognize here. Still, we can leave no endowment behind. And we cannot imagine the parking. So, perhaps, the garden dies with us.

We are not without precedent, for we know that the great garden designer Beatrix Farrand stood on her porch and watched her garden being bulldozed into the ground before her death. And Linc Foster, our good friend, whose beautiful garden, Millstream, had become a destination for rock and alpine gardeners throughout the world, wrote to us when he was near death, "The garden was young when I was young, and old when I am old, and it will die when I die." Actually, we do not find that thought uncomfortable in the least.

When we were both in our twenties, on a lovely spring morning we decided to fly a kite. We bought a kit, with balsam ribs and tissue paper and string, and we spent the whole morning assembling it. It was a very fine kite, crimson red and deep blue, and we put it together pretty well, given the fact that we had no particular expertise in construction of anything except chicken cages, at which we had done what we thought was a good job. The Public Garden across from which we lived had no free space for running up a kite, so we crossed Charles Street, and launched our kite by running up the hill of Boston Common. It went up splendidly, and soon it became a speck in the sky. But the allowance of string in the kit was meager, and so one of us ran back down Charles Street to buy another spool. When we tried to tie one end to another, the wind was strong and the kite slipped free. We watched as long as it was visible, and when we could no longer see it, we went home.

This event occurred at the very beginning of our gardening life and our life together. It seems to be a paradigm of our experience here. And we ask anyone who should visit in years to come to remember that gardens always depend on the constant care and the vigilance of their creators. After that, they are shadows. Or a speck in the sky, as our kite became.

Index

Abeliophyllum distichum, 96, 99
Aborigines, 304–305
achimenes, 262
acidanthera, 257–58
Aconitum, 309; *A. episcopale*, 179
addiction, of gardeners, 70
adonis, 309
Agapanthus, 9–13, 104; *A. africanus*, 10;
    Headbourne hybrids of, 12–13; over-
    wintering of, 12–13
agaves, 36, 52, 310
airport security, gardeners and, 102–103
Alcea: *A. ficifolia*, 54; *A. pallida*, 54; *A.*
    rosea, 52–53, 54, 57
alder-leaved mountain ash, 246–49
Allegheny spurge, 158
Allen C. Haskell & Son, 39
Allium porrum, 236
amarcrinum, 263–64
Amaryllidaceae, 166
Amaryllis belladonna, 263–64
American Horticultural Society A–Z
    Encyclopedia of Garden Plants, 266
American Magnolia Society, 153
American Primrose Society, 195, 200
American Rock Garden Society, 106, 235
A. M. Leonard, 101, 171
Andlau, Comtesse d', 164–65, 166, 167
annuals, 14–21, 80; biennials bred as, 52;
    definitions of, 15; flowering period of,
    53–54
apple trees, 96
apricot, Japanese, 208–11
arborvitae, 22–27, 113, 122
armerias, 225
Arnold Arboretum, 204, 247, 252

artichokes, 16, 28–33, 281; as ornamental,
    32–33; sauces for, 31; wine and, 31
artificiality, in gardens, 34–35, 37
Arundinaria viridistriata, 217–18
ash trees, 111, 248, 253, 291
Asklepios, 107
asparagus, 170
Asteraceae, 31–32
asters, 170
aubrietas, 225
"August slump," 17
Australia, Aborigines of, 304–305
autumn, 71–72, 111
azaleas, 4, 69, 268–69; Satsuki, 268–69

Babylonians, 189, 190
bamboos, 52, 216–18; overwintering of,
    114, 116; poles as pea supports, 171–72
banana trees, 34–37; diffusion of, 190;
    overwintering of, 35
barba di frate, 279
Barbarea vulgaris, 52–53
barberry, 46–50; medicinal uses of, 48;
    poor reputation of, 47
bark mulch, 162
battening, of hedges, 122
"Bavarian Gentians" (Lawrence),
    105–106, 109
bay leaves, fresh, 42, 45
bay trees, 38–45, 69, 191, 310; ideal shape
    of, 40–41; overwintering of, 42, 43–44;
    pots for, 41; pruning of, 42–43
Beacon Street, authors' apartment on, 3–5
beans, 16, 309
beeches, 111, 121, 248, 253, 272, 291
begonias, tuberous, 262

Begonia sutherlandii, 14, 15, 21
Berberis: *B. julianae*, 49; *B.* ×*stenophylla*,
   49; *B. thunbergii*, 49; *B. vulgaris*,
   46–50; *B. wilsoniae*, 49
biennials, 51–58, 80; definition of, 51–52;
   flowering period of, 54; planning and,
   53–54; transplanting, 57–58
birches, 248, 253
bitter melon, 7
Blake, William, 229
bloodroot, 182
Bluebeard, 17
blueberries, 170; highbush, 98–99, 121
bog, at North Hill, 107–108, 114, 154,
   221, 293
bonsai, 42, 70, 210
borders, 17, 18, 32, 55
Borghese marbles, 177
Bourbon, Isle de (Réunion Island), 231
Bowden-Cornish, Athelstan, 166
Bowles, E. A., 74
boxwoods, 23, 44, 59–63, 69, 136, 151,
   228, 310; cuttings of, 60; English,
   59–63, 116; as hedges, 122; hybrids of,
   61–62; Korean, 61, 63; overwintering
   of, 60–61, 116
branches, forcing of, 94–99
British National Trust, 311
Brooklyn Botanic Garden, 155
Brussels sprouts, 279
bulbs, in mature gardens, 275
bulbs, summer-blooming, 255–64
bunchberry, 160
Burdick, Dave, 93
Burnet, Stub, 89
butterbur, Japanese, 218–19
butterflies, 19
Buxus, 23, 44, 69, 136, 151, 228, 310; *B.*
   ×'Glencoe', 62; *B. microphylla* var.
   koreana (*B. sinica* var. *insularis*), 61, 63;
   B. sempervirens, 59–63, 116

cactus, Christmas, 304
caladiums, 262–63
California poppies, 183–84
calla lilies, 263
Caltha palustris, 197
Camellia, 64–70, 104, 209, 304; *C.*

japonica, 65; *C. sasanqua*, 44, 67;
   C. sinensis var. *sinensis*, 67, 70; Higo, 67,
   270; medicinal and cosmetic uses of,
   65; overwintering, 66–70, 95,
   136
Campanula: *C. medium*, 52; *C.*
   poscharskyana, 224–25
canaries, 306
cannas, 259, 263
Canterbury bells, 52
Capriccio (Strauss), 310
Carduus, 32
carrots, 279, 280
Catherine's wheels, 17
cattleya orchids, 4
ceanothus, 67
cedar waxwings, 134
celeriac, 281
celery, 279, 281
Chaenoemeles, 206
Charlemagne, 235–36
Charles IX, King of France, 147
Chatto, Andrew, x
Chatto, Beth, x, 47
cherries, 96; Cornelian, 204–205; 'Hally
   Jolivette', 202–207; Higan, 204;
   Yoshino, 204
Chevre de Venus, 17
Chicago Botanic Garden, 62
chickens, 4–6, 7, 39
Chinese lantern lilies, 263
chinodoxas, 138
Chino's, 279
Christina, Queen of Sweden, 177
Christmas cactus, 304
Christmas holly, 114, 135–36
Christmas rose, 126–27, 128
CITES (Convention on International
   Trade in Endangered Species), 305
Clarke, Eleanor, 24
clary sage, 52
cleistogamy, 285
clematis, 179
Clematis terniflora, 26
Cleopatra, 10
cliff green, 160–61
cogeners, 158
Colchicum, 71–75, 109, 170, 275;

C. agrippinum, 72–73; *C. autumnale*, 74, 75; *C. baytopiorum*, 75; *C. byzantinum*, 73; *C. hungaricum*, 75; *C. luteum*, 75; *C. speciosum*, 73–74; double forms of, 74–75

Colchis, 72

Coliseum, 225

collectors, gardeners as, 69, 70, 85, 87, 147, 153, 227–28, 237

Colocasia esculenta, 263

columbines, 224

conifers, 228; as privacy screens, 203–204; as wind-breaks, 113

Connecticut River, 216

conservatories, 10, 44

container gardening, 189–93

Cooking from the Garden (Creasy), 32

corn, 170

Cornelian cherry, 121

Cornus, 7, 151, 291; *C. canadensis*, 160; *C. florida*, 160; *C. mas*, 204–205

Corot, Camille, 182

Corydalis, 76–81, 225; *C. cava*, 79; *C. dyphilla*, 79; *C. flexuosa*, 79–80; *C. lutea*, 77–78, 80, 224; *C. ochroleuca*, 78; *C. sempervirens*, 80–81; *C. solida*, 79, 81; *C. turtschaninovii*, 80; hardiness of, 81; transplanting, 77–78

cottage floweres, 52–53

Country Garden, The (Nuese), 252

courage, 254

crab apples, 204

Creasy, Rosalind, 32

Crinum moorei, 263–64

crocosmia, 258–59

Crocus, 4, 11, 138, 170; *C. sativus*, 71, 109, 309; *C. speciosus*, 71, 109; *C. tommasinianus*, 139, 276

crows, 174

Cruso, Thalassa, 119, 252

cucumber, 170

Culp, David, 125–26

Cuphea lanceolata, 49

currants, 170

cuttings: of arborvitae, 22–23, 25, 26–27; of boxwoods, 60

Cuttings from a Rock Garden (Foster and Foster), x

Cyclamen, 82–87, 109, 304; *C. africanum*, 84, 86–87; *C. balearicum*, 87; *C. coum*, 84, 87; *C. creticum*, 87; *C. cyprium*, 87; *C. hederifolium*, 82, 85–86, 87, 213; *C. libanoticum*, 87; *C. persicum*, 84–85, 95; *C. rohlfsianum*, 84, 87; hardiness of, 86

Cynara: *C. cardunculus*, 32; *C. scolymus*, 28–33

Cypripedium, 219; *C. kentuckiense*, 180, 275; *C. reginae*, 180

daffodils, 7, 71, 90–93, 170, 242, 310

Dahlia, 259–60, 263; 'Bishop of Llandaff', 260

Dame aux Camellias, La (Dumas), 68

dame's rocket, 52–53, 54–55, 57–58

Daphne, 69, 225; *D. bholua*, 67

Darmera peltata, 108

deadly nightshade, 7

deer, 26

Deerfield River, 216

Dendromecon rigida, 183

Descanso Gardens, 68

devil-in-the-bush, 17

Dianthus, 225; *D. barbatus*, 52–53

Digitalis purpurea, 52–53, 55–57

dioecious plants, 219

division, of agapanthus, 11

dogwoods, 7, 151, 291

drabas, 225

Drucker, Marge, 269

Dumas, Alexandre, fils, 68

East Lambrook Manor, 292

eggplants, 281

Egypt, ancient, gardening in, 44, 189

Egyptian onions, 170

Elizabeth, Queen of France, 147

Elizabethan gardens, 17

English gardens, 56

English Rock Garden, The, 107

epimediums, 162, 228

Eryngium giganteum, 185

Eschscholzia californica, 183–84

espaliers, 7

Eucomis, 263

Everett, T. H., 237, 265

evergreens: boughs of, as protection for sensitive plants, 115–16, 233, 309; as hedges, 121, 122, 203–204; offshoots of, 25

Fargesia, 216
farmers markets, 280
farm stands, 279–81
Farrand, Beatrix, 311
Farrar, Reginald, 107
Fenderson, Kris, 187, 286
ferns, 76, 113, 225
fertilizing, of hedges, 122, 123
festivals, 169, 170; gardens as, 232–33
ficus, 3, 43, 44, 164
Fish, Margery, x, 125, 128–29, 130, 131, 292
Fishelson, Mrs., 4
Flanders fields, 186
"florists," 198–99
flowering shrubs and trees, forcing of, 94–99
forcing, of branches, 94–99
forget-me-nots, 52–53, 55, 57, 104
Forsythia, 99; *F.* ×*intermedia* 'Karl Sax', 204; *F. suspensa*, 96, 272; *F. viridissima*, 96
Foster, Laura Louise "Timmy," x
Foster, Linc, x, 198, 296, 311–12
foxgloves, 52–53, 55–57
Fritillaria meleagris, 73
Frost, Robert, 173
Fuchs, Leonard, 65
fuchsias, 65, 102
fuki, 218–19
fumitory, 76–81
future, of North Hill, 308–12

galanthophiles, 241
Galanthus, 126, 138, 139, 170, 228, 240–45; *G. koenenianus*, 241; *G. nivalis*, 242, 243; *G. nivalis* 'Blewbury Tart', 244; *G. nivalis* 'Flore Pleno', 243; *G. nivalis* 'Sandersii', 244; *G. nivalis* 'Virescens', 244; *G. nivalis* 'Viridapice', 243–44; *G. reginae-olgae*, 242; *G. reginae-olgae* subsp. *vernalis*, 242; *G.* 'S. Arnott', 245; *G.* 'William Thomson', 241
Galax, Va., 159

Galax urceolata, 159
Galtonia candicans, 260–61
Garbo, Greta, 177
Garden Conservancy, 50, 311
Gardening in the Shade (Fish), 125
gardening magazines, 303–304
garlic, 170
Gentiana, 104–109; *G. acaulis*, 106, 107; *G. andrewsii*, 108; *G. asclepiadea*, 107, 108; *G. decumbens*, 106–107; *G. scabra*, 109; *G. septemfida*, 108–109
Gentle Plea for Chaos, A (Osler), x
George, Marjorie, 5
Geranium, 17, 228; *G. robertianum*, 228
giant pandas, 217
Gladiolus, 256–57, 263; *G. callianthus* 'Murielae', 258; *G.* ×*hortulanus*, 257; *G. nanus*, 257
glasshouses, 10
Glaucidium palmatum, 180
global warming, 213, 216, 218, 285, 299
Gloriosa superba 'Rothschildiana', 263
gluttony, of gardeners, 27
goats, 90
gomphrena, 6
Goodwin, Nancy, 86
Gossler, Roger, 270
Gossler Farms, 153, 270
Great Dixter, 29, 30, 31, 124, 274
greenhouses, 44, 77, 132, 142; at North Hill, 69, 82, 104–105, 220–22, 267, 306
Green Mountains, 111, 113
grosbeaks, 134
groundcover, 10–11
groundcovers, 157–62
Guernsey, 165
Guernsey lilies, 165–66

Hamamelis, 97, 99, 115, 126, 132, 151, 294; *H.* ×'Brevipetala', 115
hardiness, 110–17, 190, 299; of magnolias, 152, 154, 156; in mature gardens, 113; ratings as rough estimate of, 112, 135, 253–54; of roses, 231; snow cover and, 115, 116; of stewartias, 252–53; water and, 114–15, 154; wind and, 112–13
Haskell, Allen C., 7, 39–40

Hassell, Adah, 146
Hawkins, Lester, 209, 210
Headbourne Worthy, 12
heathers, 115
heaths, 115
hedges, 118–24; fertilizing of, 122, 123;
    pruning, 121, 122, 123–24
Heimlich's Nursery, 66
Helleborus (hellebore), 115, 125–31,
    228; flowering season of, 126;
    H. dumetorum, 127–28; *H. ×ericsmithii*,
    128; *H. foetidus*, 127; *H. niger*, 126–27,
    128; *H. ×orientalis*, 127, 128–31
Hemerocallis fulva, 259
hemlocks, 111, 115, 122, 271–72
hens-and-chicks, 234–39
herb gardens, 7
herb Robert, 228
Heronswood, 307
Hesperis matrionalis, 52–53, 54–55, 57–58
Hidcote, 260
highbush blueberry, 98–99, 121
Himalayan blue poppy, 186–88, 299
Hinkley, Dan, 49, 179–80, 198, 307
Hippeastrums, 166
historians, gardeners as, 189
hollies, 39, 109, 114, 132–37, 151, 246, 247
hollyhocks, 52–53, 54, 57
honeysuckles, 179
hornbeam, 121
Hornig, Ellen, 83–84, 86
hostas, 108, 129, 275, 309
houseleeks, 234–39
houses, as protection for weakly hardy
    plants, 114
Houttuynia cordata, 108
hummingbirds, 20
Hunnemannia fumariifolia, 184
hyacinths, 4, 7
Hydrangea, 273; *H. anomala* subsp.
    petiolaris, 272–73
Hymenocallis, 261; *H. ×festalis*, 261

Ilex, 132–37; *I. glabra*, 136–37; *I. opaca*,
    114, 135–36, 246; *I. verticillata*, 39, 109,
    133–35, 247
Impatiens glandulifera, 214–15
impermanence, of gardens, 49–50

Impreneta pots, 193
ingenuity, in gardens, 222–23
"in the green," use of term, 242
invasive plants, 212–19
Iris pseudacorus, 108
Italian gardens, 177–78
"I Wandered Lonely as a Cloud"
    (Wordsworth), 91

Jacobean lilies, 263
jade plant, 304
January Thaw, 94–95, 97, 98, 99, 117
Japanese apricot, 208–11
Japanese butterbur, 218–19
Japanese Cooking: A Simple Art (Tsuji), 211
Japanese knotweed, 47
Japanese primrose, 199–200, 215–16, 221
jasmines, 67, 69, 95
Jekyll, Gertrude, 19, 25, 178
Johnson, Lawrence, 260
junipers, 25

Kamel, Georg Josef, 64–65
Kentia palms, 3
Kerdalo, 273–74
Kilmarnock willow, 294
King Lear (Shakespeare), 226
Korean mountain ash, 246–49
Kreutzberger, Sybille, x, 123–24

lady's slipper orchids, 180, 219, 275
late-season gardens, 17, 18–21, 71
Laughton, Johnny, 289
laurels, 7
Laurus nobilis, 38–45, 69, 191, 310
Lawrence, D. H., 105–106, 109
Lawrence, Elizabeth, 252
Leach, David, 153, 155, 266–67, 269
leeks, 236
Lemoine, Victor, 147, 148
Lenten rose, 127, 128–31
leptospermum, 67
lettuces, 16, 170 280, 283, 309
Leucojum, 138–43; *L. aestivum*, 138,
    140–41; l. a. "Gravetye Giant", 141;
    L. autumnale, 141–42; *L. nicaense*, 142;
    L. roseum, 142; *L. trichophyllum*, 142;
    L. vernum, 138–40, 141

Lexington Gardens, 6, 7
lilacs, 121, 144–50, 170, 204, 246;
    Governor Wentworth, 145; Lemoine
    hybrids, 147; longevity of, 145–46;
    Preston hybrids, 148–49
lilies: calla, 263; Chinese lantern, 263;
    Guernsey, 165–66; Jacobean, 263;
    pineapple, 263
lily of the Nile, 10
Linnaeus, 65
live oaks, 144
Lloyd, Christopher, 29, 124, 233, 274
Lloyd, Nathaniel, 124, 274
locust posts, for pergolas, 179
loosestrife, 215
Lopez, Mr., 268
Los Angeles County Arboretum, 304
love-in-a-mist, 17
Lumley, Al, 147–48
Lyman, Hitch, 242–43
Lythrum salicaria, 215

Macleaya cordata, 182
Magnolia, 107, 151–56, 170, 275, 291;
    forcing of, 96; hardiness of, 152, 154,
    156; *M. acuminata*, 155, 156; *M.
    campbellii*, 209; *M.* 'Elizabeth', 106;
    M. grandiflora, 67; *M. liliiflora*, 156;
    M. ×*loebneri* 'Leonard Messel', 99,
    154–55, 246, 247, 251; *M.* ×*loebneri*
    'Merrill', 99, 152–53, 154, 155; *M.
    macrophylla*, 156; *M. sieboldii*, 156;
    M. ×*soulangeana*, 3, 154; *M. stellata*,
    153–54; *M. tripetala*, 156; *M. virginiana*,
    114, 154
Making Things Grow Outdoors (Cruso),
    119, 252
Malus: M. sargentii, 204; *M.* 'Snowbank', 204
Manix, Jack and Karen, 279
maples, 111, 145, 248, 253, 273, 291;
    paper bark, 151
Marie Antoinette, Queen of France, 173
marigolds, 15, 16, 107
marsh marigolds, 197
Matteuccia struthiopteris, 180
mature gardens, 113, 274, 275–77
Meconopsis betonicifolia, 186–88, 299
Medes, 229

Mediterranean, 83, 141, 142
Mesopotamians, 189, 190
Middle Ages, gardens in, 44–45, 48
Millstream, 198, 296, 311–12
mock oranges, 179
Momordica balsamina, 7
Monarch butterflies, 19
monastery gardens, 229
monocarpic plants, 52
monospecific colonies, 160
Monticello, 23
Montrose, 86
Moore, Marianne, 117
Morden Experiment Station, 148
mosses, 225
mossy phloxes, 225
Mount Vernon, 23
muscat grapes, 221
Myosotidium hortensia, 104, 266
Myosotis sylvatica, 52–53, 55, 57
myrtles, 39, 44, 157, 245, 275

Naples, 177
narcissus, paperwhite, 4, 95, 163, 258
nasturtiums, 16
neatness, 100–101
Nerine, 163–68; *N. bowdenii*, 166;
    N. sarniensis, 165–66
New England, emblematic plants of,
    144–46
New Illustrated Encyclopedia of Gardening
    (Everett), 265
Nicolson, Harold, x, 273
Nicotiana, 19–21; *N. langsdorffii*, 19–20,
    114; *N. mutabilis*, 19, 20–21; *N. rustica*,
    19; *N. tabacum*, 19
Nigella damascena, 17–18
Norris, Tony, 166–67
North America, colonial, barberry in, 48
North Hill, 102, 187; bog at, 107–108,
    114, 154, 221, 293; creation of, 88–90,
    110–11, 202–203; daffodil meadow at,
    88–93, 119, 155, 178, 181; future of,
    308–12; greenhouse at, 69, 82,
    104–105, 220–22, 267, 306; growing
    zone of, 60, 112; Holly Court at,
    136; magnolia walk at, 155–56;
    pergola walk at, 176–81, 233, 295;

rhododendron garden at, 137, 296;
rock garden at, 24, 105, 106, 108, 155,
220–21, 222, 293; Rose Alley at, 233,
288; seasons at, 309–11; terraces at, 25,
108, 148, 233, 286, 296; vegetable
garden at, 119, 126, 155, 170, 178,
181, 283, 293, 309–10; winter
garden at, 66–70, 95, 203, 217, 267,
286, 300
Nuccio, Guillio, 269
Nuccio's Nursery, 269
Nuese, Josephine, 252

Oakes, Mrs., 195
oaks, 145, 291
Oconee bells, 158–59
"Ode: Intimations of Immortality"
(Wordsworth), 277
Olbrich, Marshall, 63, 178, 209, 210, 295
old-fashioned gardens, 54, 57
Olga, Queen of Greece, 242
onions, Egyptian, 170
opium poppies, 184–86
orangeries, 45, 191
orchids, 69, 180
Ornithogalum saundersiae, 263
Osler, Michael, x
Osler, Mirabel, x
Osmanthus fragrans, 39
ostrich fern, 180
outbuildings, 104–105
overwintering: of agapanthus, 12–13; of
banana trees, 35; of bay trees, 42,
43–44; of boxwoods, 60–61
oxalis, 262

Pachysandra, 157; *P. procumbens*, 158;
P. terminalis, 158
Pacific Horticulture, 267
Paestum, 231
Page, Russell, 53
Palmer, Lewis, 12
pansies, 95
Papaver: *P. commutatum*, 186; *P. rhoeas*,
182, 186; *P. rupifragum*, 186;
P. somniferum, 184–86
paperwhite narcissus, 4, 95, 163, 258
Parkinson, John, 127

passion, of gardeners, 9, 69, 147, 152, 228,
240, 270
Paxistima: *P. canbyi*, 160–61
peach trees, 96
Peale, Rembrandt, 193
Peale, Rubens, 193
peas, 169–75, 309; shelling, 174; supports
for, 171–73, 293
peonies, 53, 130, 199, 215
Pepperell, Mass., authors' house in, 6–8,
145–46
peppers, 281
perennials, 17, 32, 80, 114, 309; clumping,
36; false assumptions about, 53; half
hardy (weak), 15, 52; overwintering
of, 113, 115
pergola walk, 176–81, 233, 295
Perrault, Charles, 17
Persians, 229
Petasites japonicus var. *giganteus*, 218–19
petits pois, 172
Philippines, 64
Phlox drummondii, 6, 18
Phyllostachys aureosulcata, 217, 246
pineapple lilies, 263
pines, 113, 115, 122, 145
planning, biennials and, 53–54
plantains, 47
planted walls, 223–26, 238–39
pleasure, of gardening, 273, 274–77, 310
Pleioblastus: *P. auricomus*, 217–18;
P. variegatus, 218
Pliny the Elder, 181
Pliny the Younger, 181, 235
Podophyllum pleianthum, 180
Polianthes tuberosa, 261–62
Pollan, Michael, x
pollarding, 292–93, 295
Polygonum cuspidatum, 47
Pompeii, 177, 181
poppies, 16, 170, 182–88; California,
183–84; Himalayan blue, 186–88;
Mexican tulip, 184; opium, 184–86;
Spanish, 186; Veterans Day, 182, 186
Portsmouth, N.H., 145
pots, 192–93, 210; for bay trees, 41;
Impreneta, 193
potted plants, 189–93, 262–63, 304, 310

Preston, Isabella, 148, 149
Preston lilacs, 148–49
Prides Crossing, Mass., 271–73
primroses, 187, 194–201, 215–16, 221
Primula, 187, 194–201; *P. auricula*, 198–99;
    P. beesiana, 200; *P. ✕bulleesiana*,
    200–201, 221; *P. denticulata*, 197; *P.
    florindae*, 107; *P. japonicas*, 199–200,
    215–16, 221; *P. obconica*, 201; *P. veris*,
    198; *P. vulgaris*, 196–98; *P. vulgaris*
    subsp. *sibthorpii*, 198
privacy screens, 203–204
privet hedges, 7, 121, 149
pruning, 310; of bay trees, 42–43; of
    hedges, 121, 122, 123–24; of roots,
    42–43, 210, 301; *see also* pollarding
Prunus: *P. mume*, 208–11; *P. ✕*'Hally
    Jolivette', 202–207; *P. ✕subhirtella*,
    204; *P. ✕yedoense*, 204
pumpkins, 279, 281
puntarelle, 278–79
pussy willows, 99
"Putting in the Seed" (Frost), 173
pyracantha, 7

quinces, 7, 206

radishes, 16, 170
Ramonda myconi, 225
raspberries, 170
rat stripper, 160–61
Ravello, Italy, 177
Ray, John, 64
Readsboro, Vt., 89, 111
reference books, 265–66
Remay, 116, 233, 309
rescued plants, 164
Réunion Island (Isle de Bourbon), 231
Rhododendron, 67, 68, 117, 133, 137, 151,
    209, 265–70, 275; 'Else Frye', 269, 270;
    'Fragrantissimum', 269, 270;
    Maddenii, 268, 269–70; Old Dexter
    hybrids, 271; *R.* 'Countess of
    Haddington', 269, 270; *R. fosterianum*,
    268, 269–70
Rhododendrons of the World (Leach), 266,
    267
robins, 133–34

Robinson, William, 172
rock daphne, 225
Rock Gardening (Foster), x
rock gardens, 77, 115, 141, 142; at North
    Hill, 24, 105, 106, 108, 155, 220–21,
    222, 293
rock harlequin, 80–81
Rogers, Owen, 149
Roman Empire, 225
Roman gardens, 44, 176, 292
Romneya coulteri, 183
roots, pruning of, 42–43, 210, 301
Rosa: *R. canina*, 231; *R. chinensis*, 231;
    R. ✕damascena, 231; *R. gallica*, 231;
    R. moschata, 231
rosemary willow, 295–96
roses, 60, 149, 169–70, 227–33, 246, 309,
    310; climbing, 179, 298, 302; 'Cuisse de
    Nymphe', 232; floribunda, 230, 231;
    'Great Maiden's Blush', 232; hardiness
    of, 231; hybrids of, 229–30; 'Madame
    Hardy', 232; medicinal properties
    of, 229; overwintering of, 116;
    repeat-flowering, 231–32; 'Rose
    Edouard', 231–32; shrub, 230–33, 285;
    'Souvenir de la Malmaison', 232; tea,
    230, 231; 'Tour de Malakoff', 231
routines, of gardeners, 309–10
*Royal Horticultural Society's Color
    Dictionary of Flowering Plants*, 265–66

Sackville-West, Vita, x, 123, 148, 252, 273
sage, 228–29
sagebrush, 144
saguaro cactus, 144
Saint Barbara's weed, 52–53
salicorne, 279
Salix, 97–98, 99, 121, 172–73, 291–96;
    S. alba, 292; *S. alba* 'Britzensis', 293;
    S. alba 'Chermesina', 293; *S. alba* var.
    caerulea, 98, 293; *S. alba* var. *sericea*, 172,
    295; *S. alba* var. *vitellina*, 98, 172, 293;
    S. caprea, 98; *S. caprea* 'Pendula', 294;
    S. caprea 'Weeping Sally', 294–95;
    S. ✕chaenomeloides, 98, 293; *S. elaeagnos*,
    295–96; *S. gracilistyla*, 98; *S. gracilistyla*
    'Melanostachys', 294; *S. lindleyana*, 296
salpiglosis, 6

Salvia: *S. horminum*, 49; *S. officinalis*, 228–29; *S. sclarea*, 52
Sandersonia aurantiaca, 263
San Francisco, 208–209, 267
Sargent crab apple, 204
Sarnia, 165
Sasa: *S. palmata*, 218; *S. veitchii*, 218
Savage, Phil, 155
Sax, Karl, 204, 205
saxifrages, 225
scaffold, of hedges, 122
Schneider, Peter, 230
Schwerdt, Pamela, x, 124
scillas, 138
seasons, in gardens, 309–11
sedums, 225
Sempervivum, 234–39; *S. arachnoideum*, 237–38; *S. calcareum*, 238; *S. tectorum*, 237–38
Seneca Hills Rare Plant Nursery, 83–84, 86
Seven Deadly Sins, 27, 117
Shakespeare, William, 226
sharing, of plants, 276, 289, 306–307
Sheridan Nurseries, 61
Shortia galacifolia, 158–59
Sissinghurst, x, 124
snake's head fritillary, 73
snapdragons, 6
snow cover, hardiness and, 115, 116
snowdrops, 126, 138, 139, 170, 228, 240–45
soil: condition of, 55, 111; temperature of, 115–16
Sorbus: *S. alnifolia*, 246–49; *S. cashmiriana*, 165
Sorel boots, 234
Southern gardens, 39
Southern Vermont AIDS Project, 212
Spanish poppy, 186
Sprague, Jim, 90
Sprekelia formosissima, 263
Springer, Lauren, 184
spring snowflakes, 138–40, 141
spruces, 113, 115, 122
squash, 170, 279, 281
staghorn ferns, 3
standards, 38–40, 44, 63, 102, 204, 310; overwintering of, 43–44

Stewartia, 151, 170, 246, 247, 250–54, 275, 291; hardiness of, 252–53; *S. pseudocamellia*, 247, 252
Stokowski, Leopold, 177
stone walls, 77
stove houses, 191
stratification, 195
Strauss, Richard, 310
strawberries, 170
Strybing Arboretum, 209
"Student, The" (Moore), 117
Sugiyama, Nao, 211
summer, 83, 111, 310
summer snowflakes, 138, 140–41
sunflowers, 15
sweet olive, 39
sweet william, 52–53
Syneilesis: *S. aconitifolia*, 180; *S. palmata*, 180
Syringa, 170, 246; *S. reflexa*, 148; *S. villosa*, 148; *S. vulgaris*, 121, 144–50; *S. vulgaris* 'Alba', 204

tea plants, 65, 67, 70
tea roses, 230, 231
Temple Nursery, 242
terraces, 6–7, 120, 272; at North Hill, 25, 108, 148, 233, 286, 296
thistles, 32
Thuja, 113; *T. occidentalis*, 23–25, 26, 122; *T. plicata*, 25–26
Thunberg, Carl Peter, 49
time, 271–77, 308, 310
tomatoes, 170, 279, 281
tool sheds, 100–101, 103
tortoises, 94–95
transplanting: of biennials, 57–58; of corydalis, 77–78
Trees for American Gardens (Wyman), 247
"triennials," 52
Triteleia laxa, 263
tropical plants, as accents, 37
trowels, 100–103
Tsuji, Shizuo, 211
tuberoses, 261–62
Tudor, Tasha, 54
tulips, 7, 242
Tweedia caerulea, 18

umeboshi, 211
Union Square Market, 280

Vaccinium, 161–62; *V. corymbosum*,
98–99; *V. macrocarpon*, 161;
V. vitis-idaea minus, 161
valerians, 225
Vancouver, George, 162
Vancouveria hexandra, 162
vegetable gardens, 16, 178, 278–83;
annuals in, 16–17; design of, 282; as
hard work, 281–82; at North Hill, 119,
126, 155, 170, 178, 181, 283, 293,
309–10; paths in, 282–83
vegetables, garden vs. market, 28–29
Verbena bonariensis, 18–19
Verey, Rosemary, 13
Vermont: autumn in, 111; growing season
in, 110–11, 213; invasive plants in, 214;
January Thaw in, 94–95; laws of, 203;
summer in, 82, 83, 111, 174; winter in,
82, 95, 110–11, 211, 222, 254, 267, 306
Veterans Day poppies, 182, 186
Viburnum ×*bodnantense*, 96–97, 99, 126
Vienna Botanical Garden, 244
Villa Cimbrone, 177–78
Vinca, 157; *V. minor*, 245
Viola (violets), 114, 284–90; *V. labradorica*,
285–86; *V. rosea*, 286–87; *V. rotundifolia*,
284–85; *V. sororia*, 287–88; *V. sororia*
'Freckles', 288–90; *V.* 'Sulfurea', 287
Virgil, 231

Wakehurst Place, 228
Walker Farm, 279
walks and paths, function of, 180–81
walls, planted, 223–26
wandflower, 159
Warley, 276
Washingtonia palms, 144
water, hardiness and, 114–15, 154
Wayside Gardens, 247
We Made a Garden (Fish), x
Western Hills Rare Plant Nursery, 63,
209, 295
Weston Nurseries, 26, 118, 135, 152, 215,
247

White, E. B., 273
White, Katherine, 273
White Flower Farm, 299
white pine, 122
Willmott, Ellen, 185, 276
willows, 97–98, 99, 121, 172–73, 291–96;
Kilmarnock, 294; Rosemary, 295–96;
weeping, 291, 292, 294–95
willow twigs, 292; as pea supports,
172–73, 293
Wilson, E. H., 258
Wilt-Proof, 117
wind, hardiness and, 112–13
wine, and artichokes, 31
winter, 82, 95, 110–11, 132–33
winter gardens, 44; at North Hill, 66–70,
95, 203, 217, 267, 286, 300
winter sun, 113, 135
Wisteria, 67, 69, 297–302; as dwarf plants,
299–300; *W. floribunda*, 179, 299;
W. floribunda 'alba', 298–302;
W. macrostachya, 179; *W. sinensis*,
179, 299
witch hazels, 97, 99, 115, 126, 132, 151,
294
Wolff, Guy, 193
Wolkonsky, Prince Peter, 273–74
woodland plants, 113, 179–80, 197
wood poppy, 180
Wood and Garden (Jekyll), 25
Wordsworth, William, 91, 277
work, gardening as, 233, 281–82
World War I, 186
Wyman, Donald, 247, 252
Wyman's Garden Encyclopedia, 112, 207,
252, 265

Xanthorrhoea, 191
Xanthorrhoea quadrangulata, 303–307

yellow birch, 248
yews, 7, 133, 228; as hedges, 118–21, 122,
123–24, 274
Younger, Albert, 149
young gardens, 274–75

zinnias, 6, 15, 16